SAS Publishing

SAS® Guide to Report Writing
Examples
Second Edition

Michele M. Burlew

The Power to Know.

The correct bibliographic citation for this manual is as follows: Burlew, Michele M. 2005. *SAS® Guide to Report Writing: Examples, Second Edition*. Cary, NC: SAS Institute Inc.

SAS® Guide to Report Writing: Examples, Second Edition

Contents

Acknowledgments

I want to acknowledge the contributions that many people at SAS made in developing this book. Thanks to the technical reviewers: Janice Bloom, Paige Daniels, Davetta Dunlap, Marty Hultgren, Johnny Johnson, Bari Lawhorn, Kathryn McLawhorn, Allison McMahill, Linda Mitterling, Chevell Parker, Linda Reznikiewicz, Kevin Russell, Cynthia Zender, and Rebecca Zoellner. I want especially to thank Chevell and Cynthia for help with the ODS chapter. Thanks to my editors at SAS Press, Julie Platt and John West, for their thoughtful suggestions and management of this project. Thanks to Candy Farrell and Lisa Boone in Publishing Production, especially for the difficult work of making some of the output reports fit in the space allotted. Thanks to Joel Byrd for his skills in technical editing. To Patrice Cherry, thanks for designing such a great cover with colors I personally love. And thanks to Shelly Goodin and Liz Villani for their work in marketing this book.

To my friend, Jan Jannett, thanks for advice on IT user support statistics. To my friend, Sue Ahbe, thanks for help in setting up the logo for XYZ Marketing.

Thanks to Eilenne Boder with the Ramsey County Public Library System in Minnesota for advice on typical library circulation statistics. Thanks to David Bonter and the Cornell Lab of Ornithology for permission to use a data set extracted from the databases of the Lab's Citizen Science program, Project FeederWatch. Thanks to Brian Gray with the US Geological Survey for work that led to the example that uses ODS output objects.

CHAPTER 1

Writing Reports with SAS

Presenting information in a way that's understood by the audience is fundamentally important to anyone's job. Once you collect your data and understand its structure, you need to be able to report and summarize your findings effectively and efficiently.

With SAS procedures, SAS DATA steps, and SAS features such as the Output Delivery System (ODS) and the macro facility, you have the tools to succeed at writing programs that analyze your data and create reports.

Using This Book

This book presents examples of SAS programs that solve many common report-writing tasks. The examples range from simply listing the observations in a data set to computing summary statistics to creating customized reports with SAS DATA step statements to tailoring report output by including ODS features.

Each chapter in this book groups reports of a similar type as described in Table 1.1.

Table 1.1 List of Chapter Topics

Chapter	Topic	Description
2	Detail Reports	List observations.
3	Summary Reports	Summarize observations.
4	Customized Reports	Use SAS programming statements to customize the presentation of data.
5	Multipanel Reports	Place multiple rows of information side-by-side.
6	Enhancing Reports with ODS Features	Apply ODS features to enhance the formatting of reports.

Each example includes the following information in this order:

❑ a brief statement of the goal of the example

❑ the report output

❑ a table that lists the SAS code features found in the example

❑ a description of the process to solve the report-writing task and a description of the data set that the example uses

❑ the SAS program that creates the output with annotations of the code in the left margin

❑ other ways of solving the same report-writing task (optional)

❑ more detailed discussions of the special features of the example (optional)

The example data sets analyzed in this book were devised to be structurally simple so that the focus of each example is the report-writing tool rather than the unique characteristics of the data set. See Appendix A, "Creating the Example Data Sets," for details on the contents of each example data set.

As you read each example, keep in mind how you can adapt the code to report results from your data sets. You can access the data sets and programs presented in this book from the companion Web site for this book: support.sas.com/companionsites.

Understanding SAS Report-Writing Tools

Most SAS procedures produce output in a standard format. Two procedures, REPORT and TABULATE, allow some customization of output layout. DATA steps and ODS features provide the most flexibility in customizing and selecting report output. The examples in this book focus on the application of report-writing procedures, DATA steps, and ODS in producing reports.

When writing a program to create a report, you need to know which SAS procedures specialize in the kind of report you want to produce. Reports can be categorized as detail, summary, customized, and multipanel. Examples of each are shown in Figures 1.1 through 1.4.

❏ *Detail* reports list information at the observation level of a data set (see Figure 1.1).

❏ *Summary* reports summarize observations and produce output such as frequency counts and descriptive statistics (see Figure 1.2).

❏ *Customized* reports list information in a style that is different than the standard output from a SAS procedure. Often these are produced with DATA step programming (see Figure 1.3).

❏ *Multipanel* reports present multiple rows of information side-by-side (see Figure 1.4).

Some overlap does exist between the categories. For example, a detail report may include summaries, and a multipanel report may contain detail and summary information.

Figure 1.1 Example of a Detail Report

Study Heights and Weights							
		ID	GROUP	GENDER	HT	WT	AGE
	1	301	B	F	64	110	32
	2	302	A	M	71	142	42
	3	303	A	M	72	206	34
	4	304	B	M	69	160	43
	5	305	A	F	65	138	32
	6	306	A	F	65	196	32
	7	307	B	M	70	242	40

..... *more rows*........

Figure 1.2 Example of a Summary Report

Study Heights and Weights

Group	Gender	Height(in) Mean	Height(in) Std	Weight(lb) Mean	Weight(lb) Std	Age at Exam Mean	Age at Exam Std
A	Females	64.6	1.6	144	21.6	35.4	7.5
	Males	69.5	2.6	169	24.9	35.9	9.0
B	Females	65.9	2.6	139	21.4	36.2	7.3
	Males	69.5	2.7	169	20.0	36.6	8.5

Figure 1.3 Example of a Customized Report

Study Heights and Weights

Group A Males
Mean Weight: 169   Mean Height: 69.5
Group B Males
Mean Weight: 169   Mean Height: 69.5
TTest Results: Males Group A vs Group B Weight: No significant difference (p>0.05)
TTest Results: Males Group A vs Group B Height: No significant difference (p>0.05)

Group A Females
Mean Weight: 144   Mean Height: 64.6
Group B Females
Mean Weight: 139   Mean Height: 65.9
TTest Results: Females Group A vs Group B Weight: No significant difference (p>0.05)
TTest Results: Females Group A vs Group B Height: Significant difference (p < 0.05)

Figure 1.4 Example of a Multipanel Report

Study Heights and Weights

Group	ID	Gender	Ht	Wt	Age
B	301	F	64	110	31
A	302	M	71	142	42
A	303	M	72	206	34
B	304	M	69	160	43
A	305	F	64	138	32
A	306	F	65	196	32

Group	ID	Gender	Ht	Wt	Age
B	339	F	65	143	34
B	340	M	68	181	26
A	341	M	66	168	44
B	342	M	70	171	44
B	343	M	68	168	31
B	344	M	71	162	24

Group	ID	Gender	Ht	Wt	Age
A	377	F	66	152	33
B	378	M	69	176	53
B	379	F	64	127	41
B	380	M	66	174	52
B	381	M	69	154	39
B	382	F	66	135	41

......more rows............

Table 1.2 presents an overview of each category of report and the SAS procedures best suited to produce reports of that type.

Table 1.2 Report Types and the Procedures Used to Produce the Different Types

Report Type	Procedure/Step	Description
Detail	PRINT	Produces data listings quickly; can supply titles, footnotes, and column sums.
	REPORT	Offers more control and customization than PROC PRINT; can produce both column and row sums; has DATA step computation abilities.
	SQL	Combines Structured Query Language and SAS features such as formats; can manipulate data and create a SAS data set in the same step that creates the report; can produce column and row statistics; does not offer as much control over output as PROC PRINT and PROC REPORT.
	MEANS, SUMMARY, UNIVARIATE	Computes descriptive statistics for numeric variables; can produce a printed report and create an output data set.
Summary	PRINT	Produces only one summary report; can sum the BY variables.
	REPORT	Combines features of the PRINT, MEANS, and TABULATE procedures with features of the DATA step in a single report-writing tool; can also create an output data set.
	SQL	Computes descriptive statistics for one or more SAS data sets or DBMS tables; can produce a printed report or create a SAS data set.
	TABULATE	Produces descriptive statistics in a tabular format; can produce multidimensional tables with descriptive statistics; can also create an output data set.
Customized	DATA Step	Produces highly customized reports of all types using SAS programming statements.
Multipanel	All procedures when sending output to a nonlisting destination; REPORT when sending output to either the LISTING or a nonlisting destination	Produces side-by-side reports.

Most examples in this book use PROC REPORT and PROC TABULATE. A few examples use PROC PRINT and a few examples use DATA steps. One example uses PROC MEANS and another uses PROC FREQ. PROC FORMAT is used throughout to add labels and other information to the reports.

Integrating ODS and Report Writing

ODS is an integral part of the report-writing process. It can be used in all categories of reports to design the layout of a report, improve the look of a report, and select the contents of a report.

The default destination of your output when you start your SAS session is LISTING. The LISTING destination is the traditional monospace SAS output. The examples in Chapters 2, 3, 4, and 5 are written to send output to the LISTING destination. Several of these examples are modified in Chapter 6 to send output to nonlisting destinations such as RTF and HTML.

Associating Types of Reports and the Examples in This Book

Appendix B, "Cross-Reference of the Examples in This Book," presents a cross-reference of the examples in this book to the type of report, procedures used, data sets used, and ODS enhanced versions of the examples.

The rows of Table B.1 in Appendix B list the examples presented in Chapters 2 through 5. A table in the introduction to each of the Chapters 2 through 5 repeats the pertinent rows from Table B.1.

The examples in Chapter 6 are derived from the examples in Chapters 2 through 5, and a table linking the examples in Chapter 6 to the original versions is presented in the introduction to Chapter 6 and repeated in Table B.2 in Appendix B.

Using PROC SQL as a Report-Writing Tool

PROC SQL can also produce reports, but none of the examples in this book apply this procedure to a report-writing task. PROC SQL is a multipurpose procedure that is the SAS implementation of Structured Query Language.

You can produce detail reports with PROC SQL, but the report formatting options in the procedure are limited. In the process of creating your report, you may find PROC SQL most useful in combining your data sets and obtaining intermediate results that are included in your final reports. For more information on PROC SQL, see "The SQL Procedure" in the "Procedures" section of *Base SAS 9.1 Procedures Guide.*

Displaying Results Graphically

The examples in this book concentrate on producing text-based tables. Some images are included in the text reports in Chapter 6, and one example in Chapter 6 includes a programmatically derived graphical report.

A picture can be invaluable in conveying results. When you combine both pictures and text in a report, you can help your audience better understand your results.

While plotting data is beyond the scope of this book, do not ignore this topic. The best reference for presenting data graphically is *SAS/GRAPH 9.1 Reference.* To get started in producing graphical reports, look for SAS Press titles and SUGI conference proceedings, as described in the "References" section of this chapter. These resources will help you combine graphs with the material you've learned in this book.

Writing a Report Program in Five Steps

Writing a report can be an iterative process. You will likely find that it takes several tries to produce the report you need. Before starting your report program, make sure you understand your data and the types of information that the report should convey. Do not concentrate on the style attributes of the report until you're sure you can produce the basic output. Then after successfully establishing the structure of the report, add the formatting features that improve the look and readability of your report.

These five steps can guide you in writing your report programs.

1. *State the information that the report should convey.* Write sentences that describe and explain the contents of your report.

2. *Sketch how the report should look.* Consider these issues in planning your report:

   ❑ What type of report is this–detail, summary, customized, multipanel, a combination of types?

   ❑ What defines the columns of the report–variables, computed variables?

   ❑ What defines the rows of the report–an observation, summaries of observations, groups of observations?

   ❑ How should the rows be ordered?

   ❑ What kind of annotation is needed in the report–customized lines, titles, footnotes?

3. *Understand your data.* Consider these issues when you investigate the content and structure of your analysis data sets:

   ❑ What data sets do you need to produce the report?

   ❑ How are the analysis data sets structured? Run PROC CONTENTS or view the properties to review the attributes of the variables in the data sets and the characteristics of the data sets, such as size and sorting. List a few observations with PROC PRINT to see what the values look like. When producing a summary report, run PROC FREQ on the variables that define the categories in your reports to determine the number of levels and whether values should be grouped. This will help you predict the physical size of the final report. Consider whether PROC FORMAT would be useful in grouping the data. Run PROC MEANS to determine ranges of values.

   ❑ Is the physical structure of the data set in the same orientation as the report? Do you need to reshape the data sets? What method should you use to reshape the data–DATA steps, PROC TRANSPOSE, output data set from a procedure?

   ❑ Do you need to combine data sets? How should you combine data sets–MERGE or SET statements in DATA steps, PROC APPEND, PROC SQL?

❑ Do you need to compute new variables? If so, should you do this before you execute the report-writing procedure? If you're using PROC REPORT, you may not know the answer until you test your PROC REPORT step. When writing a DATA step to produce a report, you may be able to compute the new variables and produce the report in the same step.

❑ Do you need to rearrange the order of the data for the report? You may not know the answer to this question until you select the report-writing procedure. Say, for example, that your goal is to produce a detail report with ordered rows. If you use PROC PRINT, your data set must be sorted or indexed in the proper order before you execute PROC PRINT. If you use PROC REPORT, you may not have to sort the data set before using the procedure. Options within PROC REPORT–the ORDER or GROUP option on the DEFINE statement and the ORDER= option on the PROC REPORT statement–will order the rows of your report.

4. ***Select the report-writing procedure or decide to use a DATA step and, after reshaping the data sets as explained in Step 3, write the basic statements that construct the report.*** Ensure that your program can construct the basic layout of the report, and do not dwell on formatting the report (formatting columns, adding labels, adding style options, etc.). It may take several tries to achieve the required structure, and you may need to return to Step 3 to learn more about your data sets, reshape the data sets, or compute new variables. Refer to Table 1.2 for a list of which procedures perform best at which tasks.

5. ***Add formatting features to the report.*** Consider whether to add these items to improve the look of your report:

❑ SAS defined formats and user-defined formats

❑ titles, footnotes, labels

❑ customized lines

❑ style attributes for fonts, spacing, borders, etc.

❑ customized BY lines

❑ summary lines

❑ features specific to the output destination

Your final report program will likely be a hybrid of formatting features available within the procedure and those that can be supplied with ODS specifications.

References

The focus of this book is the presentation of examples, not the explanation of syntax. Therefore, it's important to have reference documentation available when you read this book. SAS®9 documentation is available online at support.sas.com/v9doc.

Basic references used for this book include:

❑ *SAS 9.1 Language Reference: Concepts*

❑ *SAS 9.1 Language Reference: Dictionary*

❑ *Base SAS 9.1 Procedures Guide*

❑ *SAS 9.1 Output Delivery System: User's Guide*

Additional SAS examples can be found in the many books available through SAS Press. See the back of this book for a list of titles, and access the SAS Press Web site (support.sas.com/saspress) for newly released and revised publications.

Several presentations at SUGI conferences show how SAS users apply report-writing techniques. Recent conference proceedings are available online, and they provide a wealth of additional applications and examples. You can link to them through the SAS support Web site (support.sas.com).

CHAPTER 2

Detail Reports

A detail report lists information at the observation level of a data set. The examples in this chapter show you ways in which you can prepare detail reports. Included in several reports are summaries of the detailed information. Some examples require that you order or restructure the observations in the analysis data set before executing the report procedure. The examples include explanations of these preparatory steps.

Two procedures, PRINT and REPORT, create the detail reports in this chapter. Most examples apply formats defined by PROC FORMAT, which adds explanatory information to the report. PROC SORT sorts observations before they are displayed by PROC PRINT. One example shows how to rank observations with PROC RANK.

All the examples in this chapter send output to the default LISTING destination. Examples 2.2, 2.4, and 2.7 are modified in Chapter 6 to include ODS features and send the output to nonlisting destinations.

See the back of this book for a list of titles related to the features of these examples, and access the SAS Press Web site (support.sas.com/saspress) for current information on new and revised publications.

Several presentations at SUGI conferences show how SAS users apply report-writing techniques. Recent conference proceedings, which are available online, provide a wealth of additional applications and examples. You can link to them through the SAS support Web site (support.sas.com).

Table 2.0 presents a cross-reference of the examples in this chapter to the procedures used, data sets used, and ODS enhanced versions of the examples. See Appendix A for details on the example data sets analyzed in this chapter. See Appendix B for a table that cross-references all examples in this book.

Table 2.0 Cross-Reference of Examples in Chapter 2

| Example | Report-Writing Tool Used | | | | | | ODS Enhanced Version | Data Set | Example Title |
	REPORT	TABULATE	PRINT	DATA Step	MEANS	FREQ			
2.1			X					HOUSING	Listing Selected Observations in a Specific Order
2.2	X		Related Technique				6.1	HOUSING	Ordering the Rows of a Report
2.3			X					FEEDERBIRDS	Placing Data That Is Constant for a Category in Titles
2.4	X		Related Technique				6.10	POWERUSE	Summarizing the Rows of a Report
2.5	X							POWERUSE	Summarizing Columns and Rows
2.6	X							POWERUSE	Suppressing the Display of Specific Columns
2.7	X						6.4	LIPIDS	Presenting Multiple Observations per Report Row
2.8	X							TOWNSURVEY	Presenting Long Text Fields in a Report
2.9	X							MARATHON	Listing the Rank and Percentile for Each Observation

Example 2.1 Listing Selected Observations in a Specific Order

Goal

List specific information about selected observations in a data set in a specific order. Each row in the report presents information for one observation.

Report

```
                    Selected Listing of Local Residential Properties
                              Price Range $200,000 to $350,000

Residential      House                                   Listing                        Square
Zone             Style     Address                        Price Bedrooms Bathrooms  Feet  Age

North Ridge      bungalow  6008 Brass Lantern Ct.      $344,500    3        2.5     2,416   6
Inside Beltline  capecod   100 Cumberland Green        $343,000    3        2.5     1,650   0
East Lake        ranch     8122 Maude Steward Rd.      $329,900    3        3.0     2,400   2
Roebuck          split     110 Skylark Way             $323,500    3        2.0     1,976  10
North Ridge      colonial  4000 Skipjack Ct.           $314,900    3        2.5     2,750   0
Roebuck          split     5617 Laurel Crest Dr.       $286,900    3        1.5     1,441  28
North Ridge      split     2414 Van Dyke               $285,000    3        1.0     1,245  36
Inside Beltline  townhouse 765 Crabtree Crossing       $284,000    3        2.0     1,471   1
North Ridge      split     500 E. Millbrook Rd.        $282,900    3        1.5     1,329  23
East Lake        split     6424 Old Jenks Rd.          $281,900    3        1.5     1,225  18
Inside Beltline  split     101 Meadowglade Ln.         $279,950    3        2.0     2,004   0
Inside Beltline  townhouse 108 Chattle Close           $279,900    3        2.5     2,080   4
Westend          split     Rt.5 Yarbororugh Rd.        $278,900    2        1.0       960   2
Roebuck          townhouse 8 Stonevillage              $271,000    2        2.0     1,276   6
Ensley           townhouse 409 Galashiels              $260,000    2        1.5     1,280   4
East Lake        split     4341 Rock Quarry            $260,000    3        1.0     1,010  28
Inside Beltline  townhouse 216 Concannon Ct.           $259,900    2        1.5     1,040   9
Inside Beltline  townhouse 1239 Donaldson Ct.          $249,900    2        1.5     1,150  15
Westend          split     603 Greentree Dr.           $217,800    3        2.0     1,533   5
East Lake        ranch     6509 Orchard Knoll          $207,900    3        2.0     1,526   6
Southside        townhouse 154 Montrose                $202,000    2        2.0     1,595   6
Mountain Brook   duplex    108 South Elm St.           $200,000    3        1.0     1,569  73
North Ridge      split     6324 Lakeland, Lake Park    $200,000    3        2.0     1,662  12

              Total Available Properties within Price Range: 23
```

Example Features

Data Set	HOUSING
Preparatory Step	PROC SORT
Featured Step	PROC PRINT
Featured Step Statements and Options	PROC PRINT statement: N= option VAR statement WHERE statement
Formatting Features	PROC PRINT statement: NOOBS and SPLIT= options PROC PRINT statement: UNIFORM option when sending output to the LISTING destination
Other Examples That Use This Data Set	Examples 2.2 and 6.1

Example Overview

This report lists observations from the HOUSING data set. It presents data about houses for sale within a specific price range and arranges the observations in descending order of price.

Each row in the report corresponds to one observation in the HOUSING data set. Each column corresponds to one variable.

The data set must be sorted before the PROC PRINT step. A VAR statement within the PROC PRINT step selects the variables to list in the report. A WHERE statement within the PROC PRINT step selects the observations to list in the report.

Program

Sort the observations by the descending values of PRICE.

```
proc sort data=housing;
   by descending price;
run;
```

Create a format that can associate meaningful descriptions to the numeric values of the variable ZONE.

```
proc format;
   value $zonefmt '1'='North Ridge'
                  '2'='Inside Beltline'
                  '3'='Southside'
                  '4'='East Lake'
                  '5'='Westend'
                  '6'='Mountain Brook'
                  '7'='Ensley'
                  '8'='Roebuck';
run;
```

Print the sorted data set.

```
proc print data=housing
```

Print the number of observations in the data set and specify explanatory text to print with the number.

```
   n='Total Available Properties within
       Price Range: '
```

Suppress the column in the output that identifies each observation by number.

```
   noobs
```

Specify the split character that controls line breaks in column headings. (The SPLIT= option causes variable labels to be used as column headings. If you want labels, but do not need to specify a split character, replace SPLIT= with the keyword LABEL.)

```
   split='/'
```

Format all pages of a multipage report uniformly when sending output to the LISTING destination.

```
   uniform;
```

```
   title 'Selected Listing of Local Residential
          Properties';
   title2 'Price Range $200,000 to $350,000';
```

Select the observations to include in the report.

```
   where price between 200000 and 350000;
```

List the variables in the order in which they should appear in the report.

```
   var zone type address price bedr bath sqfeet age;
```

Associate formats with variables.

```
format sqfeet comma5. price dollar9.
       zone $zonefmt.;
```

Label the variables in the report. Include the split character within the label to control line breaks in the heading for the variable.

```
label zone='Residential/Zone'
      type='House/Style'
      address='Address'
      price='Listing/Price'
      bedr='Bedrooms'
      bath='Bathrooms'
      sqfeet='Square/Feet'
      age='Age';
run;
```

Where to Go from Here

BY statement processing. See "BY Statement" in the "Statements" section of *SAS 9.1 Language Reference: Dictionary,* and "Statements with the Same Function in Multiple Procedures" in the "Concepts" section of *Base SAS 9.1 Procedures Guide.*

PROC PRINT reference, usage information, and additional examples. See "The PRINT Procedure" in the "Procedures" section of *Base SAS 9.1 Procedures Guide.*

WHERE statement processing. See "WHERE Statement" in the "Statements" section of *SAS 9.1 Language Reference: Dictionary,* and "WHERE-Expression Processing" in the "SAS System Concepts" section of *SAS 9.1 Language Reference: Concepts.*

Example 2.2   Ordering the Rows of a Report

Goal

List specific information about selected observations in a data set in a specific order. Group the rows by the values of the ordering variables. Each row in the report should present information for one observation.

Report

```
                    Listing of Local Residential Properties
                        Price Range $200,000 to $350,000
                                 Listed by Zone

                                                                       Square
Residential      Listing House                                          Feet Age
Zone             Price  Style   Address         Bedrooms Bathrooms     Feet Age
-----------------------------------------------------------------------------------
East Lake        $329,900 ranch     8122 Maude Steward Rd.    3      3.0  2,400   2
                 $281,900 split     6424 Old Jenks Rd.        3      1.5  1,225  18
                 $260,000 split     4341 Rock Quarry          3      1.0  1,010  28
                 $207,900 ranch     6509 Orchard Knoll        3      2.0  1,526   6

Ensley           $260,000 townhouse 409 Galashiels            2      1.5  1,280   4

Inside Beltline  $343,000 capecod   100 Cumberland Green      3      2.5  1,650   0
                 $284,000 townhouse 765 Crabtree Crossing     3      2.0  1,471   1
                 $279,950 split     101 Meadowglade Ln.       3      2.0  2,004   0
                 $279,900 townhouse 108 Chattle Close         3      2.5  2,080   4
                 $259,900 townhouse 216 Concannon Ct.         2      1.5  1,040   9
                 $249,900 townhouse 1239 Donaldson Ct.        2      1.5  1,150  15

Mountain Brook   $200,000 duplex    108 South Elm St.         3      1.0  1,569  73

North Ridge      $344,500 bungalow  6008 Brass Lantern Ct.    3      2.5  2,416   6
                 $314,900 colonial  4000 Skipjack Ct.         3      2.5  2,750   0
                 $285,000 split     2414 Van Dyke             3      1.0  1,245  36
                 $282,900 split     500 E. Millbrook Rd.      3      1.5  1,329  23
                 $200,000 split     6324 Lakeland, Lake Park  3      2.0  1,662  12

Roebuck          $323,500 split     110 Skylark Way           3      2.0  1,976  10
                 $286,900 split     5617 Laurel Crest Dr.     3      1.5  1,441  28
                 $271,000 townhouse 8 Stonevillage            2      2.0  1,276   6

Southside        $202,000 townhouse 154 Montrose              2      2.0  1,595   6

Westend          $278,900 split     Rt.5 Yarbororugh Rd.      2      1.0    960   2
                 $217,800 split     603 Greentree Dr.         3      2.0  1,533   5

                        Listing Produced on Dec 10, 2005
```

Example Features

Data Set	HOUSING
Featured Step	PROC REPORT
Featured Step Statements and Options	DEFINE statement: ORDER option WHERE statement BREAK AFTER statement
Formatting Features	PROC REPORT statement: SPLIT= option PROC REPORT statement: HEADLINE, SPACING=, and WIDTH= options when sending output to the LISTING destination

Additional Features	Macro functions
Related Technique	PROC SORT and PROC PRINT
🔎 A Closer Look	Comparing PROC PRINT and PROC REPORT
ODS Enhanced Version of this Example	Example 6.1
Other Examples That Use This Data Set	Examples 2.1 and 6.1

Example Overview

This detail report lists specific data about houses for sale within the price range of $200,000 to $350,000 and is similar to Example 2.1. This report, however, does not require that you sort the data set prior to producing the report. Statements within PROC REPORT order the rows first by residential zone and then within each residential zone, by descending price.

Each row in the report corresponds to one observation in the HOUSING data set. Each column corresponds to one variable.

Program

Create a format to associate meaningful descriptions to the numeric values of the variable ZONE.

```
proc format;
   value $zonefmt '1'='North Ridge'
                  '2'='Inside Beltline'
                  '3'='Southside'
                  '4'='East Lake'
                  '5'='Westend'
                  '6'='Mountain Brook'
                  '7'='Ensley'
                  '8'='Roebuck';
run;

proc report data=housing
```

Send output to the SAS procedure output destination rather than the interactive REPORT window.

```
   nowindows
```

Specify the split character to control line breaks in column headings.

```
   split='/'
```

Underline all column headers and the spaces between them when sending output to the LISTING destination.

```
   headline
```

Override the default spacing of two
blank characters between columns when
sending output to the LISTING
destination.

```
spacing=1;

title 'Listing of Local Residential Properties';
title2 'Price Range $200,000 to $350,000';
title3 'Listed by Zone';
```

Include today's date in the footnote text.
Place double quotes around the footnote
text so that the macro function obtains
today's date and formats it.

```
footnote "Listing Produced on
          %sysfunc(today(),worddate12.)";
```

Select the observations to include in the
report.

```
where price between 200000 and 350000;
```

List the columns in the order in which
they should appear in the report.

```
column zone price type address bedr bath sqfeet age;
```

Describe the order of the rows and
specify formats (FORMAT=), column
widths (WIDTH=), and column
headings (text enclosed in single quotes).
Order the detail rows first by the formatted
value of ZONE and within each ZONE,
order the detail rows in descending order
by PRICE. Include the forward slash (/) in
the column heading so that SAS inserts a
line break in the column heading at the
position of the forward slash. Specify the
column width when sending output to the
LISTING destination.

```
define   zone      / order format=$zonefmt15.
                      width=15
                      'Residential/Zone';
define   price     / order descending
                      format=dollar10. width=10
                      'Listing/Price';

define   type      / display
                      format=$9.'House/Style';

define   address   / format=$25. width=25 'Address';
define   bedr      / format=2. width=8 'Bedrooms';
define   bath      / format=3.1 width=9 'Bathrooms';
define   sqfeet    / format=comma6. width=6
                      'Square/Feet';
define   age       / format=3. 'Age';
```

Write a blank line after the last row for
each unique value of the order variable
ZONE.

```
break after zone / skip;
run;
```

Related Technique

A report similar to the one featured above can be produced with PROC SORT
and PROC PRINT as demonstrated in this section. Figure 2.2 presents the output
from a program that uses PROC SORT and PROC PRINT.

Figure 2.2 Output Produced by PROC PRINT

```
                        Listing of Local Residential Properties
                            Price Range $200,000 to $350,000
                                     Listed by Zone

                 House                                     Square            Listing
Zone             Style      Address          Bedrooms Bathrooms Feet   Age     Price

North Ridge      bungalow   6008 Brass Lantern Ct.    3    2.5    2,416   6    $344,500
                 colonial   4000 Skipjack Ct.         3    2.5    2,750   0    $314,900
                 split      500 E. Millbrook Rd.      3    1.5    1,329  23    $282,900
                 split      2414 Van Dyke             3    1.0    1,245  36    $285,000
                 split      6324 Lakeland, Lake Park  3    2.0    1,662  12    $200,000

Inside Beltline  capecod    100 Cumberland Green      3    2.5    1,650   0    $343,000
                 split      101 Meadowglade Ln.       3    2.0    2,004   0    $279,950
                 townhouse  1239 Donaldson Ct.        2    1.5    1,150  15    $249,900
                 townhouse  216 Concannon Ct.         2    1.5    1,040   9    $259,900
                 townhouse  765 Crabtree Crossing     3    2.0    1,471   1    $284,000
                 townhouse  108 Chattle Close         3    2.5    2,080   4    $279,900

Southside        townhouse  154 Montrose              2    2.0    1,595   6    $202,000

East Lake        ranch      6509 Orchard Knoll        3    2.0    1,526   6    $207,900
                 ranch      8122 Maude Steward Rd.    3    3.0    2,400   2    $329,900
                 split      4341 Rock Quarry          3    1.0    1,010  28    $260,000
                 split      6424 Old Jenks Rd.        3    1.5    1,225  18    $281,900

Westend          split      Rt.5 Yarbororugh Rd.      2    1.0      960   2    $278,900
                 split      603 Greentree Dr.         3    2.0    1,533   5    $217,800

Mountain Brook   duplex     108 South Elm St.         3    1.0    1,569  73    $200,000

Ensley           townhouse  409 Galashiels            2    1.5    1,280   4    $260,000

Roebuck          split      5617 Laurel Crest Dr.     3    1.5    1,441  28    $286,900
                 split      110 Skylark Way           3    2.0    1,976  10    $323,500
                 townhouse  8 Stonevillage            2    2.0    1,276   6    $271,000


                        Listing Produced on Dec 10, 2005
```

[handwritten annotations in left margin: "break after", "→ skip"]

The program that produced the report in Figure 2.2 follows.

Ensure that the BYLINE option is in effect when executing this program. This will keep information for multiple zones on the same page. If NOBYLINE is in effect, PROC PRINT starts a new page for each value of the BY variable, ZONE. For more about the BYLINE option, see Example 2.3.

Use the same format as shown in the main example.

```
proc format;
    value $zonefmt '1'='North Ridge'
                   '2'='Inside Beltline'
                   '3'='Southside'
                   '4'='East Lake'
                   '5'='Westend'
                   '6'='Mountain Brook'
                   '7'='Ensley'
                   '8'='Roebuck';
run;

proc sort data=housing;
    by zone type;
run;
proc print data=housing
    uniform
```

Ensure that the layout on each page of a multipage report is the same when sending output to the LISTING destination.

Define the split character for column headings.

```
split='/';

title 'Listing of Local Residential Properties';
title2 'Price Range $200,000 to $350,000';
title3 'Listed by Zone';

footnote "Listing Produced on
            %sysfunc(today(),worddate12.)";

where price between 200000 and 350000;
by zone;

id zone;
var type address bedr bath sqfeet age price;

format sqfeet comma6. price dollar10. zone
        $zonefmt15.;

label zone='Zone'
      type='House/Style'
      address='Address'
      bedr='Bedrooms'
      bath='Bathrooms'
      sqfeet='Square/Feet'
      age='Age'
      price='Listing/Price';
run;
```

Specify on the ID and VAR statements the variables to include in the report and their order of appearance. Suppress the default observation number column and replace it with the values of the variable named on the ID statement. To list the ID variable only once for each BY group and suppress the usual headings above each BY group, specify the same variable on both the BY statement and ID statement.

If you want to send the report to the LISTING destination, you can achieve the look of underlining in the headings. Revise the LABEL statement as follows to include the split character followed by dashes.

```
label zone='Zone/---------------'
      type='House/Style/--------'
      address='Address/-------------------------'
      bedr='Bedrooms/--------'
      bath='Bathrooms/---------'
      sqfeet='Square/Feet/------'
      age='Age/---'
      price='Listing/Price/----------';
```

The revised LABEL statement causes the headings to appear as if they are underlined, as shown below in the following partial listing of the report.

```
                   Listing of Local Residential Properties
                       Price Range $200,000 to $350,000
                               Listed by Zone

                  House                                      Square    Listing
     Zone         Style     Address          Bedrooms Bathrooms Feet  Age  Price
     ------------- --------  ------------------------ -------- --------- ------ --- ---------

North Ridge       bungalow  6008 Brass Lantern Ct.       3       2.5     2,416   6  $344,500
                  colonial  4000 Skipjack Ct.            3       2.5     2,750   0  $314,900
                  split     2414 Van Dyke                3       1.0     1,245  36  $285,000
                  split     500 E. Millbrook Rd.         3       1.5     1,329  23  $282,900
                  split     6324 Lakeland, Lake Park     3       2.0     1,662  12  $200,000
```

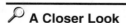 **A Closer Look**

Comparing PROC PRINT and PROC REPORT

The two reports in this example are similar. The processing of the two procedures REPORT and PRINT can differ. The differences are highlighted in Table 2.2.

Table 2.2 Comparing PROC PRINT and PROC REPORT

Feature	PROC PRINT	PROC REPORT
Ordering rows	Always orders variables by their internal values (in this case, it orders the numbers 1 to 8). You must sort the input data set and use a BY statement in the PROC PRINT step.	Gives you control over the order of the rows with the ORDER and the ORDER= options. Sorting is unnecessary. By default, PROC REPORT orders variables by their formatted values.
Printing repeated rows	Prints the value of every variable on every row of the report unless the variable is listed in both the BY and ID statements.	Does not repeat the value of an order or group variable from one row to the next if the value is the same.
Placing values and column headers	Automatically places values and column headers.	Right-aligns numeric values and their column headers and left-aligns character values and their column headers by default. You can control the alignment with options in the DEFINE statement.
Underlining column headers (applies only to the LISTING destination)	Requires hard-coding the underlining in the labels of the column headers.	Uses one option (HEADLINE) to underline all column headers.

Where to Go from Here

BY statement processing. See "BY Statement" in the "Statements" section of *SAS 9.1 Language Reference: Dictionary,* and "Statements with the Same Function in Multiple Procedures" in the "Concepts" section of *Base SAS 9.1 Procedures Guide.*

PROC PRINT reference, usage information, and additional examples. See "The PRINT Procedure" in the "Procedures" section of *Base SAS 9.1 Procedures Guide.*

PROC REPORT reference, usage information, and additional examples. See "The REPORT Procedure" in the "Procedures" section of *Base SAS 9.1 Procedures Guide.*

Example 2.3

Placing Data That Is Constant for a Category in Titles

Goal

Order a data set by categories and list the observations. Write information that is constant for a category in the page titles rather than in columns. Each row in the report presents information about one observation.

Report

```
Project FeederWatch Counts for Ten Observation Periods in Minnesota during 2002-2003
Counts for Site MN1001
Site Description: Medium (1,001-4,000 sq ft/101-375 sq m) in landscaped yard (with lawn and plantings)
Community: Rural with a population of 5,001 to 25,000
```

Species	Ever Seen	P1	P2	P3	P4	P5	P6	P7	P8	P9	P10
American crow	****	0	0	0	1	2	0	2	0	0	0
American goldfinch	****	2	2	3	6	9	7	6	8	7	6
American robin	****	1	20	1	0	0	0	1	0	0	3
American tree sparrow		0	0	0	0	0	0	0	0	0	0
Black-capped chickadee	****	3	2	2	2	1	1	2	2	1	2
Blue jay	****	2	2	1	4	2	2	1	4	3	2
Boreal chickadee		0	0	0	0	0	0	0	0	0	0
Brown creeper		0	0	0	0	0	0	0	0	0	0
Chipping sparrow .	****	0	0	0	0	0	0	0	0	1	0
Common grackle	****	0	0	0	0	0	0	0	0	0	5
Common redpoll		0	0	0	0	0	0	0	0	0	0
Cooper's hawk		0	0	0	0	0	0	0	0	0	0
Dark-eyed junco	****	1	9	1	2	3	2	5	2	20	4
Downy woodpecker	****	3	2	2	2	3	3	6	3	4	6
European starling	****	0	0	0	0	0	0	0	0	4	5
Fox sparrow		0	0	0	0	0	0	0	0	0	0
Hairy woodpecker	****	0	0	1	3	2	2	1	0	1	1
House finch	****	3	0	0	0	0	0	0	0	2	2
House sparrow	****	20	30	20	20	20	20	20	20	10	20
Loggerhead shrike		0	0	0	0	0	0	0	0	0	0
Mallard		0	0	0	0	0	0	0	0	0	0
Mourning dove	****	0	0	0	0	0	0	0	1	0	1
Northern cardinal	****	2	2	0	1	3	2	2	2	3	2
Norther flicker	****	0	0	0	0	0	0	0	2	0	0
Northern shrike		0	0	0	0	0	0	0	0	0	0
Pileated woodpecker	****	0	0	0	1	1	0	0	1	0	0
Pine siskin		0	0	0	0	0	0	0	0	0	0
Purple finch	****	1	0	0	0	0	0	0	0	0	0
Red-breasted nuthatch		0	0	0	0	0	0	0	0	0	0
Reb-bellied woodpecker	****	0	1	1	1	1	1	1	1	1	1
Red-winged blackbird		0	0	0	0	0	0	0	0	0	0
Rock dove		0	0	0	0	0	0	0	0	0	0
Sharp-shinned hawk		0	0	0	0	0	0	0	0	0	0
Song sparrow	****	0	0	0	0	0	0	1	0	0	0
Tufted titmouse		0	0	0	0	0	0	0	0	0	0
White-breasted nuthatch	****	2	1	1	1	1	1	2	1	2	1
White-throated sparrow		0	0	0	0	0	0	0	0	0	0

```
Key to Ten Observation Periods:
  1: 09nov2002-22nov2002    2: 23nov2002-06dec2002    3: 07dec2002-20dec2002    4: 21dec2002-03jan2003
  5: 04jan2003-17jan2003    6: 18jan2003-31jan2003    7: 01feb2003-14feb2003    8: 15feb2003-28feb2003
  9: 01mar2003-14mar2003   10: 15mar2003-28mar2003
```

```
Project FeederWatch Counts for Ten Observation Periods in Minnesota during 2002-2003
Counts for Site MN1002
Site Description: Medium (1,001-4,000 sq ft/101-375 sq m) in landscaped yard (with lawn and plantings)
Community: Rural with a population of 1 to 5,000

                        Ever
Species                 Seen   P1   P2   P3   P4   P5   P6   P7   P8   P9   P10

American crow           ****    0    0    0    0    0    0    0    2    2    1
American goldfinch      ****    1    0    0    2    7    0    1    7    7    0
American robin          ****    0    0    0    0    0    0    0    1    0    0
American tree sparrow           0    0    0    0    0    0    0    0    0    0
Black-capped chickadee  ****    3    3    4    4    5    5    4    4    6    4
Blue jay                ****    2    2    2    1    2    2    0    4    2    1
Boreal chickadee                0    0    0    0    0    0    0    0    0    0
Brown creeper           ****    1    3    2    2    1    3    1    2    2    1
Chipping sparrow                0    0    0    0    0    0    0    0    0    0
Common grackle          ****    2    1    2    1    0    0    0    0    0    0
Common redpoll                  0    0    0    0    0    0    0    0    0    0
Cooper's hawk           ****    0    0    1    0    0    0    0    0    0    0
Dark-eyed junco         ****   30    6    1   12    6    6    0    4    8    0
Downy woodpecker        ****    1    2    2    2    1    1    1    2    2    2
European starling       ****    0    0    0    0    4    1    0    1    0    3
Fox sparrow                     0    0    0    0    0    0    0    0    0    0
Hairy woodpecker        ****    0    0    0    1    1    0    0    1    1    1
House finch             ****    1    8    0    6    6    8    0    8    8    2
House sparrow           ****   40   50   50   50   50   50   50   25   30   20
Loggerhead shrike               0    0    0    0    0    0    0    0    0    0
Mallard                         0    0    0    0    0    0    0    0    0    0
Mourning dove           ****    0    0    0    0    0    0    0    2    2    2
Northern cardinal       ****    2    1    1    1    2    2    1    2    2    1
Norther flicker         ****    1    1    0    1    1    1    0    1    0    2
Northern shrike                 0    0    0    0    0    0    0    0    0    0
Pileated woodpecker             0    0    0    0    0    0    0    0    0    0
Pine siskin             ****    1    0    0    0    0    0    0    0    0    0
Purple finch                    0    0    0    0    0    0    0    0    0    0
Red-breasted nuthatch   ****    0    0    1    0    0    0    0    0    0    0
Reb-bellied woodpecker  ****    1    1    1    1    1    0    1    1    1    2
Red-winged blackbird    ****    0    0    0    0    0    0    0    0    0    1
Rock dove                       0    0    0    0    0    0    0    0    0    0
Sharp-shinned hawk      ****    1    1    0    1    0    0    0    1    1    0
Song sparrow                    0    0    0    0    0    0    0    0    0    0
Tufted titmouse                 0    0    0    0    0    0    0    0    0    0
White-breasted nuthatch ****    3    3    3    2    2    3    2    3    3    2
White-throated sparrow  ****   24    0    0    0    0    0    0    0    0    0

Key to Ten Observation Periods:
 1: 09nov2002-22nov2002   2: 23nov2002-06dec2002   3: 07dec2002-20dec2002   4: 21dec2002-03jan2003
 5: 04jan2003-17jan2003   6: 18jan2003-31jan2003   7: 01feb2003-14feb2003   8: 15feb2003-28feb2003
 9: 01mar2003-14mar2003  10: 15mar2003-28mar2003
```

Example Features

Data Set	FEEDERBIRDS
Featured Step	PROC PRINT
Featured Step Statements and Options	PROC PRINT statement: LABEL option BY statement
Formatting Features	OPTIONS statement: BYLINE/NOBYLINE, MISSING, and CENTER options TITLE statement with #BYVAL
🔍 A Closer Look	Working with #BYVAL, #BYVAR, and #BYLINE when Customizing Titles

Example Overview

When you want to list the observations in a data set by categories, and the values of several of the variables for a category are constant, you can place the constant information in the titles. By doing so, you make more room on the report page for information that varies within a category.

This example lists observations from the FEEDERBIRDS data set. This data set is a random sample of observations taken from a Cornell Laboratory of Ornithology data set that manages the records in the Project FeederWatch Citizen Science program. The sample contains records of the bird species seen and numbers counted at bird feeders during the 2002-2003 winter season in Minnesota.

Each observation in the data set corresponds to the maximum number of birds of one species seen at one time during ten observation periods. The data set is ordered by site ID. Several characteristics of the site are stored in the data set. These descriptions are constant for each site and their values are printed in the titles of the report. The program uses the #BYVAL feature of the TITLE statement in conjunction with the SAS system option NOBYLINE to place the site characteristics in the titles. The NOBYLINE option suppresses the BY line that normally appears in output produced with BY-group processing,

PROC PRINT lists the observations in the FEEDERBIRDS data set. If you use the BY statement and the NOBYLINE option, PROC PRINT always starts a new page for each BY group. This behavior ensures that if you create customized BY lines by putting BY-group information in a title and you suppress the default BY lines with NOBYLINE, the information in the titles matches the report on the pages.

The report that follows lists the counts for two of the ten sites in the sample data set.

Program

Suppress the automatic printing of BY lines in subsequent procedure output because the #BYVAL feature will be used to list BY-group data.

Left-align SAS procedure output.

Assign '0' as the character to print for missing numeric values.

```
options nobyline

          nocenter

          missing='0';
proc format;
   value size
      1='Very small -- a window or hanging feeder only'
      2='Small (< 1,000 sq ft/100 sq m)'
      3='Medium (1,001-4,000 sq ft/101-375 sq m)'
      4='Large (> 4,000 sq ft/375 sq m)';
   value desc
      1='no vegetation (pavement only)'
      2='garden or courtyard'
      3='mix of natural and landscaped vegetation'
      4='landscaped yard (with lawn and plantings)'
      5='natural vegetation (woods, fields)'
      6='desert: natural or landscaped'
      7='other type';
   value pop  1='1 to 5,000'
              2='5,001 to 25,000'
              3='25,001 to 100,000'
```

```
                                  4='More than 100,000';
                   value dens 1='Rural'
                              2='Rural/suburban mix'
                              3='Suburban'
                              4='Urban';
                   value $species 'amecro'='American crow'
                                  'amegfi'='American goldfinch'
                                  'amerob'='American robin'
                                  'amtspa'='American tree sparrow'
                                  'bkcchi'='Black-capped chickadee'
                                  'blujay'='Blue jay'
                                  'borchi'='Boreal chickadee'
                                  'brncre'='Brown creeper'
                                  'chispa'='Chipping sparrow'
                                  'comgra'='Common grackle'
                                  'comred'='Common redpoll'
                                  'coohaw'='Cooper''s hawk'
                                  'daejun'='Dark-eyed junco'
                                  'dowwoo'='Downy woodpecker'
                                  'eursta'='European starling'
                                  'foxspa'='Fox sparrow'
                                  'haiwoo'='Hairy woodpecker'
                                  'houfin'='House finch'
                                  'houspa'='House sparrow'
                                  'logshr'='Loggerhead shrike'
                                  'mallar'='Mallard'
                                  'moudov'='Mourning dove'
                                  'norcar'='Northern cardinal'
                                  'norfli'='Norther flicker'
                                  'norshr'='Northern shrike'
                                  'pilwoo'='Pileated woodpecker'
                                  'pinsis'='Pine siskin'
                                  'purfin'='Purple finch'
                                  'rebnut'='Red-breasted nuthatch'
                                  'rebwoo'='Reb-bellied woodpecker'
                                  'rewbla'='Red-winged blackbird'
                                  'rocdov'='Rock dove'
                                  'shshaw'='Sharp-shinned hawk'
                                  'sonspa'='Song sparrow'
                                  'tuftit'='Tufted titmouse'
                                  'whbnut'='White-breasted nuthatch'
                                  'whtspa'='White-throated sparrow';
                   value everseen 0=' '
                                  1='****';
                run;
```

Arrange the observations by site ID.
```
proc sort data=feederbirds;
  by id;
run;
```

Use the labels of the report variables in the PROC PRINT report as column headings.
```
proc print data=feederbirds label;
```

List the observations in order by site ID.
```
  by id
```

Include in the BY statement the variables with values that are constant for each site ID. The values of these variables will be inserted in the titles. Since the site characteristic variables are constant for each site, it is not necessary to sort the data set by these variables. Indicate that these variables have not been sorted by preceding each variable with the NOTSORTED keyword.
```
     notsorted countsitesize
     notsorted countsitedesc
     notsorted density
     notsorted pop;
```

(handwritten note: by Nobyline => New page for each By group)

Identify observations by the values of the variable on the ID statement rather than the observation numbers.

```
id species;


title "Project FeederWatch Counts for Ten Observation
       Periods in Minnesota during 2002-2003";
```

Substitute the current values of the BY variables in the next three TITLE statements where enclosed by #BYVAL and parentheses.

```
title2 "Counts for Site #byval(id)";
title3 "Site Description: #byval(countsitesize) in
        #byval(countsitedesc)";
title4 "Community: #byval(density) with a population
        of #byval(pop)";
footnote1 "Key to Ten Observation Periods:";
footnote2 ' 1: 09nov2002-22nov2002  '
          '2: 23nov2002-06dec2002  '
          '3: 07dec2002-20dec2002 '
          '4: 21dec2002-03jan2003';
footnote3 ' 5: 04jan2003-17jan2003 '
          '6: 18jan2003-31jan2003  '
          '7: 01feb2003-14feb2003 '
          '8: 15feb2003-28feb2003';
footnote4 ' 9: 01mar2003-14mar2003 '
          '10: 15mar2003-28mar2003';
```

List the variables whose values vary within each site.

```
var everseen p1-p10;
format countsitesize size. countsitedesc desc.
       density dens. pop pop.
       species $species. everseen everseen.;
label species='Species'
      p1='P1'
      p2='P2'
      p3='P3'
      p4='P4'
      p5='P5'
      p6='P6'
      p7='P7'
      p8='P8'
      p9='P9'
      p10='P10'
      everseen='Ever Seen';

run;
```

Reset options to their default settings.

```
options byline center missing='.';
```

🔍 A Closer Look

Working with #BYVAL, #BYVAR, and #BYLINE when Customizing Titles

When your PROC steps include a BY statement, you can customize your titles by taking advantage of the #BYVAL, #BYVAR, and #BYLINE features. These three features insert text at the position you place them in your TITLE statements.

The BYLINE/NOBYLINE SAS option controls the automatic printing of BY lines. Submit

```
options nobyline;
```

to turn off the BYLINE option before using the #BYVAL, #BYVAR, or #BYLINE features. As with other SAS options, NOBYLINE remains in effect until you reset it with

```
options byline;
```

Table 2.3 describes the #BYVAL, #BYVAR, and #BYLINE features.

Table 2.3 #BYVAL, #BYVAR, and #BYLINE features

Feature	Specification	Action
#BYVAL	#BYVAL*n*	Replaces #BYVAL in the text string with the current value of the *nth* BY variable in the BY statement.
	#BYVAL(*variable-name*)	Replaces #BYVAL in the text string with the current value of the BY variable whose name is enclosed in parentheses.
#BYVAR	#BYVAR*n*	Replaces #BYVAR in the text string with the name or label of the *nth* BY variable in the BY statement. Use the variable name only if the variable does not have a label.
	#BYVAR(*variable-name*)	Replaces #BYVAR in the text string with the name or label of the BY variable whose name is enclosed in parentheses in the BY statement. Use the variable name only if the variable does not have a label.
#BYLINE		Replaces #BYLINE in the text string with the entire BY line.

When writing TITLE statements, terminate either of the two types of #BYVAL specifications and the two types of #BYVAR specifications with a delimiting character, such as a space or other nonalphanumeric character.

If you want the #BYVAL or #BYVAR substitution to be followed immediately by other text and not the delimiter, terminate the #BYVAL or #BYVAR specification with a trailing dot, just as you would with macro variables.

Where to Go from Here

BY statement processing. See "BY Statement" in the "Statements" section of *SAS 9.1 Language Reference: Dictionary,* and "Statements with the Same Function in Multiple Procedures" in the "Concepts" section of *Base SAS 9.1 Procedures Guide.*

The BYLINE/NOBYLINE SAS system options. See "SAS System Options" in *SAS 9.1 Language Reference: Dictionary.*

Inserting BY-group information in titles. See "Creating Titles that Contain BY-Group Information" in the "Fundamental Concepts for Using Base SAS Procedures" section of *Base SAS 9.1 Procedures Guide.*

PROC PRINT reference, usage information, and additional examples. See "The PRINT Procedure" in the "Procedures" section of *Base SAS 9.1 Procedures Guide.*

Example 2.4   Summarizing the Rows of a Report

Goal

List observations in a data set and summarize selected numeric variables by groups. Present an overall summarization of the selected numeric variables at the end of the report.

Report

```
                              Regional Energy
                Quarterly Use by Residential and Commercial Customers

                         -------First Quarter--------   -------Second Quarter-------
             Service     January  February    March      April      May      June
Commercial   Area Lights    6,526   11,999    17,533    10,221    17,218     8,857
             Flood Lights  10,911   12,648    15,502     9,120     8,624    18,338
             General Service 1,203     641       728     1,039     1,156       782
             Off Peak      15,062   15,635     9,509    11,717    11,456    12,461
             Other Service  1,390    1,672     1,638     1,282     1,654     1,915
             Space Heating    111       85       121       109       125       103
             Water Heating    160      168       130       187       101       101
============                 ========  ========  ========  ========  ========  ========
Commercial                  35,363   42,848    45,161    33,675    40,334    42,557
============                 ========  ========  ========  ========  ========  ========

Residential  Area Lights      118      116        91        92        95       137
             Flood Lights      96       89        75        87        75        82
             General Service 22,281   21,505    22,556    22,784    25,977    25,371
             Off Peak       1,152    1,362       698     1,047       534     1,492
             Other Service    286      238       109        33       158       465
             Space Heating  8,280   10,984    10,111    13,234    13,723    11,072
             Water Heating  9,589   10,625    14,160    18,130     8,592     7,654
============                 ========  ========  ========  ========  ========  ========
Residential                 41,802   44,919    47,800    55,407    49,154    46,273
============                 ========  ========  ========  ========  ========  ========

                            ========  ========  ========  ========  ========  ========
                            77,165   87,767    92,961    89,082    89,488    88,830
                            ========  ========  ========  ========  ========  ========
```

Example Features

Data Set	POWERUSE
Featured Step	PROC REPORT
Featured Step Statements and Options	DEFINE statement: ANALYSIS, ORDER, and SUM options BREAK AFTER statement: SUMMARIZE option RBREAK AFTER statement: SUMMARIZE option
Formatting Features	Placing a heading over the headings of several variables (spanned header) Padding column headings with a character when sending output to the LISTING destination DEFINE statement: WIDTH option when sending output to the LISTING destination. Controlling line breaks in column headings BREAK and RBREAK statements: DOL, DUL, and SKIP options when sending output to the LISTING destination
Related Technique	PROC SORT and PROC PRINT

Related Technique Features	PROC PRINT statements: ID and SUM
ODS Enhanced Version of Related Technique	Example 6.10
Other Examples That Use This Data Set	Examples 2.5, 2.6, and 6.10

Example Overview

Some detail reports contain a lot of numbers. Summing these numbers for selected rows can make a report more meaningful without removing any of the detail.

This report lists the energy usage for several types of service over a six-month period. In addition to listing the detail usage by type of service, the report totals energy usage by residential customers, by commercial customers, and overall.

Each detail row in the report—those with a value for SERVICE—corresponds to one observation in the POWERUSE data set. The other rows, which are summaries of the detail rows, were created by the PROC REPORT statements BREAK and RBREAK.

Each column in the report corresponds to one variable in the POWERUSE data set.

Program

Create formats for TYPE and SERVICE.

```
proc format;
     value $type    'res'='Residential'
                    'com'='Commercial';
     value $service 'gen'='General Service'
                    'wtr'='Water Heating'
                    'op' ='Off Peak'
                    'spc'='Space Heating'
                    'fld'='Flood Lights'
                    'area'='Area Lights'
                    'oth'='Other Service';
run;

title 'Regional Energy';
title2 'Quarterly Use by Residential and Commercial
        Customers';

proc report data=poweruse nowindows;
```

List the columns in the order in which they should appear in the report.

```
   column type service
```

Place a column heading—a spanned header—above a group of variables. Enclose within parentheses the quoted column heading followed by the list of variables above which the text should be placed. If sending the report to the LISTING destination, pad the header to the left and to the right of the header text with dashes (Remove the pad character when sending output to a nonlisting destination.)

```
          ('-First Quarter-' jan feb mar)
          ('-Second Quarter-' apr may jun);
```

Order the detail rows according to the ascending, formatted values of the order variables. Establish the order of the detail rows by sorting the order variables from left to right according to their position in the COLUMN statement.

```
define type    / order format=$type. width=11 ' ';
define service / order format=$service. width=15
                 'Service';
```

Enhance the report. For each column variable: assign a format; specify a column width (LISTING destination only); and specify a column heading. Suppress the column heading for TYPE by writing the label as a blank.

Calculate the SUM statistic for each of the analysis variables.

```
define jan    / analysis sum 'January' width=8
                format=comma6.;
define feb    / analysis sum 'February' width=8
                format=comma6.;
define mar    / analysis sum 'March' width=8
                format=comma6.;
define apr    / analysis sum 'April' width=8
                format=comma6.;
define may    / analysis sum 'May' width=8
                format=comma6.;
define jun    / analysis sum 'June' width=8
                format=comma6.;
```

Write a summary line after the last row for each value of TYPE. Sum the analysis variables over all observations with the same value of TYPE. When sending output to the LISTING destination, place a double overline and a double underline above and below the summary row, and skip a line after the double underline.

```
break after type / summarize dol dul skip;
```

Write a summary line at the end of the report. Sum the analysis variables over all observations. When sending output to the LISTING destination, place a double overline and a double underline above and below the summary row, and skip a line after the double underline.

```
break after / summarize dol dul skip;
run;
```

Related Technique

The report in Figure 2.4 is produced by PROC PRINT and looks similar to the one produced by PROC REPORT. Before PROC PRINT executes, however, you must first sort the data set.

Figure 2.4 Output Produced by PROC PRINT

```
                              Regional Energy
                  Quarterly Use by Residential and Commercial Customers

               Service        January   February   March    April      May      June

Commercial     Area Lights     6,526    11,999    17,533   10,221    17,218    8,857
               Flood Lights   10,911    12,648    15,502    9,120     8,624   18,338
               General Service 1,203       641       728    1,039     1,156      782
               Off Peak       15,062    15,635     9,509   11,717    11,456   12,461
               Other Service   1,390     1,672     1,638    1,282     1,654    1,915
               Space Heating     111        85       121      109      125      103
               Water Heating     160       168       130      187      101      101
-----------                   -------   --------   ------   ------   ------   ------
Commercial                     35,363    42,848    45,161   33,675    40,334   42,557

Residential    Area Lights      118       116        91       92       95      137
               Flood Lights      96        89        75       87       75       82
               General Service 22,281    21,505    22,556   22,784    25,977   25,371
               Off Peak        1,152     1,362       698    1,047      534    1,492
               Other Service     286       238       109       33      158      465
               Space Heating   8,280    10,984    10,111   13,234    13,723   11,072
               Water Heating   9,589    10,625    14,160   18,130     8,592    7,654
-----------                   -------   --------   ------   ------   ------   ------
Residential                    41,802    44,919    47,800   55,407    49,154   46,273
                              =======   ========   ======   ======   ======   ======
                               77,165    87,767    92,961   89,082    89,488   88,830
```

The program that produced the report in Figure 2.4 follows.

```
proc format;
  value $type    'res'='Residential'
                 'com'='Commercial';
  value $service 'gen'='General Service'
                 'wtr'='Water Heating'
                 'op' ='Off Peak'
                 'spc'='Space Heating'
                 'fld'='Flood Lights'
                 'area'='Area Lights'
                 'oth'='Other Service';
run;
```

Sort the data set in the order you want the rows to appear in the PROC PRINT report.

```
proc sort data=poweruse out=sorted;
  by type service;
run;

title 'Regional Energy';
title2 'Quarterly Use by Residential and Commercial
         Customers';
```

Use variable labels as column headings.

```
proc print data=sorted label;
```

Specify the variables in the report and their order from left to right with the ID and VAR statements. Specify the same variable on both the ID and BY statements so that PROC PRINT lists the ID variable only once for each BY group, suppresses the usual BY-group headings, and identifies subtotals by the value of the BY variable rather than by variable name.

```
  id type;
  by type;
  var service jan feb mar apr may jun;
```

Sum the values of the numeric variables for each BY group and overall.

Enhance the report. Assign labels and formats to each variable. Assign hexadecimal zero as the label text for type so that the column heading prints as a blank.

```
   sum jan feb mar apr may jun;

label type='00'x
      service='Service'
      jan='January'
      feb='February'
      mar='March'
      apr='April'
      may='May'
      jun='June';
format type $type. service $service.
       jan--jun comma6.;
run;
```

Where to Go from Here

BY statement processing. See "BY Statement" in the "Statements" section of *SAS 9.1 Language Reference: Dictionary,* and "Statements with the Same Function in Multiple Procedures" in the "Concepts" section of *Base SAS 9.1 Procedures Guide.*

PROC PRINT reference, usage information, and additional examples. See "The PRINT Procedure" in the "Procedures" section of *Base SAS 9.1 Procedures Guide.*

PROC REPORT reference and usage information. For complete syntax and additional examples for PROC REPORT, see "The REPORT Procedure" in the "Procedures" section of *Base SAS 9.1 Procedures Guide.*

Example 2.5   Summarizing Columns and Rows

Goal

List observations in a data set, one observation per row, and summarize selected numeric variables. Summarize over all observations and summarize observations within groups. Summarize specific variables within an observation and add these summaries as columns in the report.

Report

```
                                     Regional Energy
                      Quarterly Use by Residential and Commercial Customers

                      ------------First Quarter------------   ------------Second Quarter------------
                                          Quarter                                 Quarter
            Service    January  February   March    Total    April     May      June     Total    Total
Commercial  Area Lights  6,526   11,999   17,533   36,058   10,221   17,218    8,857   36,296   72,354
            Flood Lights 10,911  12,648   15,502   39,061    9,120    8,624   18,338   36,082   75,143
            General Service 1,203   641      728    2,572    1,039    1,156      782    2,977    5,549
            Off Peak    15,062   15,635    9,509   40,206   11,717   11,456   12,461   35,634   75,840
            Other Service 1,390   1,672    1,638    4,700    1,282    1,654    1,915    4,851    9,551
            Space Heating  111      85      121      317      109      125      103      337      654
            Water Heating  160     168      130      458      187      101      101      389      847
            ===========  ========  ========  ========  ========  ========  ========  ========  ========  ========
Commercial              35,363   42,848   45,161  123,372   33,675   40,334   42,557  116,566  239,938
===========             ========  ========  ========  ========  ========  ========  ========  ========  ========

Residential Area Lights   118      116       91      325       92       95      137      324      649
            Flood Lights   96       89       75      260       87       75       82      244      504
            General Service 22,281  21,505   22,556   66,342   22,784   25,977   25,371   74,132  140,474
            Off Peak     1,152    1,362      698    3,212    1,047      534    1,492    3,073    6,285
            Other Service  286      238      109      633       33      158      465      656    1,289
            Space Heating 8,280   10,984   10,111   29,375   13,234   13,723   11,072   38,029   67,404
            Water Heating 9,589   10,625   14,160   34,374   18,130    8,592    7,654   34,376   68,750
            ===========  ========  ========  ========  ========  ========  ========  ========  ========  ========
Residential             41,802   44,919   47,800  134,521   55,407   49,154   46,273  150,834  285,355
===========             ========  ========  ========  ========  ========  ========  ========  ========  ========

                        ========  ========  ========  ========  ========  ========  ========  ========  ========
                        77,165   87,767   92,961  257,893   89,082   89,488   88,830  267,400  525,293
                        ========  ========  ========  ========  ========  ========  ========  ========  ========
```

Example Features

Data Set	POWERUSE
Featured Step	PROC REPORT
Featured Step Statements and Options	DEFINE statement: ANALYSIS, COMPUTED, ORDER, and SUM options COMPUTE blocks to create new variables BREAK AFTER statement: SUMMARIZE option RBREAK AFTER statement: SUMMARIZE option
Formatting Features	Placing a heading over the headings of several variables Padding column headings with a character when sending output to the LISTING destination DEFINE statement: WIDTH option when sending output to the LISTING destination. Controlling line breaks in column headings BREAK and RBREAK statements: DOL, DUL, and SKIP options when sending output to the LISTING destination

🔍 **A Closer Look**	Writing COMPUTE Blocks
	Referencing Report Items in COMPUTE Blocks
	Processing Missing Values in COMPUTE Blocks
	Understanding How PROC REPORT Processes COMPUTE Blocks
Other Examples That Use This Data Set	Examples 2.4, 2.6, and 6.10

Example Overview

Example 2.4 presents monthly power usage by type of service for commercial and residential customers from January to June. This report includes the same information as Example 2.4 plus three new columns: two that summarize power usage for each of the two quarters represented in the report and one that summarizes power usage over the six-month reporting period. To produce these new summary columns, the program creates temporary report variables during execution of the report step.

Each detail row in the report—those with a value for SERVICE—corresponds to one observation in the POWERUSE data set. The other rows, which are summaries of the detail rows, were created by the PROC REPORT statements BREAK and RBREAK.

All the report columns except for the quarterly totals and overall total correspond to one variable in the POWERUSE data set. PROC REPORT defines the columns containing the totals. Statements in COMPUTE blocks in PROC REPORT calculate the totals by summing variables in the POWERUSE data set.

Program

Create formats for TYPE and SERVICE.

```
proc format;
   value $type     'res'='Residential'
                   'com'='Commercial';
   value $service  'gen'='General Service'
                   'wtr'='Water Heating'
                   'op' ='Off Peak'
                   'spc'='Space Heating'
                   'fld'='Flood Lights'
                   'area'='Area Lights'
                   'oth'='Other Service';
run;

options ls=120 ps=45;

title 'Regional Energy';
title2 'Quarterly Use by Residential and Commercial
        Customers';

proc report data=poweruse nowindows
```

Specify the split character to control line breaks in column headings.

```
   split='/';
```

List the columns in the order in which they should appear in the report. Include the computed variable in the

```
column type service
```

list. Ensure that the columns used to calculate a computed variable precede the computed variable.

Place a column heading above a group of variables. Enclose within parentheses the quoted column heading and the list of variables that the heading text should be placed above. If sending the output to the LISTING destination, pad the heading to the left and to the right of the text with dashes. (Remove the pad character when sending output to a nonlisting destination.)

```
('-First Quarter-' jan feb mar quarter1)
('-Second Quarter-' apr may jun quarter2)
total;
```

Order the detail rows according to the ascending, formatted values of the order variables. Establish the order of the detail rows by sorting the order variables from left to right as specified by their position in the COLUMN statement.

```
define type    / order format=$type. width=11 ' ';
define service / order format=$service. width=15
                 'Service';
```

Enhance the report. For each column variable: assign a format; specify a column width (LISTING destination only); and specify a column header. Enclose a blank within single quotation marks to suppress a column header.

Calculate the SUM statistic for each of the analysis variables.

```
define jan     / analysis sum 'January' width=8
                 format=comma8.;
define feb     / analysis sum 'February' width=8
                 format=comma8.;
define mar     / analysis sum 'March' width=8
                 format=comma8.;
define apr     / analysis sum 'April' width=8
                 format=comma8.;
define may     / analysis sum 'May' width=8
                 format=comma8.;
define jun     / analysis sum 'June' width=8
                 format=comma8.;
```

Identify the computed columns. Split the column headers for QUARTER1 and QUARTER2 over two lines.

```
define quarter1 / computed 'Quarter/Total' width=8
                  format=comma8.;
define quarter2 / computed 'Quarter/Total' width=8
                  format=comma8.;
define total    / computed 'Total' width=8
                  format=comma8.;
```

Calculate the values of each computed variable. Define a COMPUTE block for each variable.

```
compute quarter1;
```

Sum specific analysis variables. Represent the analysis variables with a compound name. Use the SUM function so that the computed variable is equal to the sum of the nonmissing arguments; this prevents generation of missing values when at least one of the arguments is nonmissing.

```
   quarter1=sum(jan.sum,feb.sum,mar.sum);
endcomp;
compute quarter2;
   quarter2=sum(apr.sum,may.sum,jun.sum);
endcomp;

compute total;
```

Compute the value of the new report variable by summing the values of two computed variables. Do not specify the arguments to the SUM function with

```
   total=sum(quarter1,quarter2);
endcomp;
```

compound names since they are not
analysis variables.

**Summarize the analysis variables and
computed variables over all
observations with the same value of
TYPE.** Write the summaries on the line
after the last row for each value of TYPE.
When sending output to the LISTING
destination, place a double overline and a
double underline above and below the
summary row, and skip a line after the
double underline.

```
break after type / summarize dol dul skip;
```

**Sum the analysis variables and
computed variables over all
observations.** Write the summary at the
end of the report. When sending output to
the LISTING destination, place a double
overline and a double underline above and
below the summary row, and skip a line
after the double underline.

```
  rbreak after / summarize dol dul skip;
run;
```

🔍 A Closer Look

Writing COMPUTE Blocks

A COMPUTE block is a section of code that contains one or more SAS
language programming statements. In the nonwindowing PROC REPORT
environment, the COMPUTE and ENDCOMP statements enclose the code. In
the windowing PROC REPORT environment, you enter the programming
statements into the COMPUTE window.

A COMPUTE block can reference either a report item or a location. Report
items include data set variables, statistics, and computed variables. The locations
that a COMPUTE block can reference are the top of a report; the bottom of a
report; before a group of observations; and after a group of observations. The
second usage is usually associated with break lines and enables you to customize
break lines.

You can have more than one COMPUTE block per PROC REPORT step, as
shown in the previous example, but you cannot nest the COMPUTE blocks.

COMPUTE blocks can incorporate most features of the SAS language,
including the following items.

❑ DM statement

❑ %INCLUDE statement

❑ DATA step statements:

ARRAY	IF-THEN/ELSE
Assignment	LENGTH
CALL	RETURN
DO (all forms)	SELECT
END	Sum

- comments
- null statements
- macro variables and macro invocations
- all DATA step functions.

Referencing Report Items in COMPUTE Blocks
The way you reference a report item in a COMPUTE block depends on how you've defined its usage. You can reference a report item in four ways:

- by name
- by a compound name that identifies both the variable and the name of the statistic that you calculate with it. A compound name has this form

```
variable-name.statistic
```

- by an alias that you create in the COLUMN statement or in the DEFINITION window
- by column number, in the form

```
'_Cn_'
```

where *n* is the number of the column (from left to right) in the report

When you reference columns by number, remember to include in your count the columns that you define with NOPRINT and NOZERO, even though these columns do not appear in your report.

Table 2.5a shows how to use each type of reference in a COMPUTE block.

Table 2.5a Referencing Variables in COMPUTE Blocks

If the variable that you reference is this type...	Then refer to it by...	For example...
Group	Name*	department
Order	Name*	department
Computed	Name*	department
Display	Name*	department
Display sharing a column with a statistic	A compound name*	sales.sum
Analysis	A compound name*	sales.mean
Any type sharing a column with an across variable	Column number**	'_c3_'

*If the variable has an alias, then you must reference it with the alias.

**Even if the variable has an alias, you must reference it by column number.

Processing Missing Values in COMPUTE Blocks

As in DATA step programming, when you reference in a COMPUTE block a variable that has a missing value, the result is a missing value. PROC REPORT displays the current missing value designation, which by default is a blank for character variables and a period for numeric variables. Where appropriate, consider using functions in COMPUTE blocks to prevent the generation of missing values when at least one of the arguments is nonmissing. The program above uses the SUM function for this reason.

Understanding How PROC REPORT Processes COMPUTE Blocks

You can associate a COMPUTE block with a *report item* or with a *location*. The way PROC REPORT processes a COMPUTE block depends on its usage.

When a COMPUTE block is associated with a report item, PROC REPORT executes the COMPUTE block on every row of the report when it comes to the column for that report item. The value of a computed variable in any row of a report is the last value assigned to that variable during that execution of the programming statements in the COMPUTE block. PROC REPORT assigns values to the columns in a row of a report from left to right. Consequently, you cannot base the calculation of a computed variable on any variable that appears to its right in the report.

When a COMPUTE block is associated with a location, PROC REPORT executes the COMPUTE block only at that location. Because PROC REPORT calculates statistics for groups before it actually constructs the rows of the report, statistics for sets of detail rows are available before or after the rows are displayed, as are values for any variables based on these statistics.

Table 2.5b describes the processing of both types of COMPUTE blocks in a PROC REPORT step.

Table 2.5b How PROC REPORT Processes COMPUTE Blocks

When a COMPUTE block is associated with a …	PROC REPORT executes the COMPUTE block…	Example
Report item	On every row of the report when it comes to the column for that report item	```proc report data=poweruse nowindows;
   title 'Regional Energy';
   title2
'Quarterly Use by Residential and Commercial
Customers';
   column type service
      '-First Quarter-' jan feb mar quarter1);

   define type / order format=$type. width=11 ' ';
   define service / order format=$service.
                       width=15 'Service';

   define jan / analysis sum 'January' width=8
                  format=comma8.;
   define feb / analysis sum 'February'
                  width=8 format=comma8.;
   define mar/ analysis sum 'March' width=8
                  format=comma8.;
   define quarter1 / computed 'Quarter/Total'
                     width=8 format=comma8.;
   compute quarter1;
     quarter1=sum(jan.sum,feb.sum,mar.sum);
   endcomp;
``` |
| Location | Only at that location | ```compute after type;
     line '****** Total for the quarter is '
          quarter1 comma8.;
     line ' ';
   endcomp;
run;
``` |

Where to Go from Here

PROC REPORT reference, usage information, and additional examples. See, "The REPORT Procedure" in the "Procedures" section of *Base SAS 9.1 Procedures Guide.*

Example 2.6   Suppressing the Display of Specific Columns

Goal

List observations in a data set and summarize selected numeric variables. Summarize over all observations and summarize within groups. Summarize specific variables within an observation and add these summaries as columns in the report. Display the summary columns. Do not display the variables used to calculate the summaries.

Report

```
                                Regional Energy
                 Quarterly Use by Residential and Commercial Customers

                                    First      Second
                                   Quarter     Quarter
                    Service         Total       Total      Total
        Commercial  Area Lights    36,058      36,296     72,354
                    Flood Lights   39,061      36,082     75,143
                    General Service 2,572       2,977      5,549
                    Off Peak       40,206      35,634     75,840
                    Other Service   4,700       4,851      9,551
                    Space Heating     317         337        654
                    Water Heating     458         389        847
        ===========                ========    ========   ========
        Commercial                 123,372     116,566    239,938
        ===========                ========    ========   ========

        Residential Area Lights       325         324        649
                    Flood Lights      260         244        504
                    General Service 66,342      74,132    140,474
                    Off Peak        3,212       3,073      6,285
                    Other Service     633         656      1,289
                    Space Heating  29,375      38,029     67,404
                    Water Heating  34,374      34,376     68,750
        ===========                ========    ========   ========
        Residential                134,521     150,834    285,355
        ===========                ========    ========   ========

                                   ========    ========   ========
                                   257,893     267,400    525,293
                                   ========    ========   ========
```

Example Features

Data Set	POWERUSE
Featured Step	PROC REPORT
Featured Step Statements and Options	DEFINE statement: ANALYSIS, COMPUTED, NOPRINT, ORDER, and SUM options
	COMPUTE blocks to create new variables
	BREAK AFTER statement: SUMMARIZE option
	RBREAK AFTER statement: SUMMARIZE option

Formatting Features	Controlling line breaks in column headings
	DEFINE statement: WIDTH option when sending output to the LISTING destination.
	BREAK and RBREAK statements: DOL, DUL, and SKIP options when sending output to the LISTING destination
Other Examples That Use This Data Set	Examples 2.4, 2.5, and 6.10

Example Overview

This report includes only the summary columns from Example 2.5. It presents energy usage by type of service for commercial and residential customers by quarter. This example sums columns and rows. It suppresses the display of the analysis variables used to compute the quarter totals, which were displayed in Example 2.5.

Each detail row in the report—those with a value for SERVICE—corresponds to one observation in the POWERUSE data set. The other rows, which are summaries of the detail rows, were created by the PROC REPORT statements, BREAK and RBREAK.

The columns for customer group and type of service each correspond to a variable in the POWERUSE data set. PROC REPORT defines the other three columns. It calculates their values with programming statements in COMPUTE blocks. The calculations sum the monthly usage variables in the POWERUSE data set.

Program

Create formats for TYPE and SERVICE.

```
proc format;
   value $type    'res'='Residential'
                  'com'='Commercial';
   value $service 'gen'='General Service'
                  'wtr'='Water Heating'
                  'op' ='Off Peak'
                  'spc'='Space Heating'
                  'fld'='Flood Lights'
                  'area'='Area Lights'
                  'oth'='Other Service';
run;
options ls=120 ps=45;

title 'Regional Energy';
title2 'Quarterly Use by Residential and Commercial
       Customers';

proc report data=poweruse nowindows
```

Specify the split character to control line breaks in column headings

```
   split='/';
```

List the columns in the order in which they should appear in the report. Include in the list the computed variables and the variables that will not be displayed. Ensure that the columns used to calculate the value of a computed variable precede the computed variable.

```
column type service
       jan feb mar apr may jun
       quarter1 quarter2 total;
```

Order the detail rows according to the ascending, formatted values of the order variables. Establish the order of the detail rows by sorting the order variables from left to right according to their position in the COLUMN statement. Specify the column width when sending output to the LISTING destination.

```
define type    / order format=$type. width=11 ' ';
define service / order format=$service. width=15
                 'Service';
```

Enhance the report. For each column variable that will be displayed: assign a format; specify a column width (when sending output to the LISTING destination); and specify a column heading. Suppress the column heading for TYPE by enclosing a blank within single quotation marks.

Do not display the next six variables in the report. Therefore, do not include options to format these columns. Calculate the SUM statistic for each of the six analysis variables.

```
define jan    / analysis sum noprint;
define feb    / analysis sum noprint;
define mar    / analysis sum noprint;
define apr    / analysis sum noprint;
define may    / analysis sum noprint;
define jun    / analysis sum noprint;
```

Define the computed columns. Split the column headings for QUARTER1 and QUARTER2 over three lines.

```
define quarter1 / computed 'First/Quarter/Total'
                  width=8
                  format=comma8.;
define quarter2 / computed 'Second/Quarter/Total'
                  width=8
                  format=comma8.;
define total    / computed 'Total' width=8
                  format=comma8.;
```

Calculate the values of each computed variable. Define a COMPUTE block for each variable.

```
compute quarter1;
```

Sum specific analysis variables. Represent the analysis variables with a compound name. Use the SUM function so that the computed variable is equal to the sum of the nonmissing arguments; this prevents generation of missing values when at least one of the arguments is nonmissing.

```
   quarter1=sum(jan.sum,feb.sum,mar.sum);
endcomp;

compute quarter2;
   quarter2=sum(apr.sum,may.sum,jun.sum);
endcomp;
```

Compute the value of a new report variable by summing the values of two computed variables. Do not specify the arguments to the SUM function with compound names, since they are not analysis variables.

```
compute total;
   total=sum(quarter1,quarter2);
endcomp;
```

Summarize the analysis variables and computed variables over all observations with the same value of TYPE. Write the summaries on the line after the last row for each value of TYPE. When sending output to the LISTING destination, place a double overline and a double underline above and below the summary row, and skip a line after the double underline.

```
break after type / summarize dol dul skip;
```

Sum the analysis variables and computed variables over all observations. Write the summary at the end of the report. When sending output to the LISTING destination, place a double overline and a double underline above and below the summary row, and skip a line after the double underline.

```
rbreak after / summarize dol dul skip;
run;
```

Where to Go from Here

PROC REPORT reference and usage information. See "The REPORT Procedure" in the "Procedures" section of *Base SAS 9.1 Procedures Guide.*

Example 2.7   Presenting Multiple Observations per Report Row

Goal

Present in one row data from more than one observation. Use the values of a grouping variable to select the observations to present in one row.

Analyze specific variables within a row and present the results in computed columns in the report. Some of the calculations will be derived from the multiple observations in the row.

Report

```
                                  Exercise Program Results

                                                     Chol/   Chol/
                          Study  Pre Program  Post Program   HDL     HDL    Chol/HDL
        Gender              ID   Chol   HDL   Chol   HDL     Pre     Post   Change
        Males             1005   296    47    272    51      6.3     5.3    Improved
                          1006   155    31    152    33      5.0     4.6    Minimal Change
                          1007   250    55    231    60      4.5     3.9    Improved
                          1008   264    43    195    44      6.1     4.4    Improved
                          1013   183    51    192    49      3.6     3.9    Minimal Change
                          1014   256    43    235    43      6.0     5.5    Minimal Change
                          1015   235    43    216    44      5.5     4.9    Improved
                          1016   238    36    207    36      6.6     5.8    Improved
                          1017   215    50    205    52      4.3     3.9    Minimal Change
                          1018   190    31    164    32      6.1     5.1    Improved
                          1019   168    52    172    44      3.2     3.9    Worsened
                          1020   219    57    207    58      3.8     3.6    Minimal Change
                          1021   203    28    169    28      7.3     6.0    Improved
                          1022   215    51    205    52      4.2     3.9    Minimal Change
                          1023   222    32    210    32      6.9     6.6    Minimal Change

        Females           1001   156    48    150    50      3.3     3.0    Minimal Change
                          1002   151    50    139    54      3.0     2.6    Improved
                          1003   165    51    149    51      3.2     2.9    Minimal Change
                          1004   158    51    143    53      3.1     2.7    Improved
                          1009   187    71    174    69      2.6     2.5    Minimal Change
                          1010   161    64    155    66      2.5     2.3    Minimal Change
                          1011   164    72    149    73      2.3     2.0    Improved
                          1012   160    66    168    61      2.4     2.8    Worsened
                          1024   196    61    186    62      3.2     3.0    Minimal Change
                          1025   216    51    171    54      4.2     3.2    Improved
                          1026   195    60    195    60      3.3     3.3    Minimal Change
```

Example Features

Data Set	LIPIDS
Featured Step	PROC REPORT
Featured Step Statements and Options	DEFINE statement: ACROSS, COMPUTED, DESCENDING, DISPLAY, and GROUP options COMPUTE blocks Stacking one column above other columns
Formatting Features	Controlling line breaks in column headings BREAK statement: SKIP option when sending output to the LISTING destination

A Closer Look	Understanding the Processing of the BREAK Statement in This Example
	Constructing Columns from Column Specifications
	Reshaping a Report by Using GROUP and ACROSS Variables
ODS Enhanced Version	Example 6.4
Other Examples That Use This Data Set	Examples 3.3, 6.4, 6.8, and 6.9

Example Overview

This report presents test results for participants in a study that measures lipids before and after participation in an exercise program. The goal of the study is to reduce cholesterol and raise HDL. Results are measured by the ratio of cholesterol to HDL. The report should present an evaluation of the change in the ratio before and after participation in an exercise program.

Each observation in the LIPIDS data set corresponds to the lipid measurements for one participant during one of the two testing periods.

Simply listing the observations with PROC PRINT or with PROC REPORT produces a long listing with many rows. The structure of this simple presentation makes it difficult to draw conclusions about each participant's test results in the two time periods.

Grouping the observations by GENDER and STUDYID and specifying TESTPERIOD as an ACROSS column reshapes the long listing into a more concise report that puts each participant's results on one row. This new structure makes it easier to compare the results for a study participant. It also makes it possible to calculate changes for a participant before and after the exercise program and to include these evaluations in the report.

Each row in the report contains data from two observations in the LIPIDS data set. The two observations are the test results for a study participant before and after participation in the exercise program. The last three columns are computed columns defined by PROC REPORT, and their values are determined in COMPUTE blocks.

Program

```
proc format;
   value ratio low-<-.1='Improved'
               -.1-.1='Minimal Change'
               >.1-high='Worsened';
   value $gender 'M'='Males'
                 'F'='Females';
   value $results 'Pre'='Pre$Program$Results'
                  'Post'='Post$Program$Results';
run;

proc report data=lipids nowindows
```

Place the dollar sign character in the format label in the positions where the value label should split over lines.

Replace the default split character (/)
with another character because some of
the column labels in the report contain
the slash (/).

```
      split='$';
```

Stack one column above two other
columns.

```
title 'Exercise Program Results';
column gender studyid
       testperiod, (chol hdl)

         ratiopre ratiopost results;
```

List the three computed columns. Ensure
that any column that is based on another
computed column follows that computed
column.

Identify the variables that group the
observations and define the rows.
Order the values of GENDER in
descending order so that the data for males
is displayed before that for females.

```
define gender / group descending 'Gender'
                    format=$gender.;
define studyid / group 'Study ID' width=5;
```

data reshape

Identify TESTPERIOD as the variable
whose values define and label the
columns.

```
define testperiod / across
```

Order the values of TESTPERIOD in
descending order so that the "PRE"
data values are displayed before the
"POST" data values.

```
       descending
```

PRE   POST

Suppress the column heading for
TESTPERIOD.

```
       ' '
       center format=$results.;
```

Specify the display variables that are
listed side-by-side beneath the values of
TESTPERIOD. Specify the column
width when sending output to the
LISTING destination.

```
define chol / display 'Chol' width=5;
define hdl / display 'HDL' width=5;
```

Specify the computed columns.

```
define ratiopre / computed format=5.1
                   'Chol/HDL Pre' center;
define ratiopost / computed format=5.1
                   'Chol/HDL Post' center;
```

Characterize the pre- and post-exercise
results by formatting the value of the
computed column.

```
define results / computed format=ratio.
                   'Chol/HDL Change' left width=14;
```

Skip a line after each section that is
grouped by GENDER when sending
output to the LISTING destination.

```
break after gender / skip;
```

Compute two columns whose values are
based on other columns. Reference these
columns explicitly by number, because
they do not have a single name to reference
them.

```
compute ratiopre;
   ratiopre=_c3_/_c4_;
endcomp;
compute ratiopost;
   ratiopost=_c5_/_c6_;
endcomp;
```

Compute an additional column based on the two computed columns, and reference these columns by name, even though their COMPUTE blocks use explicit column numbers to create them.

```
compute results;
   results=(ratiopost-ratiopre)/ratiopre;
endcomp;
run;
```

A Closer Look

Understanding the Processing of the BREAK Statement in This Example

The SAS log for this program generates the following note:

```
NOTE: Missing values were generated as a result of performing
an operation on missing values.
Each place is given by: (Number of times) at (Line):(Column).
2 at 1:15    2 at 1:16    2 at 1:20
```

Reviewing the reason for this note can further help you understand how PROC REPORT processes BREAK statements.

The BREAK statement executes before it processes the observations within a group. Since CHOL and HDL are DISPLAY variables, their values are missing when the BREAK statement executes. Thus the three COMPUTE blocks generate missing values. A missing value is generated twice in each COMPUTE block, which corresponds to each value of GENDER.

One way to suppress the note is to define CHOL and HDL as analysis variables that compute the mean statistic. Each row has an N of 1, so the means end up being equal to the actual detail value. Mean statistic values for columns 3, 4, 5, and 6 are available when the BREAK statement executes. The means, however, are not displayed, because the SUMMARIZE option is not included in the BREAK statement.

Another way to suppress the note is to test the value of the automatic variable, _BREAK_. PROC REPORT assigns specific values to _BREAK_ that you can test to control execution of the statements in the COMPUTE blocks. The value of _BREAK_ is missing when PROC REPORT is not processing a BREAK line. The COMPUTE blocks could be rewritten as follows to test the value of _BREAK_.

```
compute ratiopre;
   if _break_=' ' then ratiopre= c3 / c4 ;
endcomp;
compute ratiopost;
   if _break_=' ' then ratiopost= c5 / c6 ;
endcomp;
compute results;
   if _break_=' ' then
      results=(ratiopost-ratiopre)/ratiopre;
endcomp;
```

Example 3.8 conditionally executes COMPUTE block statements by testing the value of _BREAK_. Further discussion of _BREAK_ is included in the "A Closer Look" section in that example.

Constructing Columns from Column Specifications

The COLUMN statement in this report uses two types of column specifications. One is the simple specification of a single report item. The other is the specification of report items separated by a comma.

```
column gender studyid testperiod (chol hdl)
        ratiopre ratiopost results;
```

A third way to specify report columns is to assign an alias to a report item. If you want to use the same report item more than once in a COLUMN statement, you can assign an alias to each occurrence. This allows you to specify a different DEFINE statement for each occurrence. The Related Technique in Example 3.9 assigns aliases to multiple occurrences of the statistic N.

Table 2.7 describes three ways to specify report columns.

Table 2.7 Constructing Columns from Column Specifications

This type of column specification...	Results in this type of structure...	Corresponding report items in this example
A single report item	A single column	GENDER STUDYID RATIOPRE RATIOPOST RESULTS
Two or more report items separated by a comma	Items that collectively determine the contents of the column or columns. All items are used to create column headings with the heading for the leftmost item on top. (The heading for TESTPERIOD is a blank; the formatted values of TESTPERIOD become the column heading for TESTPERIOD.) If one of the items is an analysis variable, a computed variable, or a statistic, its values fill the cells. Otherwise, PROC REPORT fills the cells with frequency counts. The parentheses in this example's specification create a column for each of the variables within the parentheses beneath each value of the report item to the left of the comma. (In this example, the values for TESTPERIOD are "Pre" and "Post.")	TESTPERIOD,(CHOL HDL)
A single report item and an alias	A single column. The alias enables you to use two different DEFINE statements for the single report item so that you can specify different attributes for the different occurrences of the variable.	See Example 3.9

Reshaping a Report by Using GROUP and ACROSS Variables

The first option in each DEFINE statement for this report describes how PROC REPORT should use each variable in the report. This report defines four kinds of variables:

❑ group variables: GENDER and STUDYID

❑ across variables: TESTPERIOD

❑ display variables: CHOL and HDL

❑ computed variables: RATIOPRE, RATIOPOST, and RESULTS

Group and across variables affect the layout of rows and columns in the report. A variable defined as DISPLAY lists the values of the variable. (An analysis variable could be specified in the same manner as the display variable, and the values presented would be the statistic associated with the variable.) Computed variables are calculated from other items in the report. The rest of this section explains the different usages in more detail.

Group Variables

A group is a set of observations that have a unique combination of formatted values for all group variables. PROC REPORT summarizes all the observations in a group in one row of the report.

In this report, the group variables are GENDER and STUDYID. Figure 2.7a illustrates what happens when PROC REPORT creates groups for GENDER and STUDYID from the first six observations in the input data set. These six observations represent three rows in the report.

Figure 2.7a Grouping Six Observations

Input Data Set

Report

```
STUDYID GENDER
   1001     F
   1001    .F
   1002     F
   1002     F
   1003     F
   1003     F
```

```
                  Study
    Gender          ID
    Females        1001
                   1002
                   1003
```

Across Variables

PROC REPORT creates a column for each formatted value of an across variable. In this report, it creates a column for each combination of testing time period and the two tests, cholesterol and HDL. By default, the values that fill the cells created by an across variable are frequency counts. This report, however, overrides this default. The values of each test fill the cells because the test variables, CHOL and HDL, are nested underneath the across variable and are defined as display variables.

Figure 2.7b uses the first six observations to illustrate how PROC REPORT places values for TESTPERIOD, CHOL, and HDL in the report. Note that TRI is not included in the final report.

Figure 2.7b Layout Created by Across Variables

Input Data Set

```
STUDYID GENDER TESTPERIOD CHOL HDL TRI
1001       F       Pre      156  48  134
1001       F       Post     150  50  127
1002       F       Pre      151  50  102
1002       F       Post     139  54  81
1003       F       Pre      165  51  114
1003       F       Post     149  51  101
```

Report

```
    Pre          Post
  Program       Program
  Results       Results
Chol   HDL    Chol   HDL
156    48     150    50
151    50     139    54
165    51     149    51
```

Putting Together the Pieces

This example uses group and across variables together to reshape and present the data in one step. Figure 2.7a lists the first six observations in the LIPIDS data set. Figure 2.7b shows the transformation of these first six observations into three rows of the report.

The computed variables add columns to the report. The calculation of a computed variable value uses information in the row in which the value is placed. Because each row presents test values from several observations, the calculation therefore ends up being performed on data from several observations. Figure 2.7c includes the three computed variables.

Figure 2.7c Constructing the Whole Report

Input Data Set

```
STUDYID GENDER TESTPERIOD CHOL HDL TRI
1001       F       Pre      156  48  134
1001       F       Post     150  50  127
1002       F       Pre      151  50  102
1002       F       Post     139  54  81
1003       F       Pre      165  51  114
1003       F       Post     149  51  101
```

Report

| | | Pre Program Results | | Post Program Results | | Chol/ HDL | Chol/ HDL | Chol/HDL |
Gender	Study ID	Chol	HDL	Chol	HDL	Pre	Post	Change
Females	1001	156	48	150	50	3.3	3.0	Minimal Change
	1002	151	50	139	54	3.0	2.6	Improved
	1003	165	51	149	51	3.2	2.9	Minimal Change

Where to Go from Here

PROC FORMAT reference, usage information, and additional examples.
See "The FORMAT Procedure" in the "Procedures" section of *Base SAS 9.1 Procedures Guide,* and "Formatted Values" in the "Fundamental Concepts for Using Base SAS Procedures" section of *Base SAS 9.1 Procedures Guide.*

PROC REPORT reference, usage information, and additional examples.
See "The REPORT Procedure," in the "Procedures" section of *Base SAS 9.1 Procedures Guide.*

Example 2.8   Presenting Long Text Fields in a Report

Goal

List observations in a data set where at least one of the character variables has a long length. Wrap the character data in the column assigned to the lengthy character variable.

Report

```
                              Town Survey
                          Comments Received

                 Years       Children
    Residential  Lived in    Under    Adults
    Area         Town        18?      Over 65?  Comments
    -------------------------------------------------------------------------
    Lakeside     < 2          No       No       Empty the garbage cans at the
                                                parks more frequently

                 2-10         Yes      No       Too much paperwork to just remodel
                                                a kitchen

                 More than 10 Yes      No       We loved the canoe derby

                              No       No       Enforce the beach curfew


    Northwest    < 2          Yes      No       More organized sports for the kids

                 2-10         No       Yes      Replace wornout street signs

                              Yes      Yes      We want snowmobile trails

                 More than 10 Yes      No       Advertise the brush pickup earlier
                                                than two weeks before the pickup

                              No       Yes      Change the yield sign to a stop
                                                sign at W. Lake and Hilltop


    Prairie      2-10         Yes      No       Stop all outdoor burning because
                                                it aggravates my asthma

                              No       No       Enforce the leash laws. Add an off
                                                leash dog park.

                 More than 10 Yes      No       Loved the community picnic


    Town Center  < 2          No       No       Partner with neighboring
                                                communities to build a public
                                                library

                              No       No       City office is never open when I'm
                                                off work. Please expand the hours.

                              Yes      Yes      Plow the snow early and plow often

                              Yes      No       More soccer fields now!!!

                              No       Yes      Too many potholes

                 2-10         Yes      No       Please add more soccer fields

                              Yes      No       Add rink lights for lacrosse and
                                                hockey at night

                              Yes      No       Salt the roads faster after each
                                                snowfall

                 More than 10 No       Yes      Enforce the dog barking ordinance

                              Yes      No       Our kids love the new playground
                                                equipment
```

Example Features

Data Set	TOWNSURVEY
Featured Step	PROC REPORT
Featured Step Statements and Options	DEFINE statement: FLOW, NOPRINT, ORDER, and ORDER= options
	BREAK AFTER statement
	Using the ORDER option to arrange observations by the variable while suppressing the display of the ordering variable with NOPRINT
Formatting Features	PROC REPORT statement: HEADLINE option when sending output to the LISTING destination
	DEFINE statement: WIDTH option when sending output to the LISTING destination
	BREAK AFTER statement: SKIP option when sending output to the LISTING destination
Other Examples That Use This Data Set	Example 3.9

Example Overview

This report lists the comments that town residents gave in a survey of town services. Each set of lines that comprises a complete comment corresponds to one observation in the TOWNSURVEY data set. The report includes only the observations where a comment was recorded. Each column in the report corresponds to one variable in the input data set.

See Figure 3.9a in Example 3.9 for the form that collected the survey data.

Program

Create formats that can associate meaningful descriptions to values of the variables in the report.

```
proc format;
    value $yn 'Y'='Yes'
              'N'='No';
    value $area 'L'='Lakeside'
                'T'='Town Center'
                'N'='Northwest'
                'P'='Prairie';
    value yrslived 1='< 2'
                   2='2-10'
                   3='More than 10';
run;

proc report data=townsurvey nowindows
```

When sending output to the LISTING destination, underline all column headers and the spaces between them.

```
        headline;


    title 'Town Survey';
    title2 'Comments Received';
```

Select the observations to include in the report.

```
where comments ne ' ';

column area yrslived surveyid kids seniors
       comments;
```

Sort the detail rows by the order variables according to their position in the COLUMN statement, starting at the leftmost column and moving to the right. Specify the column width when sending output to the LISTING destination.

```
define area     / order format=$area. width=12
                     'Residential/Area';
define yrslived / order format=yrslived. width=12
```

Order the values by their unformatted values, which overrides the default ORDER=FORMATTED option.

```
                    order=internal
                    'Years/Lived in/Town'
                    left;
```

Suppress the display of SURVEYID, but use its values to order the rows. When sending output to the LISTING destination, also use SURVEYID in the BREAK AFTER statement to skip lines between each respondent's comment.

```
define surveyid / order noprint;

define kids     / format=$yn. 'Children/Under 18?'
                    width=8 center;
define seniors  / format=$yn. 'Adults/Over 65?'
                    width=8 center;
```

Wrap the values of this variable in its column.

```
define comments / flow
```

Ensure that the column is wide enough when sending output to the LISTING destination.

```
                    width=35 'Comments';
```

Insert a blank line after each observation in the report when sending output to the LISTING destination.

```
break after surveyid / skip;
```

Insert a blank line after the last observation in each area when sending output to the LISTING destination.

```
  break after area / skip;
run;
```

Where to Go from Here

PROC REPORT reference, usage information, and additional examples.
See "The REPORT Procedure," in the "Procedures" section of *Base SAS 9.1 Procedures Guide.*

Example 2.9   Listing the Rank and Percentile for Each Observation

Goal

Rank the observations in a data set based on the value of a numeric variable. Determine the quartile based on the value of a numeric variable. List the observations and their ranks and quartiles.

Report

```
                Official Results of Boston Marathon 1980-2004              1
              With Winning Times Ranked from Fastest(1) to Slowest(N)

                            Women's Division

       Year  Winner                  Country        Time   Order  Quartile
       1980  Jacqueline Gareau       Canada        2:34:28   25   Bottom
       1981  Allison Roe             New Zealand   2:26:46   20   Bottom
       1982  Charlotte Teske         West Germany  2:29:33   23   Bottom
       1983  Joan Benoit             United States 2:22:43    3   Top
       1984  Lorraine Moller         New Zealand   2:29:28   22   Bottom
       1985  Lisa Larsen Weidenbach  United States 2:34:06   24   Bottom
       1986  Ingrid Kristiansen      Norway        2:24:55   12   High Mid
       1987  Rosa Mota               Portugal      2:25:21   15   Low Mid
       1988  Rosa Mota               Portugal      2:24:30   10   High Mid
       1989  Ingrid Kristiansen      Norway        2:24:33   11   High Mid
       1990  Rosa Mota               Portugal      2:25:24   16   Low Mid
       1991  Wanda Panfil            Poland        2:24:18    8   High Mid
       1992  Olga Markova            Russia        2:23:43    6   Top
       1993  Olga Markova            Russia        2:25:27   17   Low Mid
       1994  Uta Pippig              Germany       2:21:45    2   Top
       1995  Uta Pippig              Germany       2:25:11   13   High Mid
       1996  Uta Pippig              Germany       2:27:12   21   Bottom
       1997  Fatuma Roba             Ethiopia      2:26:23   19   Low Mid
       1998  Fatuma Roba             Ethiopia      2:23:21    4   Top
       1999  Fatuma Roba             Ethiopia      2:23:25    5   Top
       2000  Catherine Ndereba       Kenya         2:26:11   18   Low Mid
       2001  Catherine Ndereba       Kenya         2:23:53    7   High Mid
       2002  Margaret Okayo          Kenya         2:20:43    1   Top
       2003  Svetlana Zakharova      Russia        2:25:20   14   Low Mid
       2004  Cathering Ndereba       Kenya         2:24:27    9   High Mid
```

```
                Official Results of Boston Marathon 1980-2004              2
              With Winning Times Ranked from Fastest(1) to Slowest(N)

                             Men's Division

       Year  Winner             Country        Time   Order  Quartile
       1980  Bill Rodgers       United States  2:12:11   24   Bottom
       1981  Toshihiko Seko     Japan          2:09:26   13   High Mid
       1982  Alberto Salazar    United States  2:08:52    7   High Mid
       1983  Greg Meyer         United States  2:09:00    8   High Mid
       1984  Geoff Smith        Great Britain  2:10:34   19   Low Mid
       1985  Geoff Smith        Great Britain  2:14:05   25   Bottom
       1986  Robert de Castella Australia      2:07:51    3   Top
       1987  Toshihiko Seko     Japan          2:11:50   23   Bottom
       1988  Ibrahim Hussein    Kenya          2:08:43    6   Top
       1989  Abebe Mekonnen     Ethiopia       2:09:06   10   High Mid
       1990  Gelindo Bordin     Italy          2:08:19    5   Top
       1991  Ibrahim Hussein    Kenya          2:11:06   22   Bottom
       1992  Ibrahim Hussein    Kenya          2:08:14    4   Top
       1993  Cosmas Ndeti       Kenya          2:09:33   14   Low Mid
       1994  Cosmas Ndeti       Kenya          2:07:15    1   Top
       1995  Cosmas Ndeti       Kenya          2:09:22   12   High Mid
       1996  Moses Tanui        Kenya          2:09:15   11   High Mid
       1997  Lameck Aguta       Kenya          2:10:34   19   Low Mid
```

(continued)

(*continued*)

```
1998  Moses Tanui               Kenya    2:07:34    2   Top
1999  Joseph Chebet             Kenya    2:09:52   17   Low Mid
2000  Elijah Lagat              Kenya    2:09:47   16   Low Mid
2001  Lee Bong-Ju               Korea    2:09:43   15   Low Mid
2002  Rodgers Rop               Kenya    2:09:02    9   High Mid
2003  Robert Kipkoech Cherui    Kenya    2:10:11   18   Low Mid
2004  Timothy Cherigat          Kenya    2:10:37   21   Bottom
```

Example Features

Data Set	MARATHON
Preparatory Step	PROC SORT
Featured Step	PROC RANK
Featured Step Statements and Options	PROC RANK statement: DESCENDING, GROUPS=, OUT=, and TIES= options BY statement RANKS statement
Report Step	PROC REPORT
Report Step Options and Statements	BY statement DEFINE statement: ORDER option
Formatting Features	Customizing titles with #BYVAL DEFINE statement: WIDTH option when sending output to the LISTING destination.
A Closer Look	Creating the Rank and Percentile Variables Choosing a Method for Ordering Ranks and Handling Tied Values Selecting the Number of Groups for the Percentile Categories See "Working with #BYVAL, #BYVAR, and #BYLINE when Customizing Titles" in Example 2.3

Example Overview

When comparing the values of a numeric variable, you may not be able to easily identify the high and low values or judge the position of values relative to certain percentile levels, such as the median or quartiles or deciles. This can be especially difficult when the variable values contain many digits or are formatted in a way other than standard decimal notation.

Creating variables based on ranks and percentiles provides a method for directly comparing observations. With this report, a rank variable and a quartile variable demonstrate the general trend of the winning times over many years of the Boston Marathon.

The ranks and quartiles are determined by gender. PROC RANK determines the ranks and quartiles, and the program executes PROC RANK twice, once to compute ranks and once to compute quartiles. PROC RANK saves the ranks and quartiles in output data sets that also contain the variables in the input data set. A DATA step merges the two PROC RANK output data sets. The report includes both the original data plus the new ranking statistics.

Each row in the report corresponds to one observation in the data set. The first four columns correspond to variables in the data set. The last two columns are the ranking statistics produced by PROC RANK.

Program

Sort the data set.

```
proc sort data=marathon;
  by gender;
run;
```

Create formats for GENDER and QUARTILE.

```
proc format;
  value $div    'M'="Men's Division"
                'F'="Women's Division";
  value quarter  3='Top'
                 2='High Mid'
                 1='Low Mid'
                 0='Bottom';
run;
```

Compute the rank.

```
proc rank data=marathon
```

Create an output data set containing the original observations and the ranking variable.

```
     out=ordered
```

Specify that ties should be assigned the smallest of the corresponding ranks.

```
     ties=low;
```

Compute the ranks separately for each gender.

```
  by gender;
```

Determine the rank based on the values of the variable TIME.

```
  var time;
```

Create a new variable that holds the rank.

```
  ranks order;
run;
```

Compute the quartile.

```
proc rank data=marathon
```

Create an output data set containing the original observations and the quartile variable.

```
     out=grouped
```

Partition the data within each BY group into quartiles.

```
     groups=4
```

Reverse the direction of the ranks so that the quartiles are defined from largest to smallest, to reflect that the highest quartile corresponds to the fastest times.

```
     descending
```

Specify that ties should be assigned the largest of the corresponding ranks.

```
     ties=high;
```

Compute the ranks separately for each gender.

```
  by gender;
```

Determine the quartile based on the values of the variable TIME.

```
  var time;
```

| Create a new variable that holds the quartile. | ```
  ranks quartile;
run;
``` |
| Perform a one-to-one merge of the two data sets created by PROC RANK. | ```
data combine;
  merge ordered grouped;
run;
``` |
| Suppress the automatic printing of BY lines in subsequent procedure output. | ```
options nobyline;
``` |

```
proc report data=combine nowindows;
    title1 'Official Results of Boston Marathon
            1980-2004';
    title2 'With Winning Times Ranked from Fastest(1) to
            Slowest(N)';
```

| Insert the current value of the BY variable whose name is enclosed in parentheses. | ```
    title4 '#byval(gender)';
``` |
| Create a separate report for each value of the BY variable. | ```
    by gender;
``` |
| Specify the variables that should appear in the report and the order in which they should appear. | ```
    column year winner country time order quartile;
``` |
| Order the detail rows within each BY group by the ascending values of the order variable. Specify the column width when sending output to the LISTING destination. | ```
    define year     / order format=4. 'Year';
    define winner   / width=22 'Winner';
    define country  / width=13 'Country';
    define time     / width=7 'Time' format=time7.;
    define order    / width=5 'Order';
    define quartile / width=8 'Quartile' format=quarter.;
``` |
| Format the values of the variable GENDER, which in this example is inserted in TITLE4 in the position of #BYVAL(GENDER). | ```
    format gender $div.;
run;
``` |
| Reset the option to its default settings. | ```
options byline;
``` |

🔍 A Closer Look

Creating the Rank and Percentile Variables

PROC RANK can examine a variable's values and determine individual rankings or group membership where you specify the number of groups that PROC RANK should create. PROC RANK can save these results in variables and output them along with the original data in the input data set for additional processing.

By default, PROC RANK assigns the lowest ranking to the observation with the lowest value of the variable listed in the VAR statement; it assigns the highest ranking to the observation with the highest value. The DESCENDING option reverses this by assigning high rankings to low values and low rankings to high values. With the TIES= option, you can specify whether tied values receive the highest or lowest possible ranking.

Choosing a Method for Ordering Ranks and Handling Tied Values

The first PROC RANK step in this example applies the default method for ordering rankings. It assigns the lowest ranking of 1 to the observation with the lowest value of TIME (the best time).
```

This default method of ranking, along with the specification of TIES=LOW, assures that tied values receive the best possible rank. For example, if three values are tied for second place, all three receive a rank of 2. PROC RANK always assigns the same rank to tied values, regardless of the value of the TIES= option.

```
proc rank data=marathon out=ordered ties=low;
```

The second PROC RANK step assigns group membership. With GROUPS=4, quartiles are defined and the quartile values assigned to each observation range from 0 to 3. The DESCENDING option gives the group value of 3 to the lowest set of values of TIME, the group value of 2 to the next lowest set of values, and so on. The TIES=HIGH option assures that tied values in this PROC RANK step receive the best possible rank.

```
proc rank data=marathon out=grouped groups=4
    descending ties=high;
```

Table 2.9 shows the results of using all the combinations of the DESCENDING option with the HIGH and LOW values of the TIES= option. The variables are similar to the ones in the marathon example, but the values of QUARTILE are not formatted by the QUARTER format. Table 2.9 uses only four observations, of which two have tied values for TIME.

Table 2.9 Using the DESCENDING and TIES Options in PROC RANK

| | | ORDER | | | | QUARTILE | | | |
| | | Without DESCENDING | | With DESCENDING | | Without DESCENDING | | With DESCENDING | |
RUNNER	TIME	TIES=LOW	TIES=HIGH	TIES=LOW	TIES=HIGH	TIES=LOW	TIES=HIGH	TIES=LOW	TIES=HIGH
Mike	2:34:51	1	1	4	4	0	0	3	3
Patrick	2:36:09	2	3	2	3	1	2	1	2
Glenn	2:36:09	2	3	2	3	1	2	1	2
Carl	2:40:34	4	4	1	1	3	3	0	0

Selecting the Number of Groups for the Percentile Categories

The GROUPS= option specifies the number of categories in which to group the observations. The values of the group variable go from 0 to one less than the value specified in the GROUPS= option. Formatting the values of the group variable with a descriptive label makes it easy to identify each observation's group in the report.

The formula for calculating group values is

FLOOR(*rank*k/(n+1)*)

where *FLOOR* is the FLOOR function, *rank* is the value's order rank, *k* is the value of GROUPS=, and *n* is the number of observations having nonmissing values of the ranking variable.

If the number of observations is evenly divisible by the number of groups, the result is an equal number of observations in each group, provided there are no tied values at the boundaries of the groups. However, if the number of observations is not evenly divisible by the value of GROUPS=, you can't partition observations into groups of equal sizes. In the marathon example, dividing the women's results with 25 observations into four groups places seven observations in the "High Mid" category and places six observations in each of the other three.

Where to Go from Here

BY statement processing. See "BY Statement" in the "Statements" section of *SAS 9.1 Language Reference: Dictionary,* and "Statements with the Same Function in Multiple Procedures" in the "Concepts" section of *Base SAS 9.1 Procedures Guide.*

The BYLINE/NOBYLINE SAS System Options. See "SAS System Options" in *SAS 9.1 Language Reference: Dictionary.*

The FLOOR function syntax, usage information, and additional examples. See "Floor Function" in the "Functions and CALL Routines" section of *SAS 9.1 Language Reference: Dictionary.*

Inserting BY-group information in titles. See "Creating Titles that Contain BY-Group Information" in the "Fundamental Concepts for Using Base SAS Procedures" section of *Base SAS 9.1 Procedures Guide.*

MERGE statement syntax, usage information, and additional examples. See "MERGE Statement" in the "Statements" section of *SAS 9.1 Language Reference: Dictionary.*

One-to-one merging. See "Combining SAS Data Sets: Basic Concepts" in "Reading, Combining, and Modifying SAS Data Sets" in the "DATA Step Concepts" section of *SAS 9.1 Language Reference: Concepts.*

PROC RANK reference, usage information, and additional examples. See "The RANK Procedure" in the "Procedures" section of *Base SAS 9.1 Procedures Guide.*

PROC REPORT reference, usage information, and additional examples. See "The REPORT Procedure" in the "Procedures" section of *Base SAS 9.1 Procedures Guide.*

CHAPTER 3
Summary Reports

A summary report summarizes observations in a data set. Summary reports can range from presentations of simple frequency counts to complex tables of descriptive statistics for categories defined by the combinations of several variables in the data set.

The examples in this chapter describe ways in which you can prepare summary reports. Each example presents a different style of summary report. Three procedures—REPORT, TABULATE, and MEANS—create the summary reports in this chapter. All examples use PROC FORMAT to assign labels to categories or to group categories. One example focuses on a special feature of PROC FORMAT that assigns multiple labels to categories.

All examples in this chapter send output to the default LISTING destination. Examples 3.2, 3.3, 3.5, 3.8 and 3.10 are modified in Chapter 6 to include ODS features and send the output to nonlisting destinations.

See the back of this book for a list of titles related to the features of these examples, and visit the SAS Press Web site (support.sas.com/saspress) for current information on new and revised publications.

Several presentations at SUGI conferences show how SAS users apply report-writing techniques. Recent conference proceedings that are available online provide a wealth of additional applications and examples. You can link to them through the SAS support Web site (support.sas.com).

Table 3.0 presents a cross-reference of the examples in this chapter to the procedures used, data sets used, and ODS enhanced versions of the examples. See Appendix A for details on the example data sets analyzed in this chapter. See Appendix B for a table that cross-references all examples in this book.

Table 3.0 Cross-Reference of Examples in Chapter 3

| Example | Report-Writing Tool Used | | | | | | ODS Enhanced Version | Data Set | Example Title |
	REPORT	TABULATE	PRINT	DATA Step	MEANS	FREQ			
3.1	X	Related Technique						PHONDATA	Summarizing Data
3.2		Related Technique			X		6.5, 6.15	BREAD	Computing Descriptive Statistics for Specific Groups
3.3	Related Technique	X					6.8, 6.9	LIPIDS	Displaying Descriptive Statistics in a Tabular Format
3.4		X				Related Technique		JOBCLASS	Displaying Basic Frequency Counts and Percentages
3.5		X					6.3, 6.7	JOBCLASS	Producing a Hierarchical Tabular Report
3.6		X						JOBCLASS	Creating Multipage Summary Tables
3.7		X						LIBRARIES	Assigning Multiple Labels to Categories
3.8	X						6.2, 6.6	CARSALES	Writing Customized Lines in Summary Reports
3.9	Related Technique	X						TOWNSURVEY	Reporting on Multiple-Choice Survey Data
3.10		X					6.13, 6.14	CUSTRESP	Reporting on Multiple-Response Survey Data

Example 3.1   Summarizing Data

Goal

Summarize the observations in a data set by several categories.

Report

```
              Calls Received by Technical Support on January 31, 2005

                                          Percent    Average
                               Number     within     Length of
     Hour   Status of Problems  of Calls   Hour        Calls

     9:00   Automated Troubleshooting   10     15%      0:05:19
            Resolved on Initial Call    44     68%      0:05:38
            Tracked to Specialist       11     17%      0:09:20
     -----                          --------  -------  ---------
     9:00                                65     100%     0:06:13

    10:00   Automated Troubleshooting   16     21%      0:09:26
            Resolved on Initial Call    52     68%      0:06:53
            Tracked to Specialist        8     11%      0:12:21
    -----                          --------  -------  ---------
    10:00                               76     100%     0:08:00

    11:00   Automated Troubleshooting   12     16%      0:11:44
            Resolved on Initial Call    48     64%      0:07:08
            Tracked to Specialist       15     20%      0:13:48
    -----                          --------  -------  ---------
    11:00                               75     100%     0:09:12

    12:00   Automated Troubleshooting    5      9%      0:10:07
            Resolved on Initial Call    37     66%      0:08:22
            Tracked to Specialist       14     25%      0:11:08
    -----                          --------  -------  ---------
    12:00                               56     100%     0:09:13

     1:00   Automated Troubleshooting    5      8%      0:04:20
            Resolved on Initial Call    43     70%      0:05:53
            Tracked to Specialist       13     21%      0:10:39
     -----                          --------  -------  ---------
     1:00                               61     100%     0:06:47

     2:00   Automated Troubleshooting   13     15%      0:07:44
            Resolved on Initial Call    64     74%      0:07:57
            Tracked to Specialist       10     11%      0:15:21
     -----                          --------  -------  ---------
     2:00                               87     100%     0:08:46

     3:00   Automated Troubleshooting   13     15%      0:09:59
            Resolved on Initial Call    61     72%      0:06:46
            Tracked to Specialist       11     13%      0:07:29
     -----                          --------  -------  ---------
     3:00                               85     100%     0:07:21

     4:00   Automated Troubleshooting    3      4%      0:08:00
            Resolved on Initial Call    57     75%      0:07:39
            Tracked to Specialist       16     21%      0:06:13
     -----                          --------  -------  ---------
     4:00                               76     100%     0:07:21

           ==========================  ========  =======  =========
            Total for Day               581     100%     0:07:53
```

Example Features

Data Set	PHONDATA
Featured Step	PROC REPORT
Featured Step Statements and Options	DEFINE statement: ANALYSIS, COMPUTED, GROUP, MEAN, and ORDER= options COMPUTE blocks BREAK AFTER statement: SUMMARIZE option RBREAK AFTER statement: SUMMARIZE option
Formatting Features	Customizing the RBREAK summary line BREAK AFTER statement: OL and SKIP options when sending output to the LISTING destination RBREAK AFTER statement: DOL option when sending output to the LISTING destination
Related Technique	PROC TABULATE, PCTN percentage calculation
🔍 A Closer Look	Comparing PROC REPORT and PROC TABULATE for Generating the Report in this Example

Example Overview

This report summarizes phone calls to technical support by the hour the call was received and by the status of the call. As shown in the example the status of each call is classified into one of three groups. For each combination of hour and status, the report presents the number of calls and the average length of each call. The percentage of each status grouping is computed within each hour.

The first two columns of the report correspond to variables in the PHONDATA data set. These two variables define the categories for which statistics are computed. The N statistic is presented in the third column. It is equal to the number of observations represented in the row. The fourth column is a computed column that is based on the N statistic computed in column 3. The fifth column is the MEAN statistic computed on an analysis variable in the data set.

Program

Define a format to group the types of calls.

Define a format to label the hour in which technical support received the call.

List the columns in the order in which they should appear in the report. Include in the list the statistics columns and the computed column. Ensure that the columns used to calculate the computed variable precede the computed variable in the list.

Group the observations by the values of HOUR and STATUS. Establish the order of the rows by the position of the grouping variables in the COLUMN statement.

Present the groups in their unformatted order. This overrides the default ordering of the rows by the formatted values of the group variable.

Group the values of the variable STATUS by the $STATFMT format.

When sending output to the LISTING destination, specify the width of the column.

Specify the characteristics of the column that presents the N statistic.

Define the computed column and write the results with the PERCENT format.

Compute the MEAN statistic.

```
proc format;
    value $statfmt
            'PRIM/RES'='Resolved on Initial Call'
            'AUTOMATED'='Automated Troubleshooting'
            'TOTAL'='Total for Day'
            other='Tracked to Specialist';

    value hourfmt   9='9:00'
                   10='10:00'
                   11='11:00'
                   12='12:00'
                   13='1:00'
                   14='2:00'
                   15='3:00'
                   16='4:00';
run;

proc report data=phondata nowindows;
    title1 'Calls Received by Technical Support on
            January 31, 2005';

    column hour status n hourpct primtime;

    define hour      / group format=hourfmt. center

                       order=internal
                       'Hour';

    define status    / group format=$statfmt.
                       'Status of Problems';

                       width=25

    define n         / format=3. width=8 center
                       'Number/of Calls';

    define hourpct   / computed format=percent.
                       width=7 center
                       'Percent/within/Hour';

    define primtime  / analysis mean format=time8.
                       width=9 center
                       'Average/Length of/Calls';
```

Retain the total N for each HOUR category so that this value can be used as the denominator in calculating HOURPCT for each row within the HOUR category. Determine this value *before* listing the rows in the HOUR category. Note that it is not necessary to define TOTALN in the COLUMN statement or on a DEFINE statement. By default, an undefined variable that is not in the data set is a numeric computed, nondisplay variable.

```
compute before hour;
   totaln=n;
endcomp;
```

Compute the value of HOURPCT for each row of the report. Determine the percentage of each type of call within each HOUR category. For the denominator use the TOTALN variable, which is a computed, nondisplay variable. Specify the N statistic as the numerator, which is equal to the N statistic for the current row.

```
compute hourpct;
   hourpct=n/totaln;
endcomp;
```

Create a summary line after the last row for each value of HOUR.

```
break after hour / summarize
```

When sending output to the LISTING destination, skip a line after the summary row and place a line above the summary row.

```
                         skip
                         ol;
```

Create a summary line at the end of the report.

```
rbreak after / summarize
```

When sending the report to the LISTING destination, place a double line above the summary row.

```
                       dol;
```

Modify the contents of the summary line at the end of the report.

```
compute after;
```

Specify a unique value for STATUS that reflects the summary line. Note that this value was specified in the $STATFMT format that was defined in the PROC FORMAT step.

```
   status='TOTAL';
```

Replace the calculated value of HOURPCT at the end of the report. Assign a value of 1 to HOURPCT so that the PERCENT format writes the value as 100%.

```
   hourpct=1;
endcomp;
run;
```

Related Technique

PROC TABULATE can produce a report similar to the one that PROC REPORT produced, as shown in Figure 3.1.

Figure 3.1 Output Produced by PROC TABULATE

```
                 Calls Received by Technical Support on January 31, 2005
    ---------------------------------------------------------------------------
   |                                       |Number|Percent|Average |
   |                                       |  of  |within | Length |
   |                                       |Calls | Hour  |of Calls|
   |---------------------------------------+------+-------+--------|
   |Hour           |Status                 |      |       |        |
   |---------------+-----------------------+------+-------+--------|
   |9:00           |Automated Troubleshooting |  10|    15| 0:05:19|
   |               |-----------------------+------+-------+--------|
   |               |Tracked to Specialist  |   11|    17| 0:09:20|
   |               |-----------------------+------+-------+--------|
   |               |Resolved on Initial Call|  44|    68| 0:05:38|
   |               |-----------------------+------+-------+--------|
   |               |Total for Hour         |   65|   100| 0:06:13|
   |---------------+-----------------------+------+-------+--------|
   |10:00          |Status                 |      |       |        |
   |               |-----------------------|      |       |        |
   |               |Automated Troubleshooting |  16|    21| 0:09:26|
   |               |-----------------------+------+-------+--------|
   |               |Tracked to Specialist  |    8|    11| 0:12:21|
   |               |-----------------------+------+-------+--------|
   |               |Resolved on Initial Call|  52|    68| 0:06:53|
   |               |-----------------------+------+-------+--------|
   |               |Total for Hour         |   76|   100| 0:08:00|
   |---------------+-----------------------+------+-------+--------|
   |11:00          |Status                 |      |       |        |
   |               |-----------------------|      |       |        |
   |               |Automated Troubleshooting |  12|    16| 0:11:44|
   |               |-----------------------+------+-------+--------|
   |               |Tracked to Specialist  |   15|    20| 0:13:48|
   |               |-----------------------+------+-------+--------|
   |               |Resolved on Initial Call|  48|    64| 0:07:08|
   |               |-----------------------+------+-------+--------|
   |               |Total for Hour         |   75|   100| 0:09:12|
   |---------------+-----------------------+------+-------+--------|
   |12:00          |Status                 |      |       |        |
   |               |-----------------------|      |       |        |
   |               |Automated Troubleshooting |   5|     9| 0:10:07|
   |               |-----------------------+------+-------+--------|
   |               |Tracked to Specialist  |   14|    25| 0:11:08|
   |               |-----------------------+------+-------+--------|
   |               |Resolved on Initial Call|  37|    66| 0:08:22|
   |               |-----------------------+------+-------+--------|
   |               |Total for Hour         |   56|   100| 0:09:13|
   |---------------+-----------------------+------+-------+--------|
   |1:00           |Status                 |      |       |        |
   |               |-----------------------|      |       |        |
   |               |Automated Troubleshooting |   5|     8| 0:04:20|
   |               |-----------------------+------+-------+--------|
   |               |Tracked to Specialist  |   13|    21| 0:10:39|
   |               |-----------------------+------+-------+--------|
   |               |Resolved on Initial Call|  43|    70| 0:05:53|
   |               |-----------------------+------+-------+--------|
   |               |Total for Hour         |   61|   100| 0:06:47|
   |---------------+-----------------------+------+-------+--------|
   |2:00           |Automated Troubleshooting |  13|    15| 0:07:44|
   |               |-----------------------+------+-------+--------|
   |               |Tracked to Specialist  |   10|    11| 0:15:21|
   |               |-----------------------+------+-------+--------|
   |               |Resolved on Initial Call|  64|    74| 0:07:57|
   |               |-----------------------+------+-------+--------|
   |               |Total for Hour         |   87|   100| 0:08:46|
   |---------------+-----------------------+------+-------+--------|
   |3:00           |Status                 |      |       |        |
   |               |-----------------------|      |       |        |
   |               |Automated Troubleshooting |  13|    15| 0:09:59|
   |               |-----------------------+------+-------+--------|
   |               |Tracked to Specialist  |   11|    13| 0:07:29|
   |               |-----------------------+------+-------+--------|
   |               |Resolved on Initial Call|  61|    72| 0:06:46|
   |               |-----------------------+------+-------+--------|
   |               |Total for Hour         |   85|   100| 0:07:21|
   |---------------+-----------------------+------+-------+--------|
```

(continued)

(*continued*)

```
|4:00                         |Status                |    |    |       |
|                             |----------------------|    |    |       |
|                             |Automated Troubleshooting |  3|   4| 0:08:00|
|                             |----------------------+------+-------+--------|
|                             |Tracked to Specialist |   16|  21| 0:06:13|
|                             |----------------------+------+-------+--------|
|                             |Resolved on Initial Call| 57| 75| 0:07:39|
|                             |----------------------+------+-------+--------|
|                             |Total for Hour        |   76| 100| 0:07:21|
|-----------------------------+----------------------+------+-------+--------|
|Total for Day                                        | 581| 100| 0:07:53|
 --------------------------------------------------------+-------+--------
```

The following program produces the report shown in Figure 3.1.

```
proc format;
    value $statfmt
          'AUTOMATED'='Automated Troubleshooting'
          'PRIM/RES'='Resolved on Initial Call'
          other='Tracked to Specialist';
    value hourfmt  9='9:00'
                  10='10:00'
                  11='11:00'
                  12='12:00'
                  13='1:00'
                  14='2:00'
                  15='3:00'
                  16='4:00';
run;
proc tabulate data=phondata;
```

Specify the classification variables.

```
class hour status;
```

Specify the analysis variable.

```
var primtime;
```

Place HOUR as the major classification variable of the report and put it in the row dimension.

```
table hour='Hour'*
```

Nest the formatted values of STATUS within each formatted value of HOUR. Summarize the information over all values of STATUS within one formatted value of HOUR by using the ALL keyword.

```
        (status='Status' all='Total for Hour')
```

Compute an overall summary of the data and place this summary as the last row in the report.

```
all='Total for Day',
```

Place the analyses of PRIMTIME in the column dimension.

```
primtime=' '*
```

Compute three statistics on PRIMTIME.

```
(n='Number of Calls'*f=6.
```

Override the default denominator for computing percentages by specifying a different denominator in angle brackets. (The default denominator is the total number of observations analyzed in the report.) To compute the percentages within each HOUR category, use as the denominator the total number of observations analyzed over all values of STATUS for that category of HOUR. (Specify STATUS within the angle brackets.) To compute the overall percentages presented in the last row of the report, use as the denominator the total number of observations analyzed in the report. (Specify ALL within the same set of angle brackets.)

```
          pctn<status all>='Percent within Hour'*f=7.
          mean='Average Length of Calls'*f=time8.)
```

When sending output to the LISTING destination, override the default determination of the amount of space to allocate to the row titles (HOUR and STATUS).

```
       / rts=55;
    format status $statfmt. hour hourfmt.;
  run;
```

🔍 A Closer Look

Comparing PROC REPORT and PROC TABULATE for Generating the Report in This Example

As demonstrated in the previous sections, either PROC REPORT or PROC TABULATE can summarize data by categories. Each procedure has strengths and weaknesses.

Strengths of PROC REPORT

In this example, you might prefer PROC REPORT for these reasons:

❑ *More control over spacing between groups.* When sending output to the LISTING destination, you can add options to skip lines between groups as well as underline them and overline them. This helps you distinguish between lower-level and higher-level summaries in the report. PROC TABULATE inserts a separator line between each row of the report in this example, whether or not it's sent to the LISTING destination. You can remove these lines by specifying NOSEPS on the PROC TABULATE statement. However, NOSEPS removes all lines, and some of these may be useful in making the report easier to understand.

❏ *Less space required to display the report.* This advantage relates to the advantage described above and also applies to the LISTING destination. The output from the PROC REPORT step does not have any separator lines between the three types of calls within each hour, and it labels the STATUS column only once at the top of each page. The PROC TABULATE report separates the three types of call status within each hour with a line and repeats the label for STATUS within each hour. You could save a line within each hour by suppressing the column heading for STATUS in the PROC TABULATE step, but then you would not have a column heading anywhere else for STATUS. To suppress the heading for STATUS, use `status=' '` in the PROC TABULATE TABLE statement instead of `status='Status'`.

Strengths of PROC TABULATE

You might prefer PROC TABULATE for these reasons:

❏ *Easier to specify the calculation of percentages.* PROC REPORT includes percentage statistics, but the denominator for these calculations is based on the total number of observations presented in the report. To compute percentages using other denominator definitions requires the use of COMPUTE blocks. The options in PROC TABULATE allow you to base your percentage calculations on the combinations of classification variables or report dimensions that are appropriate for the information you want to convey, without adding programming statements.

❏ *Less coding required to produce summary rows and columns.* The placement of the keyword ALL in a PROC TABULATE TABLE statement summarizes all of the categories for class variables in the same parenthetical group or dimension. With PROC REPORT, you must include BREAK and RBREAK statements to summarize information.

Where to Go from Here

PROC REPORT reference, usage information, and additional examples. See "The REPORT Procedure" in the "Procedures" section of *Base SAS 9.1 Procedures Guide.*

PROC TABULATE reference, usage information, and additional examples. See "The TABULATE Procedure" in the "Procedures" section of *Base SAS 9.1 Procedures Guide.*

Example 3.2   Computing Descriptive Statistics for Specific Groups

Goal

Compute specific descriptive statistics for specific combinations of several classification variables. Omit unneeded combinations of the classification variables from the report.

Save in a data set the minimum and maximum values for specific variables for use in a later example. Save record identifiers with the results.

Report

```
        Nutritional Information about Breads Available in the Region
           Values Per Bread Slice, Calories in kcal, Fiber in Grams

                          The MEANS Procedure

        Variable          N      Mean    Minimum    Maximum
        ----------------------------------------------------------
        calories         124     87.59     56.00     138.00
        dietary_fiber    124      2.01      0.00       4.80
        ----------------------------------------------------------


 Type of
 Bread        Variable         N      Mean    Minimum    Maximum
 --------------------------------------------------------------------
 Specialty    calories         68     89.44     71.00     138.00
              dietary_fiber    68      2.02      0.00       4.80

 Sandwich     calories         56     85.34     56.00     111.00
              dietary_fiber    56      1.99      0.50       3.90
 --------------------------------------------------------------------


 Primary Flour
 Ingredient   Variable         N      Mean    Minimum    Maximum
 --------------------------------------------------------------------
 Multigrain   calories         29     88.83     76.00     108.00
              dietary_fiber    29      2.37      0.00       3.90

 Oatmeal      calories          5     93.00     84.00     111.00
              dietary_fiber     5      3.30      2.80       3.90

 Rye          calories         20     86.70     71.00     105.00
              dietary_fiber    20      2.16      1.00       4.20

 White        calories         45     87.42     56.00     138.00
              dietary_fiber    45      1.11      0.00       2.90

 Whole Wheat  calories         25     86.08     72.00     101.00
              dietary_fiber    25      2.82      1.00       4.80
 --------------------------------------------------------------------


 Source       Variable         N      Mean    Minimum    Maximum
 --------------------------------------------------------------------
 Bakery       calories         48     92.88     71.00     138.00
              dietary_fiber    48      2.10      0.30       4.40

 Grocery      calories         76     84.25     56.00     112.00
              dietary_fiber    76      1.95      0.00       4.80
 --------------------------------------------------------------------
```

(continued)

(continued)

Source	Type of Bread	Variable	N	Mean	Minimum	Maximum
Bakery	Specialty	calories	31	93.16	71.00	138.00
		dietary_fiber	31	1.99	0.30	4.40
	Sandwich	calories	17	92.35	73.00	111.00
		dietary_fiber	17	2.31	0.50	3.90
Grocery	Specialty	calories	37	86.32	72.00	112.00
		dietary_fiber	37	2.05	0.00	4.80
	Sandwich	calories	39	82.28	56.00	101.00
		dietary_fiber	39	1.85	0.50	3.50

Source	Brand	Variable	N	Mean	Minimum
Bakery	Aunt Sal Bakes	calories	10	91.30	74.00
		dietary_fiber	10	1.84	0.50
	Demeter	calories	15	96.67	71.00
		dietary_fiber	15	2.29	0.50

Source	Brand	Variable	N	Mean	Minimum
Bakery	Downtown Bakers	calories	10	96.90	82.00
		dietary_fiber	10	2.35	1.00
	Pain du Prairie	calories	13	86.62	74.00
		dietary_fiber	13	1.89	0.30
Grocery	BBB Brands	calories	5	81.80	65.00
		dietary_fiber	5	1.76	1.20
	Choice 123	calories	6	80.67	71.00
		dietary_fiber	6	1.52	0.50
	Fabulous Breads	calories	15	82.80	71.00
		dietary_fiber	15	1.84	0.00
	Five Chimneys	calories	10	86.60	75.00
		dietary_fiber	10	2.55	1.20
	Gaia's Hearth	calories	11	89.00	77.00
		dietary_fiber	11	1.83	0.00
	Mill City Bakers	calories	9	85.33	66.00
		dietary_fiber	9	1.92	0.50
	Owasco Ovens	calories	12	83.33	72.00
		dietary_fiber	12	2.20	0.80
	RiseNShine Bread	calories	8	81.88	56.00
		dietary_fiber	8	1.65	0.90

Source	Brand	Variable	Maximum
Bakery	Aunt Sal Bakes	calories	105.00
		dietary_fiber	3.90
	Demeter	calories	111.00
		dietary_fiber	4.20

(continued)

(continued)

```
                     Downtown Bakers    calories        138.00
                                        dietary_fiber     4.30

                     Pain du Prairie    calories        108.00
                                        dietary_fiber     4.40
             Grocery BBB Brands         calories         90.00
                                        dietary_fiber     2.60

                     Choice 123         calories         92.00
                                        dietary_fiber     2.30

                     Fabulous Breads    calories         97.00
                                        dietary_fiber     3.20

                     Five Chimneys      calories         98.00
                                        dietary_fiber     3.80

                     Gaia's Hearth      calories        101.00
                                        dietary_fiber     3.60

                     Mill City Bakers   calories        112.00
                                        dietary_fiber     3.10

                     Owasco Ovens       calories         92.00
                                        dietary_fiber     4.80

                     RiseNShine Bread   calories        100.00
                                        dietary_fiber     3.10
             ----------------------------------------------------
```

Example Features

Data Set	BREAD
Featured Step	PROC MEANS
Featured Step Statements and Options	PROC MEANS statement: NONOBS option CLASS statement TYPES statement
Formatting Features	PROC MEANS statement: MAXDEC= option; FW= option when sending output to the LISTING destination
Related Technique	PROC TABULATE
🔍 **A Closer Look**	Viewing the Output Data Set Created by This Example Creating Categories for Analysis with PROC MEANS Comparing the BY Statement and CLASS Statement in PROC MEANS Taking Advantage of the CLASS Statement in PROC MEANS
ODS Enhanced Version of Related Technique	Example 6.5
ODS Enhanced Version of Output Data Set from this Example	Example 6.15
Other Examples That Use This Data Set	Examples 6.5 and 6.15

Example Overview

This example summarizes nutritional information for a sample of bread products that are available either from grocery stores or from bakeries. The goal is to identify products with the lowest calories and highest dietary fiber in several categories. The data are categorized by four variables:

❑   source (grocery store vs. bakery)

❑   brand

❑   primary flour ingredient in the product

❑   type of bread (sandwich and a variety of specialty products)

The program computes statistics only for specific combinations of the four classification variables, not for all possible combinations of the four variables. It also computes the overall statistics. The results are saved in an output data set.

The following list shows the combinations for which this example saves statistics. One request computes overall statistics, three requests compute statistics for categories defined by a single classification variable, and two requests compute statistics for the categories defined by crossing two classification variables.

❑   overall

❑   type of bread

❑   primary flour ingredient in the product

❑   source

❑   source and type of bread

❑   source and brand

PROC MEANS saves the results of the six requests in one data set. Each observation in the output data set contains the results for one category. With the exception of the request for overall statistics, this yields multiple observations per request; the request for overall statistics is saved in the output data set in one observation.

The output data set saves statistics on calories and dietary fiber and it saves information that identifies the category and request. Each observation also contains identifying information for the three breads with the lowest calories and for the three breads with the highest dietary fiber for the category that the observation represents. The identifying information for these rankings includes the brand, the primary flour ingredient, and the type. The rankings are shown in Example 6.15. See Figure 3.2b for a listing of the output data set.

Program

Define a format to group the types of products. Specify the missing value level, which will exist in the output data set.

```
proc format;
   value $type 'Sandwich'='Sandwich'
               ' '=' '
                   other='Specialty';
run;
```

Compute specific statistics.

```
proc means data=bread n mean min max
```

Specify the maximum number of decimal places to display the statistics.

```
   maxdec=2
```

When sending output to the LISTING destination, specify the width of the field in which to display each statistic in the output.

```
   fw=7
```

Suppress the column that displays the total number of observations for each category ("N Obs"). (Because there is no missing data in this data set, the "N Obs" column is identical to the "N" column. When analyzing your own data, verify this condition before applying this option.)

```
   nonobs;
```

N ⇒ how to define this N if there is missing in the data set

```
title 'Nutritional Information about Breads
       Available in the Region';
title2 'Values Per Bread Slice, Calories in
        kcal, Fiber in Grams';
```

Specify the variables whose values define the categories for the analysis.

```
class source brand flour type;
```

Include the overall statistics in the report.

```
types ()
```

List the specific combinations of the classification variables that define the categories for the analyses.

```
      type flour source source*type
      source*brand;
```

```
var calories dietary_fiber;
```

Create an output data set containing specific statistics.

```
output out=breadstats
```

Save the three extreme minimum calorie values for each category specified in the TYPES statement.

```
      idgroup(min(calories) out[3]
```

Save identifying information as well as the calorie values for the three selected observations per category.

```
         (brand flour type calories)=
```

Specify the variable name prefix for each of the identifying variables and for the minimum calorie value.

```
         wherecal flourcal typecal mincal)
```

Save the three extreme maximum fiber values for each category specified in the TYPES statement.

```
      idgroup(max(dietary_fiber) out[3]
```

=??

	Specify the variable name prefix for each of the identifying variables and for the maximum fiber value.	

```
                                          (brand flour type dietary_fiber)=
                                            wherefiber flourfiber typefiber
                                            maxfiber);
```

Suppress the variable labels for the two analysis variables in the PROC MEANS output display.

```
                              label calories=' '
                                    dietary_fiber=' ';

                              format type $type.;
                        run;
```

Related Technique

A similar report can be produced easily with PROC TABULATE, as shown in Figure 3.2a. The advantage of PROC TABULATE is that it provides you with more formatting options than PROC MEANS. The PROC MEANS step constructed six separate tables. With all six table specifications on one TABLE statement, PROC TABULATE combines the six tables into one large report. If you want PROC TABULATE to generate six separate tables, replace the single TABLE statement with a TABLE statement for each table.

The advantages of PROC MEANS are in the features associated with the CLASS statement, such as the TYPES and WAYS statements and their options, and in the ease with which you can create output data sets that can then be processed by other procedures. While you can create data sets with PROC TABULATE, you cannot save information about minimum and maximum values with the output data set as you can with PROC MEANS.

Figure 3.2a Output Produced by PROC TABULATE

```
                   Nutritional Information about Breads Available in the Region
                      Values Per Bread Slice, Calories in kcal, Fiber in Grams
```

	Calories per Slice				Dietary Fiber(g) per Slice			
	N	Mean	Min	Max	N	Mean	Min	Max
Overall	124	87.59	56.00	138.00	124	2.01	0.00	4.80
Source								
Bakery	48	92.88	71.00	138.00	48	2.10	0.30	4.40
Grocery	76	84.25	56.00	112.00	76	1.95	0.00	4.80
Primary Flour Ingredient								
Multigrain	29	88.83	76.00	108.00	29	2.37	0.00	3.90
Oatmeal	5	93.00	84.00	111.00	5	3.30	2.80	3.90
Rye	20	86.70	71.00	105.00	20	2.16	1.00	4.20
White	45	87.42	56.00	138.00	45	1.11	0.00	2.90
Whole Wheat	25	86.08	72.00	101.00	25	2.82	1.00	4.80
Type of Bread								
Specialty	68	89.44	71.00	138.00	68	2.02	0.00	4.80
Sandwich	56	85.34	56.00	111.00	56	1.99	0.50	3.90

(continued)

(continued)

Source	Type of Bread	N	Mean	Min	Max	N	Mean	Min	Max
Bakery	Specialty	31	93.16	71.00	138.00	31	1.99	0.30	4.40
	Sandwich	17	92.35	73.00	111.00	17	2.31	0.50	3.90
Grocery	Specialty	37	86.32	72.00	112.00	37	2.05	0.00	4.80
	Sandwich	39	82.28	56.00	101.00	39	1.85	0.50	3.50

Source	Brand	N	Mean	Min	Max	N	Mean	Min	Max
Bakery	Aunt Sal Bakes	10	91.30	74.00	105.00	10	1.84	0.50	3.90
	Demeter	15	96.67	71.00	111.00	15	2.29	0.50	4.20
	Downtown Bakers	10	96.90	82.00	138.00	10	2.35	1.00	4.30
	Pain du Prairie	13	86.62	74.00	108.00	13	1.89	0.30	4.40
Grocery	BBB Brands	5	81.80	65.00	90.00	5	1.76	1.20	2.60
	Choice 123	6	80.67	71.00	92.00	6	1.52	0.50	2.30
	Fabulous Breads	15	82.80	71.00	97.00	15	1.84	0.00	3.20
	Five Chimneys	10	86.60	75.00	98.00	10	2.55	1.20	3.80
	Gaia's Hearth	11	89.00	77.00	101.00	11	1.83	0.00	3.60
	Mill City Bakers	9	85.33	66.00	112.00	9	1.92	0.50	3.10
	Owasco Ovens	12	83.33	72.00	92.00	12	2.20	0.80	4.80
	RiseNShine Bread	8	81.88	56.00	100.00	8	1.65	0.90	3.10

The following PROC TABULATE step produces the output shown in Figure 3.2a.

```
proc tabulate data=bread;
   title  'Nutritional Information about Breads
            Available in the Region';
   title2 'Values Per Bread Slice, Calories in
            kcal, Fiber in Grams';
```

Specify the same CLASS variables as in the PROC MEANS step.

```
   class source brand flour type;
   var calories dietary_fiber;
```

Compute an overall statistics table.

```
   table all='Overall'
```

Compute the one-way statistics tables.

```
       source flour type
```

Compute the two-way statistics tables.

```
       source*type source*brand,
```

Place the analysis variables in the column dimension and nest the statistics under each variable.

```
       (calories dietary_fiber)*
       (n*f=3. (mean min max)*f=7.2) / rts=30;

   format type $type.;
run;
```

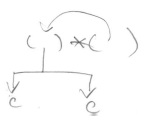

🔍 **A Closer Look**

Viewing the Output Data Set Created by This Example

The statistics computed by PROC MEANS in this example are saved in an output data set. The TYPES statement specified six requests, which results in the statistics for the six requests saved in the output data set BREADSTATS.

SAS identifies each request with a unique number and saves this value in the variable _TYPE_ that it defines. (Note that the values of _TYPE_ are numeric by default; specifying the PROC MEANS statement option CHARTYPE defines these values as character values.)

Submitting the following PROC PRINT step lists the contents of the output data set BREADSTATS. The values of _TYPE_ are formatted in the report as shown in Figure 3.2b. The variables identifying items with minimum calories and highest fiber are saved in the data set.

```
proc format;
   value _type_  0='0: Overall'
                 1='1: Type'
                 2='2: Flour'
                 8='8: Source'
                 9='9: Source*Type'
                12='12: Source*Brand';
run;

proc print data=breadstats;
   title 'Nutritional Information about Breads Available in the
      Region';
   title2 'Values Per Bread Slice, Calories in kcal, Fiber in
      Grams';
   title3 'Breads with Fewest Calories and Most Dietary Fiber';

   by _type_;
   format _type_ _type_.;
run;
```

Figure 3.2b shows the PROC PRINT output. The _FREQ_ variable, which is another variable that PROC MEANS defines, contains the number of observations that the given category represents.

Figure 3.2b PROC PRINT Listing of the BREADSTATS Data Set Created by PROC MEANS

```
                   Nutritional Information about Breads Available in the Region
                     Values Per Bread Slice, Calories in kcal, Fiber in Grams
                        Breads with Fewest Calories and Most Dietary Fiber

-------------------------------- _TYPE_=0: Overall --------------------------------

Obs  source   brand   flour   type   _FREQ_      wherecal_1       wherecal_2       wherecal_3

  1                                    124     RiseNShine Bread  BBB Brands    Mill City Bakers

Obs flourcal_1 flourcal_2 flourcal_3 typecal_1 typecal_2 typecal_3 mincal_1 mincal_2 mincal_3

  1   White      White      White    Sandwich Sandwich Sandwich     56       65       66

Obs wherefiber_1      wherefiber_2       wherefiber_3    flourfiber_1 flourfiber_2 flourfiber_3

  1 Owasco Ovens  Pain du Prairie  Downtown Bakers  Whole Wheat  Whole Wheat  Whole Wheat

Obs typefiber_1    typefiber_2     typefiber_3     maxfiber_1    maxfiber_2     maxfiber_3


  1 Specialty      Specialty      Specialty        4.8          4.4           4.3


-------------------------------- _TYPE_=1: Type --------------------------------

Obs  source  brand  flour    type     _FREQ_   wherecal_1       wherecal_2       wherecal_3

  2                        Specialty   68     Demeter         Owasco Ovens  Fabulous Breads
  3                        Sandwich    56     RiseNShine Bread BBB Brands    Mill City Bakers

Obs  flourcal_1 flourcal_2  flourcal_3   typecal_1 typecal_2 typecal_3 mincal_1 mincal_2

  2    White     Whole Wheat Whole Wheat Specialty Specialty Specialty    71       72
  3    White     White       White       Sandwich  Sandwich  Sandwich     56       65

Obs  mincal_3   wherefiber_1     wherefiber_2      wherefiber_3      flourfiber_1   flourfiber_2

  2    74      Owasco Ovens   Pain du Prairie   Downtown Bakers   Whole Wheat    Whole Wheat
  3    66      Aunt Sal Bakes Demeter           Gaia's Hearth     Multigrain     Oatmeal

Obs  flourfiber_3   typefiber_1   typefiber_2    typefiber_3    maxfiber_1   maxfiber_2   maxfiber_3

  2  Whole Wheat   Specialty     Specialty      Specialty      4.8          4.4          4.3
  3  Oatmeal       Sandwich      Sandwich       Sandwich       3.9          3.9          3.5


-------------------------------- _TYPE_=2: Flour --------------------------------

Obs source brand flour       type  _FREQ_    wherecal_1       wherecal_2        wherecal_3

  4                Multigrain        29    RiseNShine Bread Choice 123     Mill City Bakers
  5                Oatmeal           5     Five Chimneys    Fabulous Breads Owasco Ovens
  6                Rye               20    Mill City Bakers Five Chimneys   Fabulous Breads
  7                White             45    RiseNShine Bread BBB Brands      Mill City Bakers
  8                Whole Wheat       25    Owasco Ovens     Fabulous Breads Owasco Ovens


Obs flourcal_1    flourcal_2    flourcal_3    typecal_1  typecal_2  typecal_3  mincal_1 mincal_2

  4 Multigrain    Multigrain    Multigrain    Sandwich   Sandwich   Sandwich      76       76
  5 Oatmeal       Oatmeal       Oatmeal       Sandwich   Sandwich   Sandwich      84       85
  6 Rye           Rye           Rye           Sandwich   Sandwich   Sandwich      71       77
  7 White         White         White         Sandwich   Sandwich   Sandwich      56       65
  8 Whole Wheat   Whole Wheat   Whole Wheat   Specialty  Specialty  Sandwich      72       74
```

(continued)

(continued)

```
Obs  mincal_3  wherefiber_1      wherefiber_2       wherefiber_3      flourfiber_1    flourfiber_2
  4    77      Aunt Sal Bakes    Demeter            Demeter           Multigrain      Multigrain
  5    90      Demeter           Gaia's Hearth      Five Chimneys     Oatmeal         Oatmeal
  6    78      Demeter           Gaia's Hearth      Five Chimneys     Rye             Rye
  7    66      Downtown Bakers   Five Chimneys      Aunt Sal Bakes    White           White
  8    75      Owasco Ovens      Pain du Prairie    Downtown Bakers   Whole Wheat     Whole Wheat


Obs  flourfiber_3  typefiber_1    typefiber_2    typefiber_3    maxfiber_1    maxfiber_2    maxfiber_3

  4  Multigrain     Sandwich       Sandwich       Specialty        3.9           3.5           3.3
  5  Oatmeal        Sandwich       Sandwich       Sandwich         3.9           3.5           3.3
  6  Rye            Specialty      Specialty      Specialty        4.2           3.6           3.5
  7  White          Specialty      Sandwich       Specialty        2.9           2.3           2.3
  8  Whole Wheat    Specialty      Specialty      Specialty        4.8           4.4           4.3


------------------------------------- _TYPE_=8: Source -------------------------------------

Obs   source   brand  flour  type  _FREQ_   wherecal_1        wherecal_2        wherecal_3

  9  Bakery                          48     Demeter           Demeter          Pain du Prairie
 10  Grocery                         76     RiseNShine Bread  BBB Brands       Mill City Bakers

Obs  flourcal_1  flourcal_2  flourcal_3  typecal_1  typecal_2  typecal_3  mincal_1  mincal_2

  9    White       White       White      Specialty  Sandwich   Specialty     71        73
 10    White       White       White      Sandwich   Sandwich   Sandwich      56        65

Obs  mincal_3  wherefiber_1      wherefiber_2      wherefiber_3      flourfiber_1    flourfiber_2

  9    74      Pain du Prairie   Downtown Bakers   Demeter           Whole Wheat     Whole Wheat
 10    66      Owasco Ovens      Owasco Ovens      Five Chimneys     Whole Wheat     Whole Wheat

Obs   flourfiber_3  typefiber_1    typefiber_2    typefiber_3    maxfiber_1    maxfiber_2    maxfiber_3

  9  Rye            Specialty      Specialty      Specialty        4.4           4.3           4.2
 10  Whole Wheat    Specialty      Specialty      Specialty        4.8           4.0           3.8


------------------------------------- _TYPE_=9: Source*Type -------------------------------------

Obs  source  brand  flour   type    _FREQ_  wherecal_1        wherecal_2        wherecal_3

 11  Bakery                Specialty   31   Demeter           Pain du Prairie  Aunt Sal Bakes
 12  Bakery                Sandwich    17   Demeter           Pain du Prairie  Aunt Sal Bakes
 13  Grocery               Specialty   37   Owasco Ovens      Fabulous Breads  RiseNShine Bread
 14  Grocery               Sandwich    39   RiseNShine Bread  BBB Brands       Mill City Bakers


Obs  flourcal_1   flourcal_2    flourcal_3   typecal_1   typecal_2   typecal_3   mincal_1  mincal_2

 11  White        White         White        Specialty   Specialty   Specialty      71        74
 12  White        Whole Wheat   Rye          Sandwich    Sandwich    Sandwich       73        80
 13  Whole Wheat  Whole Wheat   White        Specialty   Specialty   Specialty      72        74
 14  White        White         White        Sandwich    Sandwich    Sandwich       56        65


Obs  mincal_3   wherefiber_1     wherefiber_2      wherefiber_3     flourfiber_1    flourfiber_2

 11    74       Pain du Prairie  Downtown Bakers   Demeter          Whole Wheat     Whole Wheat
 12    81       Aunt Sal Bakes   Demeter           Demeter          Multigrain      Oatmeal
 13    74       Owasco Ovens     Owasco Ovens      Five Chimneys    Whole Wheat     Whole Wheat
 14    66       Gaia's Hearth    Five Chimneys     Fabulous Breads  Oatmeal         Oatmeal
```

(continued)

(continued)

Obs	flourfiber_3	typefiber_1	typefiber_2	typefiber_3	maxfiber_1	maxfiber_2	maxfiber_3
11	Rye	Specialty	Specialty	Specialty	4.4	4.3	4.2
12	Multigrain	Sandwich	Sandwich	Sandwich	3.9	3.9	3.5
13	Whole Wheat	Specialty	Specialty	Specialty	4.8	4.0	3.8
14	Whole Wheat	Sandwich	Sandwich	Sandwich	3.5	3.3	3.1

```
--------------------------------- _TYPE_=12: Source*Brand ---------------------------------
```

Obs	source	brand	flour	type	_FREQ_	wherecal_1	wherecal_2
15	Bakery	Aunt Sal Bakes			10	Aunt Sal Bakes	Aunt Sal Bakes
16	Bakery	Demeter			15	Demeter	Demeter
17	Bakery	Downtown Bakers			10	Downtown Bakers	Downtown Bakers
18	Bakery	Pain du Prairie			13	Pain du Prairie	Pain du Prairie
19	Grocery	BBB Brands			5	BBB Brands	BBB Brands
20	Grocery	Choice 123			6	Choice 123	Choice 123
21	Grocery	Fabulous Breads			15	Fabulous Breads	Fabulous Breads
22	Grocery	Five Chimneys			10	Five Chimneys	Five Chimneys
23	Grocery	Gaia's Hearth			11	Gaia's Hearth	Gaia's Hearth
24	Grocery	Mill City Bakers			9	Mill City Bakers	Mill City Bakers
25	Grocery	Owasco Ovens			12	Owasco Ovens	Owasco Ovens
26	Grocery	RiseNShine Bread			8	RiseNShine Bread	RiseNShine Bread

Obs	wherecal_3	flourcal_1	flourcal_2	flourcal_3	typecal_1	typecal_2	typecal_3	mincal_1
15	Aunt Sal Bakes	White	Whole Wheat	Rye	Specialty	Specialty	Sandwich	74
16	Demeter	White	White	Rye	Specialty	Sandwich	Sandwich	71
17	Downtown Bakers	Rye	White	Whole Wheat	Sandwich	Specialty	Specialty	82
18	Pain du Prairie	White	Whole Wheat	Whole Wheat	Specialty	Specialty	Sandwich	74
19	BBB Brands	White	Rye	Rye	Sandwich	Sandwich	Specialty	65
20	Choice 123	White	White	Multigrain	Sandwich	Sandwich	Sandwich	71
21	Fabulous Breads	White	Whole Wheat	White	Sandwich	Specialty	Specialty	71
22	Five Chimneys	White	Rye	White	Specialty	Sandwich	Specialty	75
23	Gaia's Hearth	White	Whole Wheat	Multigrain	Specialty	Specialty	Specialty	77
24	Mill City Bakers	White	Rye	Multigrain	Sandwich	Sandwich	Sandwich	66
25	Owasco Ovens	Whole Wheat	Whole Wheat	Whole Wheat	Specialty	Sandwich	Specialty	72
26	RiseNShine Bread	White	White	Multigrain	Sandwich	Specialty	Sandwich	56

Obs	mincal_2	mincal_3	wherefiber_1	wherefiber_2	wherefiber_3	flourfiber_1
15	81	81	Aunt Sal Bakes	Aunt Sal Bakes	Aunt Sal Bakes	Multigrain
16	73	94	Demeter	Demeter	Demeter	Rye
17	82	85	Downtown Bakers	Downtown Bakers	Downtown Bakers	Whole Wheat
18	76	80	Pain du Prairie	Pain du Prairie	Pain du Prairie	Whole Wheat
19	82	84	BBB Brands	BBB Brands	BBB Brands	Whole Wheat
20	71	76	Choice 123	Choice 123	Choice 123	Multigrain
21	74	77	Fabulous Breads	Fabulous Breads	Fabulous Breads	Multigrain
22	77	82	Five Chimneys	Five Chimneys	Five Chimneys	Whole Wheat
23	80	81	Gaia's Hearth	Gaia's Hearth	Gaia's Hearth	Rye
24	71	77	Mill City Bakers	Mill City Bakers	Mill City Bakers	Multigrain
25	75	79	Owasco Ovens	Owasco Ovens	Owasco Ovens	Whole Wheat
26	74	76	RiseNShine Bread	RiseNShine Bread	RiseNShine Bread	Multigrain

Obs	flourfiber_2	flourfiber_3	typefiber_1	typefiber_2	typefiber_3	maxfiber_1	maxfiber_2	maxfiber_3
15	Rye	Whole Wheat	Sandwich	Specialty	Sandwich	3.9	3.5	2.4
16	Whole Wheat	Oatmeal	Specialty	Specialty	Sandwich	4.2	3.9	3.9
17	Whole Wheat	Rye	Specialty	Sandwich	Specialty	4.3	3.0	3.0
18	Whole Wheat	Whole Wheat	Specialty	Sandwich	Specialty	4.4	2.9	2.8
19	Rye	Rye	Sandwich	Specialty	Sandwich	2.6	2.0	1.5
20	Multigrain	Whole Wheat	Specialty	Sandwich	Sandwich	2.3	2.0	1.8
21	Whole Wheat	Rye	Specialty	Sandwich	Specialty	3.2	3.1	3.1
22	Rye	Oatmeal	Specialty	Specialty	Sandwich	3.8	3.5	3.3
23	Oatmeal	Whole Wheat	Specialty	Sandwich	Sandwich	3.6	3.5	2.3
24	Multigrain	Whole Wheat	Specialty	Sandwich	Sandwich	3.1	2.9	2.6
25	Whole Wheat	Rye	Specialty	Specialty	Specialty	4.8	4.0	2.9
26	Whole Wheat	White	Specialty	Sandwich	Specialty	3.1	2.0	1.7

Creating Categories for Analysis with PROC MEANS

PROC MEANS provides several ways to define categories in generating statistics tables. The remaining topics in this section describe some of the ways you can create categories in PROC MEANS.

When you save PROC MEANS results in a data set, you can then go on to produce customized reports using other SAS procedures, DATA steps, and ODS. Understanding your choices for defining categories for analysis will help you more efficiently use PROC MEANS to create data sets that can in turn be used to generate your final reports.

Example 6.15 uses DATA steps and ODS features to produce a report summarizing some of the information saved in the output data set created by PROC MEANS in this example.

Comparing the BY Statement and CLASS Statement in PROC MEANS

The two main ways to tell PROC MEANS you want your analyses done by categories are the BY statement and the CLASS statement.

When you use a BY statement, you request a separate analysis of each BY group. Your analysis data set must be sorted or indexed by the variables on the BY statement, or you must add the NOTSORTED option to the BY statement in the PROC MEANS step.

When you use the CLASS statement, you specify the variables whose values define the categories for the analysis. If the PROC MEANS step includes no other statements or options associated with the CLASS statement, the categories are defined by all the possible combinations of the CLASS variables, with all CLASS variables represented in each category. For example, if you have four CLASS variables, the categories for analysis are all the four-way combinations of the values of the four variables.

You do not have to sort or index your analysis data set by the CLASS variables before executing a PROC MEANS step that contains a CLASS statement, but no BY statement.

If you have several CLASS variables or your CLASS variables have many values, your report can be quite lengthy and may require additional computing resources because of the complexity. PROC MEANS must keep a copy of each unique value of each CLASS variable in memory. So in situations of limited computing resources, you may want to change some of your CLASS variables to BY variables. Also, you can adjust the PROC MEANS option SUMSIZE= to provide potentially more memory for your PROC MEANS step.

You can use a BY statement and a CLASS statement in the same PROC MEANS step. When you do, SAS analyzes the data by each BY group and applies the CLASS statement to each BY group.

Taking Advantage of the CLASS Statement in PROC MEANS

Several statements and options can be used in conjuction with the CLASS statement. These features allow you to produce tables of statistics for specific combinations of the CLASS variables as well as for specific values of the CLASS variables. You can also create output data sets that contain only these specific tables.

Understanding the choices in how to define categories will help you more efficiently focus only on the tables and categories that you need.

The BREAD data set contains two values for SOURCE, twelve values for BRAND, two values for TYPE when the TYPE format has been applied, and five values for FLOUR. To obtain the statistics shown in the preceding PROC MEANS report, without using the TYPES statement, add the PRINTALLTYPES to the PROC MEANS statement, and delete the TYPES statement. A modified version of the featured PROC MEANS step that does this follows:

```
proc means data=bread n mean min max maxdec=2 fw=7
          nonobs printalltypes;

     title 'Nutritional Information about Breads Available
            in the Region';
     title2 'Values Per Bread Slice, Calories in kcal,
             Fiber in Grams';

     class source brand flour type;

     var calories dietary_fiber;
     output out=breadstats
            idgroup (min(calories) out[3]
               (brand flour type calories)=
                wherecal flourcal typecal mincal)
            idgroup (max(dietary_fiber) out[3]
               (brand flour type dietary_fiber)=
                wherefiber flourfiber typefiber maxfiber);

     label calories=' '
           dietary_fiber=' ';

     format type $type.;
run;
```

The PROC MEANS step above produces tables for all one-way, two-way, three-way, and four-way combinations of the values of the four class variables. It also produces an overall table. This yields sixteen tables when the original request as specified on the TYPES statement specified six: five requests with classification variables plus one overall table. The output data set created by the PROC MEANS step that computes all sixteen tables contains 405 observations, whereas the output data set from the PROC MEANS step that computes the six specific tables contains 26 observations.

The four-way table alone in the PROC MEANS step that includes the PRINTALLTYPES option could generate statistics for a maximum of 240 categories: 2 sources*12 brands*2 formatted values of type*5 flours=240. (The BREAD data set, however, does not contain data for all combinations. The total number of categories in the four-way table for this data set is 89.)

Table 3.2a illustrates several ways to define categories when you use the CLASS statement in combination with other PROC MEANS features.

Table 3.2a does not describe the process of defining categories in which some of the values are represented multiple times. You can do this by creating multilabel formats with PROC FORMAT. See Example 3.7 for an example of applying multilabel formats.

Table 3.2a Combining the CLASS Statement with PROC MEANS to Define Categories

Purpose	Specification	Description and Example
Produce a table of statistics for the most complete combination of the CLASS variables	Additional statement: none PROC MEANS statement options: none CLASS statement options: none	```proc means data=bread; class source brand flour type; var calories dietary_fiber; run;``` Result: Table with statistics for each combination of the values of the four variables taken four variables at a time. Restrictions: The one-, two-, and three-way combinations are not evaluated. If many CLASS variables exist and/or the CLASS variables have many values, the report can be lengthy and can require additional computing resources.
Produce tables of statistics for all possible combinations of the CLASS variables at all levels, plus an overall table	Additional statement: none PROC MEANS statement options: PRINTALLTYPES CLASS statement options: none	```proc means data=bread printalltypes; class source brand flour type; var calories dietary_fiber; run;``` Result: Tables with statistics for each combination of the values of the four variables taken one variable at a time, two variables a time, three variables at a time, and four variables at a time. Also includes a table of overall statistics. Restrictions: If many CLASS variables exist and/or the CLASS variables have many values, the report can be lengthy and can require additional computing resources.
Produce tables for selected combinations of the CLASS variables	Additional statement: TYPES PROC MEANS statement options: none CLASS statement options: none	```proc means data=bread; class source brand flour type; types () type flour source source*type source*brand; var calories dietary_fiber; run;``` Result: Six tables of statistics: overall; three 1-way, and two 2-way. The one-way tables: categories defined by TYPE; by FLOUR; and by SOURCE. The two-way tables: categories defined by the combinations of SOURCE and TYPE; and by SOURCE and BRAND. Note: The text () specifies the computation of an overall summary.

(continued)

> what is result *(handwritten annotation)*

| Produce tables for selected levels of combinations of the CLASS variables | Additional statement: WAYS<br><br>PROC MEANS statement options: none<br><br>CLASS statement options: none | ```
proc means data=bread;
   class source brand flour type;
   ways 2 4;
   var calories dietary_fiber;
run;
```<br><br>Result: Seven tables of statistics: six 2-way tables and one 4-way table. The 2-way tables: categories defined by the combination of SOURCE and BRAND; SOURCE and FLOUR; SOURCE and TYPE; BRAND and FLOUR; BRAND and TYPE; and FLOUR and TYPE. The 4-way table: categories defined by the combination of the values of SOURCE, BRAND, FLOUR, and TYPE.<br><br>Restrictions: If many CLASS variables exist and/or the CLASS variables have many values, the report can be lengthy and can require additional computing resources. |
| Produce a table of statistics for the most complete combination of the CLASS variables. Included in the output are the categories defined in the CLASSDATA= data set, even if the categories are not present in the analysis data set. These categories have an N of 0. | Additional statement: None<br><br>PROC MEANS statement options: CLASSDATA=<br><br>CLASS statement options: none | ```
proc means data=bread classdata=complex;
   class source flour;
   var calories dietary_fiber;
run;

PROC PRINT of data set COMPLEX:
 Obs    source        flour
  1    Grocery    Whole Wheat
  2    Bakery     Whole Wheat
  3    Other      Whole Wheat
  4    Grocery    Multigrain
  5    Bakery     Multigrain
  6    Other      Multigrain
```<br><br>Result: Twelve categories in the output. One table that contains all combinations of the values of SOURCE and FLOUR that are in the BREAD data set plus two additional rows. These two rows are SOURCE='Other' and FLOUR='Whole Wheat', and SOURCE='Other' and FLOUR='Multigrain'. These two rows have an N of 0, because of no representation in the BREAD data set.<br><br>Restrictions: Must include all CLASS variables in the CLASSDATA= data set.<br><br>CLASS variables in the CLASSDATA= data set must be defined exactly as they are in the analysis data set. |

⟹ I don't understand *(handwritten annotation)*

(continued)

| Produce a table of statistics for all possible combinations of CLASS variables, including those in the analysis data set as well as those represented in the CLASSDATA= data set, even if the categories are not present in the analysis data set. Categories without representation in the analysis data set have an N of 0. | Additional statement: none<br><br>PROC MEANS statement options: CLASSDATA=, COMPLETETYPES<br><br>CLASS statement options: none | ```
proc means data=bread classdata=complex
     completetypes;
  class source flour;
  var calories dietary_fiber;
run;
```<br><br>This example uses the same COMPLEX data set as listed in the previous row in this table.<br><br>Result: Fifteen categories in the output. One table that contains all the combinations of the values of SOURCE and FLOUR that are present in the BREAD data set and in the COMPLEX data set (3 values of SOURCE and 5 values of FLOUR=15 categories). The five rows where SOURCE='Other' have an N of 0.<br><br>Restrictions: Must include all CLASS variables in the CLASSDATA= data set.<br><br>CLASS variables in the CLASSDATA= data set must be defined exactly as they are in the analysis data set.<br><br>If specifications in the CLASSDATA= data set are not in the analysis data set, there are potentially many rows in the table with no statistics other than N=0. This example has five rows with N=0. |
| Produce a table of statistics for the most complete combination of the CLASS variables for which categories are defined in the CLASSDATA= data set, even if the categories are not present in the analysis data set. These categories have an N of 0. Do not include categories that are only in the analysis data set and not in the CLASSDATA= data set. | Additional statement: none<br><br>PROC MEANS statement options: CLASSDATA=, EXCLUSIVE<br><br>CLASS statement options: none | ```
proc means data=bread classdata=complex
     exclusive;
  class source flour;
  var calories dietary_fiber;
run;
```<br><br>This example uses the same COMPLEX data set as used in the previous two rows of this table.<br><br>Result: Six categories in one table in the output. The table contains only the combinations of the values of SOURCE and TYPE that are present in the CLASSDATA= data set. Combinations that are present only in the analysis data set are excluded from the results. Two categories are generated for each of the three values of SOURCE that are present in COMPLEX, one for TYPE='Whole Wheat' and one for TYPE='Multigrain'. The two rows for SOURCE='Other' have an N of 0.<br><br>Restrictions: Must include all CLASS variables in the CLASSDATA= data set.<br><br>CLASS variables in the CLASSDATA= data set must be defined exactly as they are in the analysis data set. |

(continued)

1, 2, 3, 4, 5 =

othe

| Produce tables for all combinations of the CLASS variables as specified by the formats associated with them, even if the combinations are not in the analysis data set | Additional statement: FORMAT, if formats not already assigned to CLASS variables

PROC MEANS statement options: COMPLETETYPES

CLASS statement options: PRELOADFMT | ```
proc format;
   value $texture
         'Multigrain','Oatmeal','Whole
          Wheat'='Whole Grain'
         'White','Bleached White'='Refined'
         'Garbanzo','Soy'='Beans';
run;

proc means data=bread completetypes;
   class flour / preloadfmt;
   var calories dietary_fiber;
   format flour $texture.;
run;
```

all

Result: Four categories in one table in the output. The table contains the categories in the variable FLOUR as formatted by $TEXTURE. Values not represented in $TEXTURE are included in the analysis as their unformatted values. Values that are in $TEXTURE, but not in the BREAD data set, are included in the analysis. The report will show a row for "Beans" with N=0, because there are no products in the BREAD data set whose primary flour ingredient is garbanzo bean flour or soy flour. The report will show a row for "Rye," the one value in the BREAD data set that is not included in $TEXTURE.

Restrictions: Need to define formats for the CLASS variables before the PROC MEANS step. |
| Produce tables for all combinations of the CLASS variables as specified by the formats associated with them. Omit combinations that are in the associated format, but not in the data set. Omit combinations that are in the data set and not in the associated format. | Additional statement: FORMAT, if formats not already assigned to CLASS variables

PROC MEANS statement options: none

CLASS statement options: PRELOADFMT, EXCLUSIVE | ```
proc format;
   value $texture
         'Multigrain','Oatmeal','Whole
          Wheat'='Whole Grain'
         'White','Bleached White'='Refined'
         'Garbanzo','Soy'='Beans';
run;

proc means data=bread;
   class flour / preloadfmt exclusive;
   var calories dietary_fiber;
   format type $texture.;
run;
```

exclse no OBs

Result: One table that contains the categories in the variable FLOUR as formatted by $TEXTURE and restricted by the EXCLUSIVE option: one category for "Whole Grain" and one for "Refined." The one value of FLOUR not represented in $TEXTURE ("Rye") is not included in the report. The one formatted value in $TEXTURE ("Beans") that does not have any corresponding values in FLOUR is not included in the report.

Restrictions: Need to define formats for the CLASS variables before the PROC MEANS step.

Note: This discussion places the EXCLUSIVE option on the CLASS statement. If you place the EXCLUSIVE option on the PROC MEANS statement instead, your report will contain the same results plus a row for "RYE." |

**Where to Go from
Here**

PROC FORMAT reference, usage information, and additional examples.
See "The FORMAT Procedure" in the "Procedures" section of *Base SAS 9.1
Procedures Guide.*

PROC MEANS reference, usage information, and additional examples. See
"The MEANS Procedure" in the "Procedures" section of *Base SAS 9.1
Procedures Guide.*

PROC TABULATE reference, usage information, and additional examples.
See, "The TABULATE Procedure" in the "Procedures" section of *Base SAS 9.1
Procedures Guide.*

Example 3.3   Displaying Descriptive Statistics in a Tabular Format

Goal

Compute descriptive statistics for several categories and arrange the statistics in a tabular format.

classical

Report

```
                              Exercise Program Results
-------------------------------------------------------------------------------------------
|                  |              |                      Lipid Profile                     |
|                  |              |-------------------------------------------------------|
|                  |              |           Cholesterol          |          HDL          |
|                  |              |-------------------------------------+-----------------|
|                  |       | Std |     |     |     |   | Std |     |     |     |
|                  | N |Mean | Dev | P25 | P50 | P75 | N |Mean | Dev | P25 | P50 | P75 |
|------------------+---+-----+-----+-----+-----+-----+---+-----+-----+-----+-----+-----|
|Gender  |Testing  |   |     |     |     |     |     |   |     |     |     |     |     |
|--------|Period   |   |     |     |     |     |     |   |     |     |     |     |     |
|Males   |---------|   |     |     |     |     |     |   |     |     |     |     |     |
|        |Pre      | 15|220.6| 37.8|190.0|219.0|250.0| 15| 43.3|  9.6| 32.0| 43.0| 51.0|
|        |---------+---+-----+-----+-----+-----+-----+---+-----+-----+-----+-----+-----|
|        |Post     | 15|202.1| 30.8|172.0|205.0|216.0| 15| 43.9|  9.9| 33.0| 44.0| 52.0|
|--------+---------+---+-----+-----+-----+-----+-----+---+-----+-----+-----+-----+-----|
|Females |Pre      | 11|173.5| 21.2|158.0|164.0|195.0| 11| 58.6|  8.9| 51.0| 60.0| 66.0|
|        |---------+---+-----+-----+-----+-----+-----+---+-----+-----+-----+-----+-----|
|        |Post     | 11|161.7| 18.3|149.0|155.0|174.0| 11| 59.4|  7.7| 53.0| 60.0| 66.0|
|--------+---------+---+-----+-----+-----+-----+-----+---+-----+-----+-----+-----+-----|
|Both    |Pre      | 26|200.7| 39.3|164.0|195.5|222.0| 26| 49.8| 11.9| 43.0| 51.0| 57.0|
|Genders |---------+---+-----+-----+-----+-----+-----+---+-----+-----+-----+-----+-----|
|        |Post     | 26|185.0| 32.8|155.0|180.0|207.0| 26| 50.4| 11.8| 44.0| 51.5| 60.0|
-------------------------------------------------------------------------------------------


              -----------------------------------------------------------
              |                  |              |     Lipid Profile      |
              |                  |              |------------------------|
              |                  |              |      Triglycerides     |
              |                  |              |------------------------|
              |                  |       | Std |     |     |     |
              |                  | N |Mean | Dev | P25 | P50 | P75 |
              |------------------+---+-----+-----+-----+-----+-----|
              |Gender  |Testing  |   |     |     |     |     |     |
              |--------|Period   |   |     |     |     |     |     |
              |Males   |---------|   |     |     |     |     |     |
              |        |Pre      | 15|156.9| 81.9| 95.0|145.0|198.0|
              |        |---------+---+-----+-----+-----+-----+-----|
              |        |Post     | 15|140.5| 71.3| 83.0|136.0|174.0|
              |--------+---------+---+-----+-----+-----+-----+-----|
              |Females |Pre      | 11| 82.7| 36.2| 57.0| 65.0|114.0|
              |        |---------+---+-----+-----+-----+-----+-----|
              |        |Post     | 11| 75.0| 30.9| 56.0| 69.0|101.0|
              |--------+---------+---+-----+-----+-----+-----+-----|
              |Both    |Pre      | 26|125.5| 75.4| 65.0|108.0|150.0|
              |Genders |---------+---+-----+-----+-----+-----+-----|
              |        |Post     | 26|112.8| 65.7| 61.0| 95.5|141.0|
              -----------------------------------------------------------
```

Gender * Testing   all

(Gender all) x Testing , Lipid * (chol HDL Trig) * (N*F=

                          (Mean) * F =
                                     st

Example Features

Data Set	LIPIDS
Featured Step	PROC TABULATE
Featured Step Statements and Options	CLASS statement: DESCENDING option
Formatting Features	TABLE statement: NOCONTINUED option TABLE statement: CONDENSE and RTS= options when sending output to the LISTING destination
Related Technique	PROC REPORT, DEFINE statement: GROUP option
🔍 A Closer Look	Comparing PROC TABULATE and PROC REPORT for Generating the Report in this Example
ODS Enhanced Version of This Example	Example 6.8 and 6.9
Other Examples That Use This Data Set	Examples 2.7, 6.4, 6.8, and 6.9

Example Overview

Presenting descriptive statistics in a tabular format can help you quickly review your data set. The report in this example presents several descriptive statistics for the blood tests in the LIPIDS data set. It groups the observations in the data set by gender and testing period, and it also computes the statistics with genders combined.

Each observation in the LIPIDS data set corresponds to the lipid measurements for one participant during one of the two testing periods.

See the related technique in Example 3.1 for another example of displaying statistics in a tabular format.

Program

Define a format for one of the CLASS variables in the PROC TABULATE step.

```
proc format;
  value $gender 'M'='Males'
                'F'='Females';
run;

proc tabulate data=lipids;
  title 'Exercise Program Results';
```

To display males before females and "Pre" program results before "Post" program results, specify that the categories of the two class variables, GENDER and TIME, should be listed in descending order.

```
  class gender testperiod / descending;
```

Specify the analysis variables.	`var chol hdl tri;`
	`table`
Define the arrangement of the class variables in the row dimension.	`(gender='Gender'`
Compute statistics for both genders combined.	`all='Both Genders')*`
Nest the categories of TESTPERIOD beneath the categories of GENDER and the summary variable ALL.	`testperiod='Testing Period',`
Place a heading over the following three analysis variables.	`all='Lipid Profile'*`
Nest the three analysis variables beneath the heading specified in the preceding ALL= specification.	`(chol='Cholesterol' hdl='HDL'` `tri='Triglycerides')*`
Specify the statistics that should be computed for each analysis variable, and specify the display format of the statistics.	`(n*f=3. (mean std='Std Dev' p25 p50` `p75)*f=5.1) /`
Place as many logical pages as possible on one physical page when sending output to the LISTING destination.	`condense`
Omit the default printing of the "(Continued)" message.	`nocontinued`

When sending output to the LISTING destination, specify the space allocated to row titles.	`rts=20;`
	`format gender $gender.;`
	`run;`

Related Technique

PROC REPORT can also produce a tabular report of descriptive statistics, as shown in Figure 3.3. Here are some differences in the output in Figure 3.3 compared to the output from the main example:

❑ The summary by time period is omitted.

❑ Cholesterol and HDL results are on one page.

❑ Triglycerides results are on the second page.

Figure 3.3 Output from PROC REPORT

```
                               Exercise Program Results

----------------------------------------------------------------------------------
|           ------------Cholesterol------------   ----------------HDL----------------|
|        Testing               Std                               Std                |
|Gender  Period   N   Mean     Dev   P25   P50   P75   N   Mean   Dev   P25   P50   P75|
|------------------------------------------------------------------------------------|
|Males  | Pre    | 15| 220.6| 37.8| 190.0| 219.0| 250.0| 15| 43.3|  9.6| 32.0| 43.0| 51.0|
|       |--------+----+------+------+------+------+------+----+------+------+------+------+------|
|       | Post   | 15| 202.1| 30.8| 172.0| 205.0| 216.0| 15| 43.9|  9.9| 33.0| 44.0| 52.0|
|-------+--------+----+------+------+------+------+------+----+------+------+------+------+------|
|Females| Pre    | 11| 173.5| 21.2| 158.0| 164.0| 195.0| 11| 58.6|  8.9| 51.0| 60.0| 66.0|
|       |--------+----+------+------+------+------+------+----+------+------+------+------+------|
|       | Post   | 11| 161.7| 18.3| 149.0| 155.0| 174.0| 11| 59.4|  7.7| 53.0| 60.0| 66.0|
----------------------------------------------------------------------------------


-------------------------------------------page break--------------------------------------------

                               Exercise Program Results

         -------------------------------------------------------------
         |           ------------Triglycerides------------|
         |        Testing               Std                |
         |Gender  Period   N   Mean     Dev   P25   P50   P75|
         |---------------------------------------------------|
         |Males  | Pre    | 15| 156.9| 81.9|  95.0| 145.0| 198.0|
         |       |--------+----+------+------+------+------+------|
         |       | Post   | 15| 140.5| 71.3|  83.0| 136.0| 174.0|
         |-------+--------+----+------+------+------+------+------|
         |Females| Pre    | 11|  82.7| 36.2|  57.0|  65.0| 114.0|
         |       |--------+----+------+------+------+------+------|
         |       | Post   | 11|  75.0| 30.9|  56.0|  69.0| 101.0|
         -------------------------------------------------------------
```

The following PROC REPORT step produces the report shown in Figure 3.3.

```
proc format;

  value $gender 'M'='Males'
                'F'='Females';
run;

proc report data=lipids nowindows box;
   title 'Exercise Program Results';

column gender testperiod

     chol,(n mean std p25 p50 p75)
     hdl,(n mean std p25 p50 p75)
     tri,(n mean std p25 p50 p75);

define gender / group format=$gender. left id
               descending 'Gender';
define testperiod / group left id descending
               'Testing Period' width=7;

define chol / '-Cholesterol-';
define hdl / '-HDL-';
define tri / '-Triglycerides-';
```

Specify the same format as was used in the main example to label the values of GENDER.

Specify the columns in the report.

List within parentheses the statistics that are to be computed on each analysis variable. Nest the set of statistics beneath the heading for the analysis variable.

Group the data by gender and time of testing. Arrange the values of the two grouping variables in descending order so that data for males prints before females, and data for the "Pre" testing period prints before the "Post" testing period.

Specify the analysis variables. When sending output to the LISTING destination, pad the heading for each analysis variable with dashes.

Specify the attributes of the statistics.

```
          define n / format=4. 'N';
          define mean / format=5.1 'Mean';
          define std / format=5.1 'Std Dev';
          define p25 / format=5.1 'P25';
          define p50 / format=5.1 'P50';
          define p75 / format=5.1 'P75';
run;
```

A Closer Look

Comparing PROC TABULATE and PROC REPORT for Generating the Report in this Example

Both PROC TABULATE and PROC REPORT can summarize data by categories. Each procedure has its strengths and weaknesses.

Strengths of PROC TABULATE

In this example, you might prefer PROC TABULATE for these reasons:

❑ *Ability to summarize the classification variables in specific ways within one step.* PROC TABULATE provides the flexibility to construct summarization requests within the TABLE statement. The PROC TABULATE step analyzes the data by gender and overall for each testing period, whereas the PROC REPORT step did not. For PROC REPORT to produce the overall summarization for each testing period and have it included as the last two rows of the report requires COMPUTE blocks and programming statements. Alternatively, you could issue two PROC REPORT steps. The first would be the same as the program in the related technique. The second step would drop GENDER as a group variable.

❑ *Ability to condense multiple logical pages onto fewer physical pages when sending the report to the LISTING destination.* Both reports above were sent to the LISTING destination. The CONDENSE option on the PROC TABULATE TABLE statement caused the report to be displayed on one page. If this option was omitted, the triglyceride results and the overall results would be on a second page. PROC REPORT does not have an option similar to CONDENSE. Therefore, it sends the triglycerides results to a second page. (When you send the report to a nonlisting destination, such as RTF, the PROC REPORT report is placed on one page.)

Strengths of PROC REPORT

You might prefer PROC REPORT for these reasons:

❑ *Ability to add text to the report and add text that is based on the results in the report.* With PROC REPORT COMPUTE blocks and programming statements, you can add information to your report and control its placement. The information you add can be derived from the results obtained in the report step.

PROC TABULATE does not have statements or options that give you as much control over content and placement of text as PROC REPORT. The BOX= option on the TABLE statement enables you to add text to the upper left box of a PROC TABULATE table. You can add headings to the report as demonstrated by the placement of the text "Lipid Profile" above the statistics for the three analysis variables.

Condense

Both PROC REPORT and PROC TABULATE can use ODS features to add text in specific locations of a report. For further information, see *SAS 9.1 Output Delivery System: User's Guide.* For updates to the reference and new developments in ODS, see online resources at support.sas.com/v9doc.

❑ *Ability to compute new columns.* COMPUTE blocks and programming statements enable you to create new columns in a report produced by PROC REPORT. PROC TABULATE does not have this functionality. You would have to add these variables to your input data set prior to the PROC TABULATE step.

Where to Go from Here

PROC REPORT reference, usage information, and additional examples. See "The REPORT Procedure" in the "Procedures" section of *Base SAS 9.1 Procedures Guide.*

PROC TABULATE reference, usage information, and additional examples. See "The TABULATE Procedure" in the "Procedures" section of *Base SAS 9.1 Procedures Guide.*

Example 3.4   Displaying Basic Frequency Counts and Percentages

Goal

Compute frequency counts and percentages for categories in a data set.

Report

```
                          Gender Distribution within Job Classes
                                    for Four Regions
  -----------------------------------------------------------------------------
  |                                        |     Gender      |        |
  |                                        |-----------------|  All   |
  |                                        | Female |  Male  |Employees|
  |----------------------------------------+--------+--------+--------|
  |Job Class                   |           |        |        |        |
  |----------------------------+-----------|        |        |        |
  |Technical                   |Number of employees |     16|     18|     34|
  |                            |--------------------+--------+--------+--------|
  |                            |Percent of row total |   47.1|   52.9|  100.0|
  |                            |--------------------+--------+--------+--------|
  |                            |Percent of column total|  26.2|   29.0|   27.6|
  |                            |--------------------+--------+--------+--------|
  |                            |Percent of total    |   13.0|   14.6|   27.6|
  |----------------------------+--------------------+--------+--------+--------|
  |Manager/Supervisor          |Number of employees |     20|     15|     35|
  |                            |Percent of row total |   57.1|   42.9|  100.0|
  |                            |Percent of column total|  32.8|   24.2|   28.5|
  |                            |Percent of total    |   16.3|   12.2|   28.5|
  |----------------------------+--------------------+--------+--------+--------|
  |Clerical                    |Number of employees |     14|     14|     28|
  |                            |Percent of row total |   50.0|   50.0|  100.0|
  |                            |Percent of column total|  23.0|   22.6|   22.8|
  |                            |Percent of total    |   11.4|   11.4|   22.8|
  |----------------------------+--------------------+--------+--------+--------|
  |Administrative              |Number of employees |     11|     15|     26|
  |                            |Percent of row total |   42.3|   57.7|  100.0|
  |                            |Percent of column total|  18.0|   24.2|   21.1|
  |                            |Percent of total    |    8.9|   12.2|   21.1|
  |----------------------------+--------------------+--------+--------+--------|
  |All Jobs                    |Number of employees |     61|     62|    123|
  |                            |Percent of row total |   49.6|   50.4|  100.0|
  |                            |Percent of column total| 100.0|  100.0|  100.0|
  |                            |Percent of total    |   49.6|   50.4|  100.0|
  -----------------------------------------------------------------------------
```

Example Features

Data Set	JOBCLASS
Featured Step	PROC TABULATE
Featured Step Statements and Options	TABLE statement: ROWPCTN, COLPCTN, and REPPCTN statistics
Formatting Features	PROC TABULATE statement: FORMAT= option TABLE statement: RTS= option when sending output to the LISTING destination
Related Technique	PROC FREQ
🔍 A Closer Look	Analyzing the Structure of the Report Understanding the Percentage Statistics in PROC TABULATE Specifying a Denominator for a Percentage Statistic
Other Examples That Use This Data Set	Examples 3.5, 3.6, 6.3, and 6.7

Example Overview

Crosstabulation tables (also called contingency tables) show combined frequency distributions for two or more variables.

This report shows frequency counts for females and males within each of four job classes. The table also shows the percentage of the following totals that each frequency count represents:

❑ the total women and men in that job class (row percentage)

❑ the total for that gender in all job classes (column percentage)

❑ the total number of employees

Each observation in JOBCLASS corresponds to the information for one employee.

Program

Define formats to associate with the variables GENDER and OCCUPAT.

```
proc format;
   value gendfmt 1='Female'
                 2='Male';
   value occupfmt 1='Technical'
                  2='Manager/Supervisor'
                  3='Clerical'
                  4='Administrative';
run;
```

Specify a default format for each table cell.

```
proc tabulate data=jobclass format=8.1;
   title 'Gender Distribution within Job
          Classes';
   title2 'for Four Regions';
```

Specify the classification variables.	`class gender occupat;`
Establish the layout of the table.	`table`
Specify the row dimension of the table. Enclose the row classifications in parentheses so that the expression for the set of statistics that follows the asterisk has to be written only once. Specify headings for columns, rows, and statistics.	`(occupat='Job Class'`
Summarize at the bottom of the report the rows defined by the values of OCCUPAT.	`all='All Jobs')`
Nest statistics beneath each category defined by the row classifications. Enclose in parentheses the set of statistics that should be computed for each category.	`*(n='Number of employees'*f=9.`
Specify the percentage statistics that PROC TABULATE should calculate. Place these percentages in the row dimension. Calculate the percentage of females and males within a job class, since JOBCLASS is in the row dimension.	`rowpctn='Percent of row total'`
Calculate the percentage of job classes within each gender, which is in the column dimension.	`colpctn='Percent of column total'`
Calculate the percentage each cell contributes to the total in the report. Terminate the row specification with a comma and begin the column dimension specification.	`reppctn='Percent of total'),`
Specify the column dimension of the table.	`gender='Gender'`
Summarize in the rightmost column of the report the columns defined by the values of GENDER.	`all='All Employees' /`
When sending output to the LISTING destination, specify the space allocated to row titles with the RTS= option.	`rts=50;`

```
        format gender gendfmt. occupat occupfmt.;
run;
```

Related Technique

PROC FREQ can also produce crosstabular reports of counts and percentages. Although this procedure does not provide the customization and formatting features of PROC TABULATE, it does automatically calculate totals as well as row, column, and total percentages. You can also request a wider range of statistics with PROC FREQ, including several chi-square and odds ratios statistics.

Figure 3.4 shows the output from PROC FREQ. By default, when PROC FREQ computes a two-way table (row*column), four values are presented in each cell of the report. The key to the values in each cell is shown in the upper-left corner of the table.

Figure 3.4 Output from PROC FREQ

```
              Gender Distribution within Job Classes
                         for Four Regions

                       The FREQ Procedure

                    Table of occupat by gender

        occupat(Job class)        gender

        Frequency        |
        Percent          |
        Row Pct          |
        Col Pct          |Female  |Male     |  Total
                         |        |         |
                         |        |         |
        -----------------+--------+--------+
        Technical        |     16 |     18 |     34
                         |  13.01 |  14.63 |  27.64
                         |  47.06 |  52.94 |
                         |  26.23 |  29.03 |
        -----------------+--------+--------+
        Manager/Supervis |     20 |     15 |     35
        or               |  16.26 |  12.20 |  28.46
                         |  57.14 |  42.86 |
                         |  32.79 |  24.19 |
        -----------------+--------+--------+
        Clerical         |     14 |     14 |     28
                         |  11.38 |  11.38 |  22.76
                         |  50.00 |  50.00 |
                         |  22.95 |  22.58 |
        -----------------+--------+--------+
        Administrative   |     11 |     15 |     26
                         |   8.94 |  12.20 |  21.14
                         |  42.31 |  57.69 |
                         |  18.03 |  24.19 |
        -----------------+--------+--------+
        Total                  61       62      123
                            49.59    50.41   100.00
```

The following PROC FREQ step produces the report in Figure 3.4.

```
proc format;
   value gendfmt 1='Female'
                 2='Male';
   value occupfmt 1='Technical'
                  2='Manager/Supervisor'
                  3='Clerical'
                  4='Administrative';
run;

proc freq data=jobclass;
   title 'Gender Distribution within Job
          Classes';
   title2 'for Four Regions';
   tables occupat*gender;


   label occupat='Job class';
   format gender gendfmt. occupat occupfmt.;
run;
```

Place the row dimension to the left of the column dimension. Separate the dimensions with an asterisk (*).

🔎 **A Closer Look**

Analyzing the Structure of the Report

The combinations of the row and column classifications define the categories of the report. The two classification variables in the row dimension of the report are OCCUPAT and the universal class variable ALL. The two classification variables in the column dimension of the report are GENDER and the universal class variable ALL.

The PROC TABULATE step computes frequency percentages for each of the four possible combinations that result from crossing the two row and two column classifications. Table 3.4a describes the combinations.

Table 3.4a Combinations of the Classification Variables

Class Variables (row and column)	Description	Number of Categories
OCCUPAT and GENDER	Number of females in each job or number of males in each job	8
ALL and GENDER	Total number of females or total number of males	2
OCCUPAT and ALL	Number of employees in each job	4
ALL and ALL	Total number of employees in all jobs	1

You can think of each combination of a row and a column classification as a subtable. Figure 3.4 illustrates this concept as applied to this example's report.

Figure 3.4 Illustration of the Four Subtables

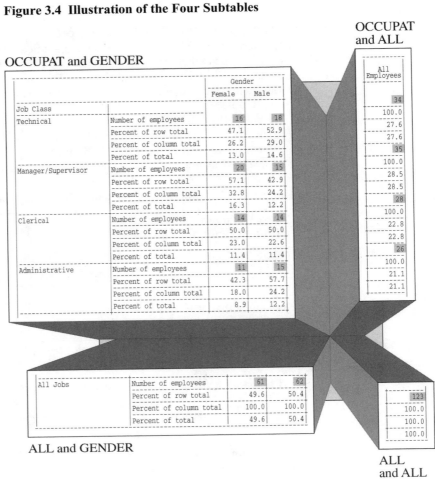

Understanding the concept of viewing a PROC TABULATE table as a collection of subtables is especially useful when you need to specify denominator definitions. See "Specifying a Denominator for a Percentage Statistic" later in this section for a discussion of how to form denominator definitions.

Understanding the Percentage Statistics in PROC TABULATE

Table 3.4b lists the eight dimension-specific percentages that PROC TABULATE can compute: four percentages are computed based on the N statistic, and four are computed based on the SUM statistic.

The total (or denominator) on which a percentage is based is the total of the statistic in the specific dimension.

Table 3.4b Dimension-Specific Percentages That PROC TABULATE Can Compute

Statistic	Dimension	Description
REPPCTN	Entire report	Percentage of the frequency count in a table cell in relation to the total frequency count in the report
REPPCTSUM	Entire report	Percentage of the sum of an analysis variable in a table cell in relation to the total sum of the analysis variable in the report
COLPCTN	Column	Percentage of the frequency count in a table cell in relation to the total frequency count in the column of the table cell
COLPCTSUM	Column	Percentage of the sum of an analysis variable in a table cell in relation to the total sum in the column of the table cell
ROWPCTN	Row	Percentage of the frequency count in a table cell in relation to the total frequency count in the row of the table cell
ROWPCTSUM	Row	Percentage of the sum of an analysis variable in a table cell in relation to the total sum in the row of the table cell
PAGEPCTN	Page	Percentage of the frequency count in a table cell in relation to the total frequency count on the page of the table cell
PAGEPCTSUM	Page	Percentage of the sum of an analysis variable in a table cell in relation to the total sum on the page of the table cell

When selecting a dimension-specific percentage, make sure that your table includes the dimension of the statistic. In the example above, the TABLE statement specifies a row and a column dimension. Including the PAGEPCTN statistic in this example's TABLE statement generates an error, because no page dimension was specified.

Two additional percentages, PCTN and PCTSUM, allow you to specify the denominators of the percentage calculations explicitly. The next section briefly discusses ways to write denominator definitions and applies this to writing the denominator definitions for the percentages in the main example.

Specifying a Denominator for a Percentage Statistic

The main example computes percentages by simply using the dimension-specific percentages. When your tables are more complex, however, the dimension-specific percentages might not produce the percentages required for your report. In those situations, using the PCTN and PCTSUM statistics enables you to specify the denominator of your percentage calculation.

When coding a PCTN or PCTSUM statistic that requires a denominator definition, follow the PCTN or PCTSUM keyword with the denominator definition enclosed in angle brackets. The denominator definition specifies the classifications to tally in order to calculate the denominator.

Table 3.4c shows how to code the denominator definition for the PCTN statistic so that PROC TABULATE calculates the *same* percentages as the corresponding dimension-specific percentages in the above example.

Table 3.4c Constructing Denominator Definitions for Percentage Calculations That Are Equivalent to Percentage Statistics in This Example

Statistic	Equivalent Statistic Using PCTN with a Denominator Definition
ROWPCTN	PCTN<GENDER ALL>
COLPCTN	PCTN<OCCUPAT ALL>
REPPCTN	PCTN or PCTN<OCCUPAT*GENDER ALL>

A version of the TABLE statement that uses the PCTN statistic follows:

```
table (occupat='Job Class' all='All Jobs')*
      (n='Number of employees'*f=9.
       pctn<gender all>='Percent of row total'
       pctn<occupat all>='Percent of column total'
       pctn='Percent of total'),
       gender='Gender' all='All Employees'
       / rts=50;
```

Table 3.4c shows that the ROWPCTN statistic is equivalent to the PCTN statistic with a denominator definition of GENDER and ALL. The report has two classification variables in the row dimension: OCCUPAT and ALL. For each level of the classification variable OCCUPAT, which is presented in a row in this report, PROC TABULATE computes the N for all the columns in this level (or row). The columns in this level are GENDER and ALL, and these are concatenated columns in the table. Therefore, "GENDER ALL" becomes the denominator definition of the PCTN statistic to compute the row percentages.

Example 3.5 features a program that uses denominator definitions.

Interpreting Denominator Definitions

The TABLE statement in the preceding topic defines denominator definitions for computing percentages. Each use of PCTN in the TABLE statement nests a row of statistics within each value of OCCUPAT and ALL. Each denominator definition tells PROC TABULATE the frequency counts to sum for the denominators in that row. This section explains how PROC TABULATE interprets these denominator definitions.

Row Percentages

The following part of the TABLE statement calculates the row percentages and labels the row:

```
pctn<gender all>='Percent of row total'
```

Consider how PROC TABULATE interprets this denominator definition for each of the four subtables.

OCCUPAT and GENDER

PROC TABULATE looks at the first element in the denominator definition, GENDER, and asks if GENDER contributes to the subtable. Because GENDER does contribute to the subtable, PROC TABULATE uses it as the denominator definition. This denominator definition tells PROC TABULATE to sum the frequency counts for all occurrences of GENDER within the same value of OCCUPAT.

For example, the denominator for the category `female, technical` is the sum of all frequency counts for all categories in this subtable for which the value of OCCUPAT is `technical`. There are two such categories: `female, technical` and `male, technical`. The corresponding frequency counts are 16 and 18. Therefore, the denominator for this category is 16+18=34.

ALL and GENDER

PROC TABULATE looks at the first element in the denominator definition, GENDER, and asks if GENDER contributes to the subtable. Because GENDER does contribute to the subtable, PROC TABULATE uses it as the denominator definition. This denominator definition tells PROC TABULATE to sum the frequency counts for all occurrences of GENDER in the subtable.

For example, the denominator for the category `all, female` is the sum of the frequency counts for `all, female` and `all, male`. The corresponding frequency counts are 61 and 62. Therefore, the denominator for cells in this subtable is 61+62=123.

OCCUPAT and ALL

PROC TABULATE looks at the first element in the denominator definition, GENDER, and asks if GENDER contributes to the subtable. Because GENDER does not contribute to the subtable, PROC TABULATE looks at the next element in the denominator definition, which is ALL. ALL does contribute to this subtable, so PROC TABULATE uses it as the denominator definition. ALL is a reserved class variable with only one category. Therefore, this denominator definition tells PROC TABULATE to use the frequency count of ALL as the denominator.

For example, the denominator for the category `clerical, all` is the frequency count for that category, 28.

Note: In these table cells, because the numerator and denominator are the same, the row percentages in this subtable are all 100.

ALL and ALL

PROC TABULATE looks at the first element in the denominator definition, GENDER, and asks if GENDER contributes to the subtable. Because GENDER does not contribute to the subtable, PROC TABULATE looks at the next element in the denominator definition, which is ALL. ALL does contribute to this subtable, so PROC TABULATE uses it as the denominator definition. ALL is a reserved class variable with only one category. Therefore, this denominator definition tells PROC TABULATE to use the frequency count of ALL as the denominator.

There is only one category in this subtable: `all, all`. The denominator for this category is 123.

Note: In this table cell, because the numerator and denominator are the same, the row percentage in this subtable is 100.

Column Percentages
The following part of the TABLE statement calculates the column percentages and labels the row:

```
pctn<occupat all>='Percent of column total'
```

Consider how PROC TABULATE interprets this denominator definition for each subtable.

OCCUPAT and GENDER
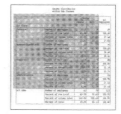
PROC TABULATE looks at the first element in the denominator definition, OCCUPAT, and asks if OCCUPAT contributes to the subtable. Because OCCUPAT does contribute to the subtable, PROC TABULATE uses it as the denominator definition. This denominator definition tells PROC TABULATE to sum the frequency counts for all occurrences of OCCUPAT within the same value of GENDER.

For example, the denominator for the category **manager/supervisor, male** is the sum of all frequency counts for all categories in this subtable for which the value of GENDER is **male**. There are four such categories: **technical, male**; **manager/supervisor, male**; **clerical, male**; and **administrative, male**. The corresponding frequency counts are 18, 15, 14, and 15. Therefore, the denominator for this category is 18+15+14+15=62.

ALL and GENDER

PROC TABULATE looks at the first element in the denominator definition, OCCUPAT, and asks if OCCUPAT contributes to the subtable. Because OCCUPAT does not contribute to the subtable, PROC TABULATE looks at the next element in the denominator definition, which is ALL. Because ALL does contribute to this subtable, PROC TABULATE uses it as the denominator definition. ALL is a reserved class variable with only one category. Therefore, this denominator definition tells PROC TABULATE to use the frequency count for ALL as the denominator.

For example, the denominator for the category **all, female** is the frequency count for that category, 61.

Note: In these table cells, because the numerator and denominator are the same, the column percentages in this subtable are all 100.

OCCUPAT and ALL

PROC TABULATE looks at the first element in the denominator definition, OCCUPAT, and asks if OCCUPAT contributes to the subtable. Because OCCUPAT does contribute to the subtable, PROC TABULATE uses it as the denominator definition. This denominator definition tells PROC TABULATE to sum the frequency counts for all occurrences of OCCUPAT in the subtable.

For example, the denominator for the category **technical, all** is the sum of the frequency counts for **technical, all**; **manager/supervisor, all**; **clerical, all**; and **administrative, all**. The corresponding frequency counts are 34, 35, 28, and 26. Therefore, the denominator for this category is 34+35+28+26=123.

ALL and ALL

PROC TABULATE looks at the first element in the denominator definition, OCCUPAT, and asks if OCCUPAT contributes to the subtable. Because OCCUPAT does not contribute to the subtable, PROC TABULATE looks at the next element in the denominator definition, which is ALL. Because ALL does contribute to this subtable, PROC TABULATE uses it as the denominator definition. ALL is a reserved class variable with only one category. Therefore, this denominator definition tells PROC TABULATE to use the frequency count of ALL as the denominator.

There is only one category in this subtable: **all, all**. The frequency count for this category is 123.

Note: In this calculation, because the numerator and denominator are the same, the column percentage in this subtable is 100.

Total Percentages

The following part of the TABLE statement calculates the total percentages and labels the row:

```
pctn='Percent of total'
```

If you do not specify a denominator definition, PROC TABULATE obtains the denominator for a cell by totaling all the frequency counts in the subtable. Table 3.4d summarizes the process for all subtables in this example.

Table 3.4d Denominators for Total Percentages

Class Variables Contributing to the Subtable	Frequency Counts	Total
OCCUPAT and GENDER	16, 18, 20, 15 14, 14, 11, 15	123
OCCUPAT and ALL	34, 35, 28, 26	123
GENDER and ALL	61, 62	123
ALL and ALL	123	123

Consequently, the denominator for total percentages is always 123.

Where to Go from Here

PROC FREQ reference, usage information, and additional examples. See "The FREQ Procedure" in the "Procedures" section of *Base SAS 9.1 Procedures Guide.*

PROC TABULATE reference, usage information, and additional examples. See "The TABULATE Procedure" in the "Procedures" section of *Base SAS 9.1 Procedures Guide.*

Example 3.5   Producing a Hierarchical Tabular Report

Goal

Compute statistics on analysis variables by categories defined by the combinations of classification variables in a data set. Nest some of the categories under each other in the same dimension of the report so that the report has a hierarchical appearance.

Report

```
                          Regional Gender Distribution
                             among Job Classes
     ----------------------------------------------------------------------
    |Job Class          |                      Region                      |
    |                   |--------------------------------------------------|
    |                   |         North          |         South           |
    |                   |------------------------+-------------------------|
    |                   |  Female    |    Male    |  Female    |    Male    |
    |                   |------------+-----------+------------+------------|
    |                   |Count|   %   |Count|   %   |Count|   %   |Count|   %   |
    |-------------------+-----+-------+-----+-------+-----+-------+-----+-------|
    |Technical          |   7|  50.0|    7|  50.0|    3|  75.0|    1|  25.0|
    |Manager/Supervisor |   7|  58.3|    5|  41.7|    6| 100.0|    0|    0|
    |Clerical           |   7|  70.0|    3|  30.0|    2|  28.6|    5|  71.4|
    |Administrative     |   0|    0|    6| 100.0|    6|  54.5|    5|  45.5|
    |All Employees      |  21|  50.0|   21|  50.0|   17|  60.7|   11|  39.3|
     ----------------------------------------------------------------------


     ----------------------------------------------------------------------
    |Job Class          |                      Region                      |
    |                   |--------------------------------------------------|
    |                   |         East           |         West            |
    |                   |------------------------+-------------------------|
    |                   |  Female    |    Male    |  Female    |    Male    |
    |                   |------------+-----------+------------+------------|
    |                   |Count|   %   |Count|   %   |Count|   %   |Count|   %   |
    |-------------------+-----+-------+-----+-------+-----+-------+-----+-------|
    |Technical          |   5|  50.0|    5|  50.0|    1|  16.7|    5|  83.3|
    |Manager/Supervisor |   7|  50.0|    7|  50.0|    0|    0|    3| 100.0|
    |Clerical           |   4|  66.7|    2|  33.3|    1|  20.0|    4|  80.0|
    |Administrative     |   5|  62.5|    3|  37.5|    0|    0|    1| 100.0|
    |All Employees      |  21|  55.3|   17|  44.7|    2|  13.3|   13|  86.7|
     ----------------------------------------------------------------------


              -----------------------------------------------
             |Job Class          |    All Regions Combined    |
             |                   |---------------------------|
             |                   |  Female    |    Male        |
             |                   |------------+--------------|
             |                   |Count|   %   |Count|   %     |
             |-------------------+-----+-------+-----+--------|
             |Technical          |  16|  47.1|   18|  52.9|
             |Manager/Supervisor |  20|  57.1|   15|  42.9|
             |Clerical           |  14|  50.0|   14|  50.0|
             |Administrative     |  11|  42.3|   15|  57.7|
             |All Employees      |  61|  49.6|   62|  50.4|
              -----------------------------------------------
```

Example Features

Data Set	JOBCLASS
Featured Step	PROC TABULATE
Featured Step Statements and Options	TABLE statement: PCTN statistic with denominator definition
Formatting Features	PROC TABULATE statement: FORMAT= option
	PROC TABULATE statement: NOSEPS option when sending output to the LISTING destination
	TABLE statement: BOX=, MISSTEXT=, and NOCONTINUED options
	TABLE statement: CONDENSE and RTS= options when sending output to the LISTING destination
ODS Enhanced Versions of This Example	Examples 6.3 and 6.7
Other Examples That Use This Data Set	Examples 3.4, 3.6, 6.3, and 6.7

Example Overview

Hierarchical tables define table cells that represent multiple class variables in the same dimension (row, column, or page). This example first presents the frequencies and percentages for each gender within each region and job class and for each gender and job class. The latter part of the report removes the top level of the hierarchy, which is the region. It summarizes the frequencies and percentages over all regions for each category defined by the combinations of the values of GENDER and JOBCLASS.

This example differs from Example 3.4 by adding REGION as a classification variable.

Each observation in JOBCLASS corresponds to the information for one employee.

Program

Define formats to associate with the classification variables.

```
proc format;
   value gendfmt 1='Female'
                 2='Male';
   value occupfmt 1='Technical'
                  2='Manager/Supervisor'
                  3='Clerical'
                  4='Administrative';
   value regfmt 1='North'
                2='South'
                3='East'
                4='West';
run;

proc tabulate data=jobclass
```

Specify a default format for each cell in the table.

```
format=5.
```

Eliminate horizontal separator lines from the row titles and the body of the table when sending output to the LISTING destination.

```
noseps;
```

```
title 'Regional Gender Distribution';
title2 'among Job Classes';
```

Identify the classification variables whose values define the categories for which PROC TABULATE calculates statistics.

```
class gender region occupat;
```

Specify the row dimension.

```
table occupat=' '
```

Add a summary row at the bottom of the report.

```
    all='All Employees',
```

Specify the column dimension. Place REGION and the universal CLASS variable ALL side-by-side at the top of the hierarchy.

```
    (region='Region'
    all='All Regions Combined')*
```

Place GENDER next in the hierarchy. Do not label GENDER.

```
    gender=' '*
```

Place the statistics, N and PCTN, at the bottom of the hierarchy. Specify GENDER as the denominator of the percentage calculation. Cells formed by the combinations of the values of REGION, GENDER, and OCCUPAT use as the denominator the sum of the frequency counts for GENDER within each combination of REGION and OCCUPAT. Cells formed by the combinations of the values of GENDER and OCCUPAT use as the denominator the sum of the frequency counts for GENDER for each value of OCCUPAT. (See "Interpreting Denominator Definitions" on page 100 for more information on using denominator definitions.)

```
    (n='Count' pctn<gender>='%'*f=7.1)
```

When sending output to the LISTING destination, specify the space allocated to row titles.

```
    / rts=20
```

Since the report is wide and not long, print as many tables as possible on one page instead of starting each table on a new page when sending output to the LISTING destination.

```
    condense
```

Suppress the continuation message for tables that span multiple physical pages.

```
    nocontinued
```

Specify the text to print in cells that
contain missing values.

```
misstext='0'
```

Specify the text to place in the empty box
above the row titles.

```
          box='Job Class';

     format gender gendfmt. occupat occupfmt.
            region regfmt.;
run;
```

Where to Go from Here

PROC TABULATE reference, usage information, and additional examples.
See "The TABULATE Procedure," in the "Procedures" section of *Base SAS 9.1
Procedures Guide.*

Example 3.6   Creating Multipage Summary Tables

Goal

Compute statistics for the combinations of classification variables in a data set. Create a separate page for each value of one of the classification variables so that each page becomes a complete report for the observations with that value. Add a last page that summarizes the separate pages.

Report

```
                        Summarization of Jobs by Region                              1
                     for Each Gender and for All Employees

 --------------------------------------------------------------------------------------
 |Gender: Female    |                       Region                         |         |
 |                  |------------------------------------------------------|         |
 |                  |   North    |   South    |   East     |   West    | All Regions |
 |                  |------------+------------+------------+-----------+-------------|
 |                  |     | % of |     | % of |     | % of |    | % of |    | % of  |
 |                  |Count|Category|Count|Category|Count|Category|Count|Category|Count|Category|
 |------------------+-----+--------+-----+--------+-----+--------+-----+--------+-----+--------|
 |Technical         |  7| 50.0|  3| 75.0|  5| 50.0|  1| 16.7| 16| 47.1|
 |------------------+-----+--------+-----+--------+-----+--------+-----+--------+-----+--------|
 |Manager/Supervisor|  7| 58.3|  6|100.0|  7| 50.0|  0|  0| 20| 57.1|
 |------------------+-----+--------+-----+--------+-----+--------+-----+--------+-----+--------|
 |Clerical          |  7| 70.0|  2| 28.6|  4| 66.7|  1| 20.0| 14| 50.0|
 |------------------+-----+--------+-----+--------+-----+--------+-----+--------+-----+--------|
 |Administrative    |  0|  0|  6| 54.5|  5| 62.5|  0|  0| 11| 42.3|
 |------------------+-----+--------+-----+--------+-----+--------+-----+--------+-----+--------|
 |All Jobs          | 21| 50.0| 17| 60.7| 21| 55.3|  2| 13.3| 61| 49.6|
 --------------------------------------------------------------------------------------
```

```
                        Summarization of Jobs by Region                              2
                     for Each Gender and for All Employees

 --------------------------------------------------------------------------------------
 |Gender: Male      |                       Region                         |         |
 |                  |------------------------------------------------------|         |
 |                  |   North    |   South    |   East     |   West    | All Regions |
 |                  |------------+------------+------------+-----------+-------------|
 |                  |     | % of |     | % of |     | % of |    | % of |    | % of  |
 |                  |Count|Category|Count|Category|Count|Category|Count|Category|Count|Category|
 |------------------+-----+--------+-----+--------+-----+--------+-----+--------+-----+--------|
 |Technical         |  7| 50.0|  1| 25.0|  5| 50.0|  5| 83.3| 18| 52.9|
 |------------------+-----+--------+-----+--------+-----+--------+-----+--------+-----+--------|
 |Manager/Supervisor|  5| 41.7|  0|  0|  7| 50.0|  3|100.0| 15| 42.9|
 |------------------+-----+--------+-----+--------+-----+--------+-----+--------+-----+--------|
 |Clerical          |  3| 30.0|  5| 71.4|  2| 33.3|  4| 80.0| 14| 50.0|
 |------------------+-----+--------+-----+--------+-----+--------+-----+--------+-----+--------|
 |Administrative    |  6|100.0|  5| 45.5|  3| 37.5|  1|100.0| 15| 57.7|
 |------------------+-----+--------+-----+--------+-----+--------+-----+--------+-----+--------|
 |All Jobs          | 21| 50.0| 11| 39.3| 17| 44.7| 13| 86.7| 62| 50.4|
 --------------------------------------------------------------------------------------
```

```
                        Summarization of Jobs by Region                           3
                      for Each Gender and for All Employees
------------------------------------------------------------------------------------
|All Employees      |                         Region                          |       |
|                   |----------------------------------------------------------|       |
|                   |   North    |   South    |    East    |    West    | All Regions |
|                   |------------+------------+------------+------------+-----------|
|                   |    | % of  |    | % of  |    | % of  |    | % of  |    | % of  |
|                   |Count|Category|Count|Category|Count|Category|Count|Category|Count|Category|
|-------------------+-----+-------+-----+-------+-----+-------+-----+-------+-----+-------|
|Technical          | 14 | 100.0| 4 | 100.0| 10 | 100.0| 6 | 100.0| 34 | 100.0|
|-------------------+-----+-------+-----+-------+-----+-------+-----+-------+-----+-------|
|Manager/Supervisor | 12 | 100.0| 6 | 100.0| 14 | 100.0| 3 | 100.0| 35 | 100.0|
|-------------------+-----+-------+-----+-------+-----+-------+-----+-------+-----+-------|
|Clerical           | 10 | 100.0| 7 | 100.0| 6 | 100.0| 5 | 100.0| 28 | 100.0|
|-------------------+-----+-------+-----+-------+-----+-------+-----+-------+-----+-------|
|Administrative     | 6 | 100.0| 11 | 100.0| 8 | 100.0| 1 | 100.0| 26 | 100.0|
|-------------------+-----+-------+-----+-------+-----+-------+-----+-------+-----+-------|
|All Jobs           | 42 | 100.0| 28 | 100.0| 38 | 100.0| 15 | 100.0| 123 | 100.0|
------------------------------------------------------------------------------------
```

Example Features

Data Set	JOBCLASS
Featured Step	PROC TABULATE
Featured Step Statements and Options	TABLE statement: PCTN statistic with denominator definition
Formatting Features	PROC TABULATE statement: FORMAT= option
	TABLE statement: BOX= and MISSTEXT= options
	TABLE statement: RTS= option when sending output to the LISTING destination
Related Technique	OPTIONS NOBYLINE, PROC TABULATE with a BY statement, and a TITLE statement with #BYLINE
🔍 A Closer Look	Comparing PROC TABULATE's Use of the BY Statement and the Page Dimension
Other Examples That Use This Data Set	Examples 3.4, 3.5, 6.3, and 6.7

Example Overview

Presenting tables on separate pages can clarify the differences among tables and make it easier to compare the tables.

The first two pages of this report show by gender the frequency counts and percentages for each job class in each region. The last page summarizes the first two and shows for all employees the frequency counts and percentages for each job class in each region.

The percentage in each table cell compares the corresponding frequency count for that table cell to the frequency count for all employees in the category represented by that table cell. On the first two pages, the percentage represents the proportion of each gender in the specific category defined by job class and region. Since the last page summarizes over gender, the percentage cells are all 100%.

Each observation in JOBCLASS corresponds to the information for one employee.

Program

Define formats to associate with the classification variables.

```
proc format;
   value gendfmt 1='Female'
                 2='Male';
   value occupfmt 1='Technical'
                  2='Manager/Supervisor'
                  3='Clerical'
                  4='Administrative';
   value regfmt 1='North'
                2='South'
                3='East'
                4='West';
run;

proc tabulate data=jobclass
```

Specify a default format for each cell in the table.

```
     format=5.;

title 'Summarization of Jobs by Region';
title2 'for Each Gender and for All
        Employees';

class gender region occupat;
table
```

Start with the classifications in the page dimension. Supply headings to elements of the table by enclosing text within quotation marks.

```
     gender='Gender: '
```

Produce a page that summarizes the other pages by including ALL as one of the class variables in the page dimension.

```
     all='All Employees',
```

Specify the classifications in the row dimension.

```
     occupat=' '
```

Summarize over OCCUPAT in the last row on each page by including ALL as one of the class variables in the row dimension.

```
     all='All Jobs',
```

Conclude with the column dimension.

```
     (region='Region'
```

Summarize over REGION in the last column on each page by including ALL as one of the class variables in the column dimension.

```
     all='All Regions')
```

Nest the statistics under the class variables in the column dimension. As the denominator of the percentage calculation, use the sum of the frequency counts for males and females for each combination of OCCUPAT and REGION.

```
     *(n='Count' pctn<gender all>=
        '% of Category'*f=8.1)
```

When sending output to the LISTING destination, specify the space allocated to row titles.	`/ rts=20`
Specify the text to print in cells that contain missing values.	`misstext='0'`
Place the default page heading in the empty box above the row titles.	`box=_page_;`

Since GENDER is in the page dimension, write the formatted values of GENDER in the empty box above the row titles.	`format gender gendfmt. occupat occupfmt.`
	`region regfmt.;`
	`run;`

Related Technique

You can use BY processing with PROC TABULATE to produce a report that is similar to the one featured in this example.

The program that follows produces a basic crosstabulation of OCCUPAT and REGION, with totals for each value of the BY variable, GENDER. Figure 3.6 shows the output from this program.

Figure 3.6 Output from PROC TABULATE Using BY Processing

```
                        Summarization of Jobs by Region                              1

                           Data for Gender=Female

--------------------------------------------------------------------------------
|                    |                          Region                |           |
|                    |-------------------------------------------------|           |
|                    |   North   |   South   |   East    |   West    |All Regions|
|                    |-----------+-----------+-----------+-----------+-----------|
|                    |Count|  %  |Count|  %  |Count|  %  |Count|  %  |Count|  %  |
|--------------------+-----+-----+-----+-----+-----+-----+-----+-----+-----+------|
|Technical           |   7| 11.48|   3| 4.92|   5| 8.20|   1| 1.64|  16| 26.23|
|--------------------+-----+-----+-----+-----+-----+-----+-----+-----+-----+------|
|Manager/Supervisor  |   7| 11.48|   6| 9.84|   7|11.48|   0|   0|  20| 32.79|
|--------------------+-----+-----+-----+-----+-----+-----+-----+-----+-----+------|
|Clerical            |   7| 11.48|   2| 3.28|   4| 6.56|   1| 1.64|  14| 22.95|
|--------------------+-----+-----+-----+-----+-----+-----+-----+-----+-----+------|
|Administrative      |   0|    0|   6| 9.84|   5| 8.20|   0|   0|  11| 18.03|
|--------------------+-----+-----+-----+-----+-----+-----+-----+-----+-----+------|
|All Jobs            |  21| 34.43|  17|27.87|  21|34.43|   2| 3.28|  61|100.00|
--------------------------------------------------------------------------------
-----------------------------------page break -------------------------------------
                                                                                     2
                        Summarization of Jobs by Region

                            Data for Gender=Male

--------------------------------------------------------------------------------
|                    |                          Region                |           |
|                    |-------------------------------------------------|           |
|                    |   North   |   South   |   East    |   West    |All Regions|
|                    |-----------+-----------+-----------+-----------+-----------|
|                    |Count|  %  |Count|  %  |Count|  %  |Count|  %  |Count|  %  |
|--------------------+-----+-----+-----+-----+-----+-----+-----+-----+-----+------|
|Technical           |   7| 11.29|   1| 1.61|   5| 8.06|   5| 8.06|  18| 29.03|
|--------------------+-----+-----+-----+-----+-----+-----+-----+-----+-----+------|
|Manager/Supervisor  |   5| 8.06|   0|   0|   7|11.29|   3| 4.84|  15| 24.19|
|--------------------+-----+-----+-----+-----+-----+-----+-----+-----+-----+------|
|Clerical            |   3| 4.84|   5| 8.06|   2| 3.23|   4| 6.45|  14| 22.58|
|--------------------+-----+-----+-----+-----+-----+-----+-----+-----+-----+------|
|Administrative      |   6| 9.68|   5| 8.06|   3| 4.84|   1| 1.61|  15| 24.19|
|--------------------+-----+-----+-----+-----+-----+-----+-----+-----+-----+------|
|All Jobs            |  21| 33.87|  11|17.74|  17|27.42|  13|20.97|  62|100.00|
```

When you use a BY statement instead of the page dimension, your report can compute percentages only for a table within a BY group. You cannot summarize information over all BY groups, because PROC TABULATE processes each BY group individually. Table 3.6 compares the usage of the page dimension and the BY statement in PROC TABULATE.

The following program generated the output in Figure 3.6.

Define formats to associate with the classification variables and the BY variable.

```
proc format;
   value gendfmt 1='Female'
                 2='Male';
   value occupfmt 1='Technical'
                  2='Manager/Supervisor'
                  3='Clerical'
                  4='Administrative';
   value regfmt 1='North'
                2='South'
                3='East'
                4='West';
run;
```

Sort the data set by the variable that defines the BR groups in the report.

```
proc sort data=jobclass;
   by gender;
run;
```

Prevent BY lines from being printed above each BY group of the report.

```
options nobyline;

proc tabulate data=jobclass format=5.;
   title 'Summarization of Jobs by Region';
```

Put the default BY line text in the title in the position taken by #BYLINE.

```
   title3 'Data for #byline';
```

Produce a table for each value of the BY variable.

```
   by gender;
```

Do not include the BY variable as a class variable.

```
   class region occupat;
   table occupat=' ' all='All Jobs',
         (region='Region' all='All Regions')
```

Compute percentages based on totals within the BY group.

```
         *(n='Count' pctn='%'*f=7.2)

         / rts=20 misstext='0';
            label gender='Gender';
   format gender gendfmt. occupat occupfmt.
          region regfmt.;
run;
```

Reset the option to its default setting.

```
options byline;
```

🔍 **A Closer Look**

Comparing PROC TABULATE's Use of the BY Statement and the Page Dimension

Table 3.6 describes the differences between PROC TABULATE with a BY statement and PROC TABULATE with a page dimension.

Table 3.6 Comparing the Use of the BY Statement and the Page Dimension in PROC TABULATE

Issue	PROC TABULATE with a BY Statement	PROC TABULATE with a Page Dimension in the TABLE Statement
Order of observations in the input data set	The observations in the input data set must by sorted by the BY variables.	Sorting or indexing is unnecessary.
Creating one report summarizing all BY groups	You cannot create one report that summarizes over the BY groups.	Use ALL in the page dimension to create a report for all classes.
Calculating percentages	The percentages in the table are based on the frequency counts for the BY group value. You cannot calculate percentages for a BY group using the total frequency counts for all BY groups combined, because PROC TABULATE prepares the individual reports separately. Data for the report for one BY group is not available to the report for another BY group.	You can use denominator definitions to control the meaning of PCTN, or you can use the percentage statistics (ROWPCTN, COLPCTN, PAGEPCTN, and REPPCTN; ROWPCTSUM, COLPCTSUM, PAGEPCTSUM, and REPPCTSUM).
Titles	You can use the #BYVAL, #BYVAR, and #BYLINE specifications in the TITLE statements to customize the titles for each BY group. When you use these specifications, suppress the default BY line by setting the SAS system option NOBYLINE.	The BOX= option in the TABLE statement customizes the page headings, but the titles remain the same on each page.

Where to Go from Here

BY statement processing. See "BY statement" in the "Statements" section of *SAS 9.1 Language Reference: Dictionary,* and "Statements with the Same Function in Multiple Procedures" in the "Concepts" section of *Base SAS 9.1 Procedures Guide.*

The BYLINE/NOBYLINE SAS System Options. See "SAS System Options" in *SAS 9.1 Language Reference: Dictionary.*

Inserting BY-group information in titles. See "Creating Titles that Contain BY-Group Information" in the "Fundamental Concepts in Using Base SAS Procedures" section of *Base SAS 9.1 Procedures Guide.*

PROC TABULATE reference, usage information, and additional examples. See "The TABULATE Procedure," in the "Procedures" section of *Base SAS 9.1 Procedures Guide.*

Example 3.7   Assigning Multiple Labels to Categories

Goal

Generate summary statistics for categories defined by the values of variables. Define multiple labels for some of the values, resulting in multiple representation of these values in the categories of the report.

Report

```
                            Monthly Circulation Report
```

		Items Circulated				
		Adult	Juvenile	Young People's	All Youth	Total
Books	Hardcover	15816	4311	1084	5395	21211
	LargeType	131	1	2	3	134
	Paperback	4143	3218	712	3930	8073
	Total for Media	20090	7530	1798	9328	29418
Periodicals	LargeType	9	0	0	0	9
	Magazines	4162	433	134	567	4729
	Total for Media	4171	433	134	567	4738
All Print Material	Hardcover	15816	4311	1084	5395	21211
	LargeType	140	1	2	3	143
	Magazines	4162	433	134	567	4729
	Paperback	4143	3218	712	3930	8073
	Total for Media	24261	7963	1932	9895	34156
Audio	Audiocassettes	1569	546	388	934	2503
	CompactDiscs	2018	0	370	370	2388
	Total for Media	3587	546	758	1304	4891
Talking Books	Audiocassettes	483	343	24	367	850
	CompactDiscs	184	10	4	14	198
	Total for Media	667	353	28	381	1048
Video	DVD	4854	1142	0	1142	5996
	Videocassettes	6092	3540	0	3540	9632
	Total for Media	10946	4682	0	4682	15628
All Recordings	Audiocassettes	2052	889	412	1301	3353
	CompactDiscs	2202	10	374	384	2586
	DVD	4854	1142	0	1142	5996
	Videocassettes	6092	3540	0	3540	9632
	Total for Media	15200	5581	786	6367	21567
Total Items Circulated		39461	13544	2718	16262	55723

Example Features

Data Set	LIBRARIES
Featured Steps	PROC FORMAT
	PROC TABULATE
Featured Step Statements and Options	PROC FORMAT
	VALUE statement: MULTILABEL option
	PROC TABULATE
	CLASS statement: MLF option
	Use of Universal Classification Variable ALL
Formatting Features	Multiple labels for categories
	Suppressing variable labels
	PROC TABULATE TABLE statement: MISSTEXT= option; RTS= option when sending output to the LISTING destination
🔍 A Closer Look	Understanding Multiple Labels

Example Overview

The value of a report's presentation can be enhanced by grouping categories in various ways and including these additional combinations in the report.

This example report shows one month's circulation totals for a library. It organizes the totals according to the values of three classification variables: media, audience, and type.

The report includes all unique combinations of the three class variables. Additionally, the report combines some of the categories into new categories, resulting in multiple representation of specific categories in the report.

For example, the new category "All Youth" sums the circulation totals for the "Juvenile" and "Young People's" classifications.

Each observation in the LIBRARIES data set corresponds to the total number of items circulated for a specific combination of media, audience, type, category, and subcategory.

Program

Define the formats required for the report. Add the MULTILABEL option to formats that will be applied to variables that are to be multiply labeled. To control the ordering of the results, indent some of the labels a sufficient number of blanks.

Add an additional value label that combines these two values.

```
proc format;
   value $aud (multilabel)
               'Adult'            ='    Adult'
               'Juvenile'         ='   Juvenile'
               "YoungPeople's"    =" Young People's"


               'Juvenile',
               "YoungPeople's"    ='All Youth';
   value $med (multilabel)
               'Books'            ='        Books'
               'Periodicals'      ='      Periodicals'
```

Add an additional value label that combines these two values.

```
'Books',
'Periodicals'    =' All Print
 Material'
'TalkingBooks'   =' Talking Books'
'Audio'          =' Audio'
'Video'          =' Video'
```

Add an additional value label that combines these three values.

```
'TalkingBooks',
'Audio','Video' ='All Recordings';
run;

proc tabulate data=libraries
```

Order the classification values by their ascending formatted values.

```
                order=formatted;

title 'Monthly Circulation Report';
```

Specify the classification variables whose values are to be multiply labeled.

```
class media audience / mlf;
```

Specify the classification variable whose values are not to be multiply labeled.

```
class type;

var items;

table media=' '*(type=' '
    all='Total for Media')
    all='Total Items Circulated',
    all='Items Circulated'*
(audience=' ' all='Total')*
items=' '*sum=' '*f=10.
```

When sending output to the LISTING destination, specify the space allocated to row titles.

```
    / rts=35
```

Specify the text to write in cells with missing values.

```
    misstext='0';

format media $med. audience $aud.;
run;
```

🔍 A Closer Look

Understanding Multiple Labels

The only procedures in SAS 9.1 that can process multiple labels are PROC MEANS, PROC SUMMARY, and PROC TABULATE. If you do not instruct SAS to use multiple labels within these three procedures, even if the format has been defined as multilabel, the feature is ignored. SAS also ignores any reference to a multilabel format in any procedure besides the three listed above.

It is important to understand what happens when you omit the MLF option in one of the three multilabel-enabled procedures, but you reference a multilabel format in the execution of the procedure. For example, if a value is multiply referenced in a PROC FORMAT VALUE statement, SAS uses only the value label associated with the *first* occurrence in the format definition. If the value is also included in a range and the range appears later in the format definition, you may see the range's value label listed if your data set contains an observation with another value in that range. Note that if a value's first occurrence is defined by a value label before the range that includes it is defined, that value is *not* represented in that range's category.

Always use caution when interpreting reports that are based on multiple labels. The preceding example sums the analysis variable ITEMS. If you added up the cells in the rows labeled "Total for Media," your sum would be greater than the value in the "Total Items Circulated" cell in the last row of the table. This is because of the multiple representation of values in the table.

When you write a VALUE statement in PROC FORMAT and do not include the MULTILABEL option, SAS looks for repeated ranges or overlapping values. If any are detected, the format is not created. Thus, if you submit the PROC FORMAT step in the preceding example with the MULTILABEL option omitted, SAS would not create the formats.

Where to Go from Here

PROC FORMAT reference, usage information, and additional examples. See "The FORMAT Procedure" in the "Procedures" section of *Base SAS 9.1 Procedures Guide.*

PROC TABULATE reference, usage information, and additional examples. See "The TABULATE Procedure" in the "Procedures" section of *Base SAS 9.1 Procedures Guide.*

Working with Formats. See "Formats and Informats" in the "SAS Language Elements" section of *SAS 9.1 Language Reference: Concepts.*

Example 3.8   Writing Customized Lines in Summary Reports

Goal

Create a summary report that customizes the text written by the automatic summaries. Evaluate statistics produced during the summarization and add customized text to the report based on the evaulations.

Report

```
                        Quality Motor Company

                        Cars Sold    Total Sales
            Sales              by            by       Average
      Representative    Quarter  Quarter       Quarter        Sale
      ==============================================================
      Johnson           1st        6    $204,000.00    $34,000.00
                        2nd       10    $336,000.00    $33,600.00
                        3rd        7    $255,000.00    $36,428.57
                        4th       10    $407,000.00    $40,700.00
      ==============================================================
      Sales Totals for Johnson    33  $1,202,000.00    $36,424.24
      Best Quarter for Johnson: 4th
      ==============================================================


      ==============================================================
      Langlois-Peele    1st        6    $217,000.00    $36,166.67
                        2nd       20    $935,000.00    $46,750.00
                        3rd       10    $358,000.00    $35,800.00
                        4th       13    $667,000.00    $51,307.69
      ==============================================================
      Sales Totals for Langlois-Peele  49  $2,177,000.00  $44,428.57
      Best Quarter for Langlois-Peele: 2nd
      ==============================================================


      ==============================================================
      Annual Totals              82  $3,379,000.00    $41,207.32
      ==============================================================
```

Example Features

Data Set	CARSALES
Featured Step	PROC REPORT
Featured Step Statements and Options	COMPUTE blocks Computed variables DEFINE statement: ANALYSIS, COMPUTED, GROUP, NOPRINT, and SUM options LINE statement _BREAK_ automatic variable
Formatting Features	DEFINE statement: WIDTH option when sending output to the LISTING destination LINE statement options when sending output to the LISTING destination
🔍 A Closer Look	Using the PROC REPORT Automatic Variable _BREAK_ Formatting Group Variables in PROC REPORT
ODS Enhanced Versions of This Example	Examples 6.2 and 6.6
Other Examples That Use This Data Set	Examples 6.2 and 6.6

Example Overview

This report analyzes the sales information for two sales representatives. It shows their quarterly and annual sales, and it identifies each sales representative's best sales quarter. The report also summarizes the combined sales information for the two sales representatives.

The PROC REPORT step uses computed variables and COMPUTE blocks to produce the report. The rightmost column, "Average Sales," is a computed variable.

The program customizes the text shown on the summary line. It uses COMPUTE blocks to retain information across all rows so that the sales representative's best quarter can be identified in the row that follows the sales representative's summary line.

The last row in the report summarizes the sales for both sales representatives combined.

Each observation in the CARSALES data set corresponds to one sales representative's sales totals in one month.

This version of the report is designed for the LISTING destination. Positioning of summary information to column locations is controlled with programming statements. See Example 6.2 for a version of the program that sends the output to a nonlisting destination and for a comparison of the coding for the two destinations.

Program

Define a format that will group the months into quarters.

```
proc format;
    value mnthfmt 1-3 = '1st'
                  4-6 = '2nd'
                  7-9 = '3rd'
                  10-12 = '4th';
run;

proc report data=carsales nowd
```

Specify the line size that works best with the layout of the report when sending output to the LISTING destination.

```
    ls=78;
    title 'Quality Motor Company';
```

List the columns in the order in which they should appear in the report. Place AVGSALES after NUMSOLD and AMTSOLD because its value is derived from NUMSOLD and AMTSOLD. Even though it does not appear in the report, include MAXSALES on the COLUMN statement because its values are used to determine the best sales quarter.

```
column name month numsold amtsold avgsales
       maxsales;
```

Group the data by the formatted values of NAME and MONTH. Specify the column width when sending output to the LISTING destination.

```
define name       / group width=18
                    '    Sales/Representative';
define month      / group width=8 'Quarter'
                    center
                    format=mnthfmt.;

define numsold  / analysis sum 'Cars
                  Sold/by/Quarter'
                  format=2. width=9;
define amtsold  / analysis sum
                  'Total Sales/by/Quarter'
                  format=dollar13.2;
```

Designate the next two variables as computed variables.

```
define avgsales / computed 'Average/Sale'
                  format=dollar13.2;
```

Suppress the display of the MAXSALES computed variable.

```
define maxsales / computed noprint;
```

Before processing the information for a sales representative, initialize the variables that are used to determine the sales representative's best sales quarter.

```
compute before name;
  bigsales=0;
  bigqtr=0;
```

Include this separator line when sending the report to the LISTING destination.

```
  line @6 70*'=';
endcomp;
```

Calculate the value of AVGSALES. Specify the analysis variables in the calculation with their compound names that identify both the variable and the statistic associated with each.

```
compute avgsales;
  avgsales = amtsold.sum / numsold.sum;
endcomp;
```

Create a COMPUTE block for MAXSALES. This COMPUTE block executes for each row of the report and determines the quarter with the biggest sales. Retain in BIGSALES and BIGQTR the value of the biggest sales and the quarter with the biggest sales as the rows are processed. Compare the sales value in the current row to the retained sales value. If the current row's sales value is larger than the retained sales value, set the variables that retain the biggest sale and its quarter to the current row's sales and quarter values.

```
compute maxsales;
```

Execute the DO group if two conditions are true: 1) the value of the automatic variable _BREAK_ is missing, which is true when the line that is currently being processed is not part of a break, and 2) the current value of AMTSOLD is greater than the value retained in the variable BIGSALES. (BIGSALES retains the maximum sales value for the sales representative so far.)

```
  if _break_=' ' and bigsales lt amtsold.sum
    then do;
      bigsales=amtsold.sum;
      bigqtr=month;
    end;
endcomp;
```

To better control how the summaries look, write COMPUTE blocks instead of using the BREAK AFTER NAME / SUMMARIZE and RBREAK AFTER / SUMMARIZE statements. Create a customized summary for each sales representative and present it after the quarterly information for the sales representative.

```
compute after name;
```

Define a character variable that will contain the contents of the customized summary line.

```
length fullline $ 50;
```

Concatenate the elements of the customized line and assign the results to a character variable.

```
fullline=catx(' ','Best Quarter for',
          cats(name,':'),
          put(bigqtr,mnthfmt.));
```

When sending the report to the LISTING destination, specify the columns in which to write the information and add separator lines at the beginning and end of each sales representative's summary.

```
line @6 70*'=';
line @6 'Sales Totals for ' name  $14.
     @42 numsold.sum 3. @45 amtsold.sum
     dollar15.2
     @60 avgsales dollar15.2;
```

Write the customized summary line. Ensure that you specify a format for FULLLINE since the LINE statement requires a format for items such as data set variables, computed variables, and statistics.

```
line @6 fullline $50.;
line @6 70*'=';
```

Skip a line. Since the LINE statement requires a specification, write a blank.

```
   line ' ';
endcomp;
```

Create a customized summary at the end of the report that summarizes the information for both sales representatives.

```
compute after;
   line @6 70*'=';
   line @6 'Annual Totals ' @41 numsold.sum 4.
        @45 amtsold.sum dollar15.2
        @60 avgsales dollar15.2;
   line @6 70*'=';
   line ' ';
endcomp;

run;
```

🔍 A Closer Look

Using the PROC REPORT Automatic Variable _BREAK_

When customizing text for your report, you may want to execute code conditionally based on whether the current row is a break. SAS assigns specific values to the automatic variable _BREAK_ that you can test to determine the current processing location in your report.

SAS assigns these values to _BREAK_:

- ❑ a *blank* if the current line is not part of a break

- ❑ the *value of the break variable* if the current line is part of a break between sets of observations

❑ the value "RBREAK" if the current line is part of a break at the beginning or end of the report

❑ the value "_PAGE_" if the current line is part of a break at the beginning or end of a page

Formatting Group Variables in PROC REPORT

PROC REPORT considers a group to be a collection of observations with a unique combination of formatted values for all group variables. PROC REPORT summarizes all the observations in a group in one row of the report. The group variables in this report are NAME and MONTH.

If you do not apply a format to MONTH, the report will contain twelve rows of monthly sales information for each sales representative. Using the MNTHFMT. format creates groups because the format reduces the number of values for month from twelve (one for each month) to four (one for each quarter). Therefore, the number of groups is reduced to four for each sales person.

Where to Go from Here

PROC REPORT reference, usage information, and additional examples. See "The REPORT Procedure" in the "Procedures" section of *Base SAS 9.1 Procedures Guide.*

Working with Formats. See "Formats and Informats" in the "SAS Language Elements" section of *SAS 9.1 Language Reference: Concepts,* and "Formats" in *SAS 9.1 Language Reference: Dictionary.*

Example 3.9   Reporting on Multiple-Choice Survey Data

Goal

Count the different responses to each question in a set of questions from a survey. Consolidate this information into a report. Each observation in the data set contains one participant's responses to all the survey questions.

Report

```
                              Town Survey Results
                           Number of Participants: 482
```

Survey Question	Strongly Disapprove		Disapprove		Neutral		Approve		Strongly Approve		Total Responses	
	N	Row %	N	Row %	N	Row %	N	Row %	N	Row %	N	Row %
1. Road Maintenance	5	1.2	134	31.7	115	27.2	143	33.8	26	6.1	423	100.0
2. Parks Upkeep	4	1.0	86	21.0	93	22.7	195	47.6	32	7.8	410	100.0
3. Snowplowing	76	17.3	169	38.5	86	19.6	93	21.2	15	3.4	439	100.0
4. Sheriff Patrolling	0	0	94	22.3	111	26.4	180	42.8	36	8.6	421	100.0
5. Ordinance Enforcement	20	4.6	156	35.9	121	27.9	107	24.7	30	6.9	434	100.0
6. Town Office Hours	1	0.2	80	19.1	124	29.7	177	42.3	36	8.6	418	100.0
7. Community Events	1	0.2	38	9.2	51	12.3	204	49.4	119	28.8	413	100.0
8. Youth Programs	2	0.5	50	11.7	45	10.5	201	47.1	129	30.2	427	100.0
9. Senior Services	3	0.7	94	22.2	121	28.6	167	39.5	38	9.0	423	100.0

Example Features

Data Set	TOWNSURVEY
Featured Steps	PROC TRANSPOSE PROC TABULATE
Featured Step Statements and Options	PROC TABULATE TABLE statement: ROWPCTN statistic
Formatting Features	TABLE statement: MISSTEXT= option TABLE statement: RTS= option when sending output to the LISTING destination
Additional Features	Macro programming SAS file input/output functions

Related Technique	PROC REPORT:
	
	    DEFINE statement: ACROSS, GROUP, NOPRINT, and ORDER= options
	    Nesting statistics under ACROSS variable
	    COMPUTE blocks
	    Explicitly referencing table columns in a COMPUTE block
	    Using arrays in a COMPUTE block
	    Using aliases to multiply reference the same variable

🔍 A Closer Look	Reshaping Data Working with Missing Class Variable Values in PROC TABULATE
Other Examples That Use This Data Set	Example 2.8

Example Overview

This report shows the results of a survey submitted to town residents regarding their opinions of town services. The survey participants were asked to rate nine services on a scale from 1 to 5, with 1 being the least favorable and 5 being the most favorable.

Each observation in the TOWNSURVEY data set represents the responses to the nine questions for one participant. The survey also included a comment line, but this example does not include this comment variable. See Example 2.8 for a program that processes the comments.

To construct this crosstabulation of service and opinion of service, you must have a data set that contains a variable for type of service and a variable for the respondent's evaluation of the service. This will allow the five possible responses to be treated as five classifications by PROC TABULATE.

PROC TRANSPOSE reshapes the data into a new data set that contains the variables for type of service and for evaluation of the service. Each observation in the transposed data set contains the response to one question for one survey participant. The transposed data set that PROC TABULATE analyzes contains nine times as many observations as the original data set, because there are nine questions.

Open code macro language statements use SAS functions to open and close the analysis data set and determine the number of nondeleted observations in the analysis data set. This value is inserted in the title. For more information on working with SAS functions, see Example 3.10.

Collecting the Data

Figure 3.9a shows the survey form submitted to town residents.

Figure 3.9a Survey Form Used to Collect the Data Saved in Data Set TOWNSURVEY

Town Services Questionnaire

ID#: _____

Please rate the services that the town provides by circling your choice. Thank you for your participation!

	1	2	3	4	5
1. Road Maintenance	Strongly Disapprove	Disapprove	Neutral	Approve	Strongly Approve
2. Parks Upkeep	Strongly Disapprove	Disapprove	Neutral	Approve	Strongly Approve
3. Snowplowing	Strongly Disapprove	Disapprove	Neutral	Approve	Strongly Approve
4. Sheriff Patrolling	Strongly Disapprove	Disapprove	Neutral	Approve	Strongly Approve
5. Ordinance Enforcement	Strongly Disapprove	Disapprove	Neutral	Approve	Strongly Approve
6. Town Office Hours	Strongly Disapprove	Disapprove	Neutral	Approve	Strongly Approve
7. Community Events	Strongly Disapprove	Disapprove	Neutral	Approve	Strongly Approve
8. Youth Programs	Strongly Disapprove	Disapprove	Neutral	Approve	Strongly Approve
9. Senior Services	Strongly Disapprove	Disapprove	Neutral	Approve	Strongly Approve
	1	2	3	4	5

Please tell us more:

Program

Create formats that will apply to the
variables in the transposed data set.

```
proc format;
   value $q 'q1'='1. Road Maintenance'
            'q2'='2. Parks Upkeep'
            'q3'='3. Snowplowing'
            'q4'='4. Sheriff Patrolling'
            'q5'='5. Ordinance Enforcement'
            'q6'='6. Town Office Hours'
            'q7'='7. Community Events'
            'q8'='8. Youth Programs'
            'q9'='9. Senior Services';
   value response 1='Strongly Disapprove'
                  2='Disapprove'
                  3='Neutral'
                  4='Approve'
                  5='Strongly Approve'
                  .='No response';
run;
```

Arrange the observations in the data set in
the order that PROC TRANSPOSE will
use them.

```
proc sort data=townsurvey;
   by surveyid;
run;
```

Reshape the data.

```
proc transpose data=townsurvey
```

Create a new data set containing the
transposed observations. Assign a more
meaningful name to the transposed variable
COL1 (the default name). This variable
corresponds to the respondent's evaluation of
the service.

```
       out=townsurvey2(rename=(col1=choice))
```

Specify the name to assign to the variable
in the output data set that will contain the
name of the transposed variables, which
are the variables listed on the VAR
statement. This variable corresponds to type
of service, and it will have nine values that
correspond to the nine questions.

```
       name=question;
```

Transpose the data set in groups defined
by the values of the BY variable. Within
each BY group, create one observation for
each variable that you transpose.

```
   by surveyid;
```

Transpose the nine variables representing
the nine survey questions into
observations. Within each BY group, create
one observation for each evaluation variable
in the list.

```
   var q1-q9;
run;
```

Open the original data set for input.
Assign the identifier for this opened data
set to the macro variable DSID. Do not
enclose the arguments in quotation marks,
because the function is being used in macro
language.

```
%let dsid=%sysfunc(open(work.townsurvey,i));
```

Obtain the number of nondeleted observations in the original data set and save that value in the macro variable NOBS.	`%let nlobs=%sysfunc(attrn(&dsid,nlobs));`

Close the opened data set.	`%let rc=%sysfunc(close(&dsid));`
	
	`proc tabulate data=townsurvey2;`
	`   title 'Town Survey Results';`

Include the total number of participants in the title.	`title2 "Number of Participants: &nlobs";`
Specify the classification variables, which were created and named by PROC TRANSPOSE.	`class question choice;`
Establish the layout of the table. Specify the questions as the rows of the report.	`table question='Survey Question',`
Define the columns of the report as the question responses.	`(choice=' '`
Total the number of respondents to the question and place that information in the rightmost column.	`all='Total Responses')*`
Compute the N statistic.	`(n='N'*f=4.`
Compute the percentages within each row.	`rowpctn='Row %'*f=5.1) /`
Specify the text to put in cells that have missing values.	`misstext='0'`
When sending output to the LISTING destination, specify the space allocated to row titles.	`rts=20;`

	`format question $q. choice response.;`
	
	`run;`

Related Technique

PROC REPORT can produce a report similar to one produced by PROC TABULATE as shown in Figure 3.9b. The following PROC REPORT step defines QUESTION as a grouping variable. This definition causes QUESTION to act as the class variable in the row dimension. The program defines CHOICE as an across variable. This definition causes CHOICE to act as a class variable in the column dimension.

It's not quite as easy to specify row percentages in PROC REPORT as it is in PROC TABULATE. To do this in PROC REPORT requires programming statements in a COMPUTE block. If you nest the PCTN statistic underneath CHOICE, the percentages will have as their denominator the total frequency count of the response column.

Figure 3.9b Output from PROC REPORT

```
                              Town Survey Results
                          Number of Participants: 482

----------------------------------------------------------------------------------------
|                                                                                       |
|                 Strongly                                        Strongly              |
|                 Disapprove   Disapprove    Neutral     Approve    Approve    Total|
|Survey Question    N    Pct     N    Pct    N    Pct    N    Pct    N    Pct      N|
|---------------------------------------------------------------------------------------|
|1. Road Maintenance  |   5|  1.2|  134|  31.7|  115|  27.2|  143|  33.8|   26|   6.1|   423|
|---------------------+-----+-----+-----+-----+-----+-----+-----+-----+-----+-----+------|
|2. Parks Upkeep      |   4|  1.0|   86|  21.0|   93|  22.7|  195|  47.6|   32|   7.8|   410|
|---------------------+-----+-----+-----+-----+-----+-----+-----+-----+-----+-----+------|
|3. Snowplowing       |  76| 17.3|  169|  38.5|   86|  19.6|   93|  21.2|   15|   3.4|   439|
|---------------------+-----+-----+-----+-----+-----+-----+-----+-----+-----+-----+------|
|4. Sheriff Patrolling|   .|  0.0|   94|  22.3|  111|  26.4|  180|  42.8|   36|   8.6|   421|
|---------------------+-----+-----+-----+-----+-----+-----+-----+-----+-----+-----+------|
|5. Ordinance Enforcement|  20|  4.6|  156|  35.9|  121|  27.9|  107|  24.7|   30|   6.9|   434|
|---------------------+-----+-----+-----+-----+-----+-----+-----+-----+-----+-----+------|
|6. Town Office Hours |   1|  0.2|   80|  19.1|  124|  29.7|  177|  42.3|   36|   8.6|   418|
|---------------------+-----+-----+-----+-----+-----+-----+-----+-----+-----+-----+------|
|7. Community Events  |   1|  0.2|   38|   9.2|   51|  12.3|  204|  49.4|  119|  28.8|   413|
|---------------------+-----+-----+-----+-----+-----+-----+-----+-----+-----+-----+------|
|8. Youth Programs    |   2|  0.5|   50|  11.7|   45|  10.5|  201|  47.1|  129|  30.2|   427|
|---------------------+-----+-----+-----+-----+-----+-----+-----+-----+-----+-----+------|
|9. Senior Services   |   3|  0.7|   94|  22.2|  121|  28.6|  167|  39.5|   38|   9.0|   423|
----------------------------------------------------------------------------------------
```

The following program reshapes the input data set the same way as in the main example. Note that the default split character (/) has been inserted in the RESPONSE format. This was not needed in the PROC TABULATE step.

```
proc format;
   value $q 'q1'='1. Road Maintenance'
            'q2'='2. Parks Upkeep'
            'q3'='3. Snowplowing'
            'q4'='4. Sheriff Patrolling'
            'q5'='5. Ordinance Enforcement'
            'q6'='6. Town Office Hours'
            'q7'='7. Community Events'
            'q8'='8. Youth Programs'
            'q9'='9. Senior Services';
```

Insert the default PROC REPORT split character in labels that are long.

```
   value response 1='Strongly/Disapprove'
                  2='Disapprove'
                  3='Neutral'
                  4='Approve'
                  5='Strongly/Approve'
                  .='No response';
run;

proc sort data=townsurvey;
   by surveyid;
run;

proc transpose data=townsurvey
       out=townsurvey2(rename=( col1=choice))
       name=question;
   by surveyid;
   var q1-q9;
run;
```

```
%let dsid=%sysfunc(open(work.townsurvey,i));
%let nlobs=%sysfunc(attrn(&dsid,nlobs));
%let rc=%sysfunc(close(&dsid));

proc report data=townsurvey2 nowindows box;
   title 'Town Survey Results';
   title2 "Number of Participants: &nlobs";
```

Compute the total N for the row, which is needed to compute the percentages. This must appear before it's needed in the COMPUTE block. Assign this column an alias, because it's necessary to reference the N statistic in the COLUMN statement more than once.

```
   column n=totaln1
```

Specify the variable that will serve as the row dimension class variable and ensure that it is defined as a GROUP variable below in its DEFINE statement.

```
          question
```

Stack CHOICE above two variables, the N statistic and a computed variable.

```
          choice,(n pct)
```

Compute the total frequency count and assign this column an alias, because it's necessary to reference the N statistic in the COLUMN statement more than once.

```
          n=totaln2;
```

Compute the total frequency count for the row before it is referenced in the COMPUTE block. Suppress the display of its values.

```
   define totaln1 / noprint;
```

Identify the grouping variable that defines the row classifications in the report.

```
   define question / group 'Survey Question'
                     format=$q.;
```

Specify the variable that acts as the class variable in the column dimension.

```
   define choice / across ' '
```

Order the display of the values of CHOICE by its internal, unformatted values.

```
                  order=internal
                  format=response.;
```

Compute the N statistic for the cell defined by the current value of QUESTION and CHOICE.

```
   define n / format=4. 'N';
```

Specify a computed variable that will contain the frequency percentage of the current value of QUESTION and CHOICE. This percentage is based on the total frequency count in the row, which equals the total number of nonmissing responses to the question.

```
   define pct / format=5.1 computed 'Pct';
```

Determine the total frequency count in the row and display the results in the last column.

```
define totaln2 / format=5. 'Total/N';
```

Compute the frequency percentages that are nested under CHOICE.

```
compute pct;
```

Because there are five values for CHOICE, define two arrays with five elements each. Define the CN array to hold the frequency counts for each value of CHOICE within the row currently being processed. Start the explicit column reference at column 3, even though the first column of frequency counts appears in column 2 of the report. The first item on the COLUMN statement is a NOPRINT variable, and PROC REPORT counts it as a column.

```
array cn{5}   _c3_ _c5_ _c7_ _c9_ _c11_;
```

Define the CPCT array to hold the computed percentages for each value of CHOICE within the row currently being processed.

```
array cpct{5} _c4_ _c6_ _c8_ _c10_ _c12_;
```

Compute each of the five frequency count percentages for the row currently being processed.

```
do i=1 to 5;
```

Compute the percentage only when the frequency count in the array element currently being processed is not missing, and the total frequency count for the row is greater than zero. Otherwise, set the percentage to zero.

```
  if cn{i} ne .  and totaln1 gt 0
     then cpct{i}=100*(cn{i}/totaln1);
  else cpct{i}=0;
end;
endcomp;
run;
```

A Closer Look

Reshaping Data
The original input data set has all the information that you need to make the crosstabular report, but PROC TABULATE cannot process the information in that format to produce the report.

PROC TRANSPOSE rearranges the data so that each observation in the new data set contains the variable SURVEYID, a variable for question number (QUESTION), and a variable for question response (CHOICE). PROC TABULATE can process this structure to create the desired crosstabular report.

If you submit the following PROC TABULATE step using the original data set, you will obtain frequency counts and percentages, but they will not be shown in a crosstabular fashion. The questions and their responses define the rows. The two columns of the report are the N and PCTN statistics.

```
proc tabulate data=townsurvey missing;
  class q1 q2 q3 q4 q5 q6 q7 q8 q9;
  table (q1 all) (q2 all) (q3 all) (q4 all) (q5 all)
        (q6 all) (q7 all) (q8 all) (q9 all),
        n*f=4. pctn*f=5.1;
  run;
```

The first page of this report is shown in Figure 3.9c. Note that the MISSING option on the PROC TABULATE statement forces inclusion of missing values as valid categories. If you omit the MISSING option, only observations where all question responses were nonmissing are included in the report. Out of a total of 482 respondents, 146 responded to all nine questions. For more information on how PROC TABULATE works with missing values, see "Working with Missing Class Variable Values in PROC TABULATE" later in this section.

Figure 3.9c First Page of PROC TABULATE Report Run on TOWNSURVEY Data Set Before It Is Reshaped

```
                          Town Survey Results
                       Number of Participants: 482

                  ---------------------------------------
                  |                       | N   |PctN  |
                  |-----------------------+-----+------|
                  |q1                     |     |      |
                  |-----------------------|     |      |
                  |.                      |  59 | 12.2 |
                  |-----------------------+-----+------|
                  |1                      |   5 |  1.0 |
                  |-----------------------+-----+------|
                  |2                      | 134 | 27.8 |
                  |-----------------------+-----+------|
                  |3                      | 115 | 23.9 |
                  |-----------------------+-----+------|
                  |4                      | 143 | 29.7 |
                  |-----------------------+-----+------|
                  |5                      |  26 |  5.4 |
                  |-----------------------+-----+------|
                  |All                    | 482 |100.0 |
                  |-----------------------+-----+------|
                  |q2                     |     |      |
                  |-----------------------|     |      |
                  |.                      |  72 | 14.9 |
                  |-----------------------+-----+------|
                  |1                      |   4 |  0.8 |
                  |-----------------------+-----+------|
                  |2                      |  86 | 17.8 |
                  |-----------------------+-----+------|
                  |3                      |  93 | 19.3 |
                  |-----------------------+-----+------|
                  |4                      | 195 | 40.5 |
                  |-----------------------+-----+------|
                  |5                      |  32 |  6.6 |
                  |-----------------------+-----+------|
                  |All                    | 482 |100.0 |
                  |-----------------------+-----+------|
                  |q3                     |     |      |
                  |-----------------------|     |      |
                  |.                      |  43 |  8.9 |
                  |-----------------------+-----+------|
                  |1                      |  76 | 15.8 |
                  |-----------------------+-----+------|
                  |2                      | 169 | 35.1 |
                  |-----------------------+-----+------|
                  |3                      |  86 | 17.8 |
                  |-----------------------+-----+------|
                  |4                      |  93 | 19.3 |
                  |-----------------------+-----+------|
                  |5                      |  15 |  3.1 |
                  |-----------------------+-----+------|
                  |All                    | 482 |100.0 |
                  |-----------------------+-----+------|
```

(continued)

(continued)

```
|q4                       |      |      |
|-------------------------|      |      |
|.                        |   61|  12.7|
|-------------------------+----+-----|
|2                        |   94|  19.5|
|-------------------------+----+-----|
|3                        |  111|  23.0|
|-------------------------+----+-----|
|4                        |  180|  37.3|
|-------------------------+----+-----|
|5                        |   36|   7.5|
|-------------------------+----+-----|
|All                      |  482| 100.0|
|-------------------------+----+-----|
|q5                       |      |      |
|-------------------------|      |      |
|.                        |   48|  10.0|
|-------------------------+----+-----|
|1                        |   20|   4.1|
|-------------------------+----+-----|
|2                        |  156|  32.4|
 -------------------------------------

(Continued)
```

PROC TRANSPOSE restructures the data so that values that were stored in one observation are written to one variable. In this example, the values of the variables Q1 through Q9 are transposed and saved in the variable CHOICE. You can specify which variables you want to transpose. The following paragraphs illustrate how PROC TRANSPOSE reshapes the data in this example.

When you transpose with BY processing, as this example does, you create from each BY group one observation for each variable that you transpose. In this example, SURVEYID is the BY variable. Each observation in the input data set is a BY group, because the value of SURVEYID is unique for each observation.

This example transposes nine variables, Q1 through Q9. Therefore, the output data set contains nine observations from each BY group. These observations correspond to the nine questions per survey participant.

Figure 3.9d uses the first two observations in the input data set to illustrate the transposition.

Figure 3.9d Transposing Two Variables

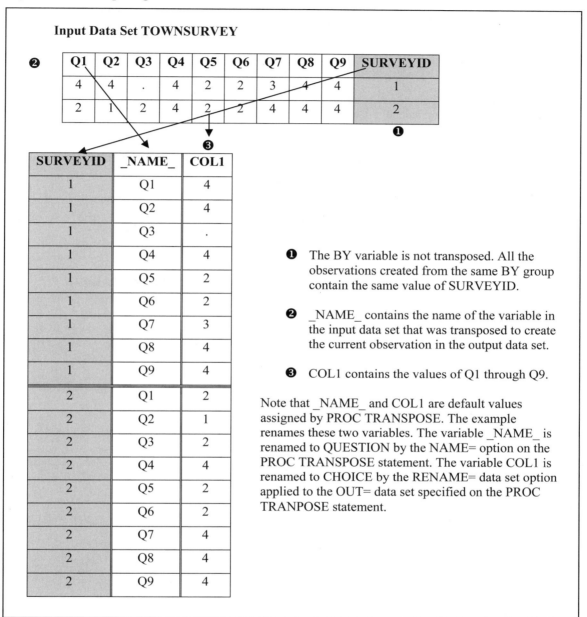

Input Data Set TOWNSURVEY

❷

Q1	Q2	Q3	Q4	Q5	Q6	Q7	Q8	Q9	SURVEYID
4	4	.	4	2	2	3	4	4	1
2	1	2	4	2	2	4	4	4	2

❶

❸

SURVEYID	_NAME_	COL1
1	Q1	4
1	Q2	4
1	Q3	.
1	Q4	4
1	Q5	2
1	Q6	2
1	Q7	3
1	Q8	4
1	Q9	4
2	Q1	2
2	Q2	1
2	Q3	2
2	Q4	4
2	Q5	2
2	Q6	2
2	Q7	4
2	Q8	4
2	Q9	4

❶ The BY variable is not transposed. All the observations created from the same BY group contain the same value of SURVEYID.

❷ _NAME_ contains the name of the variable in the input data set that was transposed to create the current observation in the output data set.

❸ COL1 contains the values of Q1 through Q9.

Note that _NAME_ and COL1 are default values assigned by PROC TRANSPOSE. The example renames these two variables. The variable _NAME_ is renamed to QUESTION by the NAME= option on the PROC TRANSPOSE statement. The variable COL1 is renamed to CHOICE by the RENAME= data set option applied to the OUT= data set specified on the PROC TRANPOSE statement.

Working with Missing Class Variable Values in PROC TABULATE

The TOWNSURVEY data set contains some missing responses. The counts in the "Total" column of the main report are the frequencies of nonmissing values. The counts, therefore, are less than 482, the total number of survey participants that was printed in the title.

By default, when you define a variable as a class variable, PROC TABULATE omits observations that have missing values for that class variable. This rule applies to all TABLE statements in the PROC TABULATE step, even if you do not include the variable in any of the TABLE statements.

To compute statistics for categories that are defined by missing values, add the MISSING option to the PROC TABULATE statement. When you add MISSING to the PROC TABULATE step in the main program of this example, PROC TABULATE adds a new column to the report that contains the N and ROWPCTN statistics for missing responses. This is shown in Figure 3.9e. The new column is the one labeled "No response."

The total N is now 482 for all questions, and the row percentages are now based on a denominator of 482, not on the total number of nonmissing responses for a question.

The PROC TABULATE statement with the MISSING option looks as follows:

```
proc tabulate data=townsurvey2 missing;
```

The output from the PROC TABULATE step that includes the MISSING option on the PROC TABULATE statement is shown in Figure 3.9e.

Figure 3.9e Output from the PROC TABULATE Step That Includes the MISSING Option

```
                              Town Survey Results
                          Number of Participants: 482

------------------------------------------------------------------------------------------------
|                    |    No    | Strongly  |           |          |         | Strongly |  Total    |
|                    | response |Disapprove |Disapprove | Neutral  | Approve | Approve  |Responses  |
|                    |----------+-----------+-----------+----------+---------+----------+-----------|
|                    | N |Row %| N |Row %| N |Row %| N |Row %| N |Row %| N |Row %| N |Row %|
|--------------------+----+-----+----+-----+----+-----+----+-----+----+-----+----+-----+----+-----|
|Survey Question     |    |     |    |     |    |     |    |     |    |     |    |     |    |     |
|--------------------|    |     |    |     |    |     |    |     |    |     |    |     |    |     |
|1. Road             |    |     |    |     |    |     |    |     |    |     |    |     |    |     |
|Maintenance         | 59| 12.2|  5|  1.0| 134| 27.8| 115| 23.9| 143| 29.7|  26|  5.4| 482|100.0|
|--------------------+----+-----+----+-----+----+-----+----+-----+----+-----+----+-----+----+-----|
|2. Parks Upkeep     | 72| 14.9|  4|  0.8|  86| 17.8|  93| 19.3| 195| 40.5|  32|  6.6| 482|100.0|
|--------------------+----+-----+----+-----+----+-----+----+-----+----+-----+----+-----+----+-----|
|3. Snowplowing      | 43|  8.9| 76| 15.8| 169| 35.1|  86| 17.8|  93| 19.3|  15|  3.1| 482|100.0|
|--------------------+----+-----+----+-----+----+-----+----+-----+----+-----+----+-----+----+-----|
|4. Sheriff          |    |     |    |     |    |     |    |     |    |     |    |     |    |     |
|Patrolling          | 61| 12.7|  0|  0.0|  94| 19.5| 111| 23.0| 180| 37.3|  36|  7.5| 482|100.0|
|--------------------+----+-----+----+-----+----+-----+----+-----+----+-----+----+-----+----+-----|
|5. Ordinance        |    |     |    |     |    |     |    |     |    |     |    |     |    |     |
|Enforcement         | 48| 10.0| 20|  4.1| 156| 32.4| 121| 25.1| 107| 22.2|  30|  6.2| 482|100.0|
|--------------------+----+-----+----+-----+----+-----+----+-----+----+-----+----+-----+----+-----|
|6. Town Office      |    |     |    |     |    |     |    |     |    |     |    |     |    |     |
|Hours               | 64| 13.3|  1|  0.2|  80| 16.6| 124| 25.7| 177| 36.7|  36|  7.5| 482|100.0|
|--------------------+----+-----+----+-----+----+-----+----+-----+----+-----+----+-----+----+-----|
|7. Community        |    |     |    |     |    |     |    |     |    |     |    |     |    |     |
|Events              | 69| 14.3|  1|  0.2|  38|  7.9|  51| 10.6| 204| 42.3| 119| 24.7| 482|100.0|
|--------------------+----+-----+----+-----+----+-----+----+-----+----+-----+----+-----+----+-----|
|8. Youth Programs   | 55| 11.4|  2|  0.4|  50| 10.4|  45|  9.3| 201| 41.7| 129| 26.8| 482|100.0|
|--------------------+----+-----+----+-----+----+-----+----+-----+----+-----+----+-----+----+-----|
|9. Senior Services  | 59| 12.2|  3|  0.6|  94| 19.5| 121| 25.1| 167| 34.6|  38|  7.9| 482|100.0|
------------------------------------------------------------------------------------------------
```

Where to Go from Here

PROC REPORT reference, usage information, and additional examples. See "The REPORT Procedure" in the "Procedures" section of *Base SAS 9.1 Procedures Guide.*

PROC TABULATE reference, usage information, and additional examples. See "The TABULATE Procedure" in the "Procedures" section of *Base SAS 9.1 Procedures Guide.*

PROC TRANSPOSE reference, usage information, and additional examples. See "The TRANSPOSE Procedure" in the "Procedures" section of *Base SAS 9.1 Procedures Guide.*

SAS File Input/Output Functions. See "Functions and CALL Routines" in *SAS 9.1 Language Reference: Dictionary.*

SAS Macro Programming. In the "Understanding and Using the Macro Facility" section of *SAS 9.1 Macro Language: Reference,* see "Macro Variables" and "Using SAS Language Functions in the DATA Step and Macro Facility" in the "Interfaces with the Macro Facility" section. Also see "Macro Language Dictionary."

Example 3.10   Reporting on Multiple-Response Survey Data

Goal

Summarize responses to survey questions for which the respondent can select one or more responses. Tally the number of times a response for a question was selected and the percentage of the total number of respondents that this count represents. Summarize fill-in-the blank numeric responses with selected statistics.

Report

```
             Customer Survey Results: 120 Respondents

             Factors Influencing the Decision to Buy

                 ------------------------------------
                 |                  | Count |Percent|
                 |------------------+-------+-------|
                 |Cost              |    87|   72.5%|
                 |------------------+-------+-------|
                 |Performance       |    62|   51.6%|
                 |------------------+-------+-------|
                 |Reliability       |    30|   25.0%|
                 |------------------+-------+-------|
                 |Sales Staff       |   120|  100.0%|
                 ------------------------------------


                      Source of Company Name

                 ------------------------------------
                 |                  | Count |Percent|
                 |------------------+-------+-------|
                 |TV/Radio          |    92|   76.6%|
                 |------------------+-------+-------|
                 |Internet          |    69|   57.5%|
                 |------------------+-------+-------|
                 |Word of Mouth     |    26|   21.6%|
                 ------------------------------------


                    Visits Resulting in Sales

                 ------------------------------------
                 |                  |       |Average |
                 |                  |       | Visits |
                 |                  | Total | Per    |
                 |                  |Visits |Customer|
                 |------------------+-------+--------|
                 |Website           |   279|     2.3|
                 |------------------+-------+--------|
                 |Store             |   327|     2.7|
                 ------------------------------------
```

Example Features

Data Set	CUSTRESP
Featured Step	PROC TABULATE
Featured Step Statements and Options	TABLE statement: PCTN statistic with denominator definition
Formatting Features	System Option: FORMDLIM when sending output to the LISTING destination Picture Format
Additional Features	Macro programming SAS file input/output functions
A Closer Look	Working with SAS Functions
ODS Enhanced Versions of This Example	Examples 6.13 and 6.14
Other Examples That Use This Data Set	Examples 6.13 and 6.14

Example Overview

The three tables in this report present information on the customers of a business where products can be purchased either in a store or online.

Each observation in CUSTRESP corresponds to one customer's responses to three questions that have a total of nine possible responses. The first question relates to influences on decisions to buy a product and asks the customer to select up to four check boxes in response. The second question relates to the customer's source in finding the company name and asks the customer to select up to three check boxes. The responses to the last question are numerical values that the customer provides for the number of visits to the company's Web site and the number of visits to the company's store.

Note that the three tables are placed on one page. When sending the report to the LISTING destination, setting the SAS option FORMDLIM keeps the tables on one page. Examples 6.13 and 6.14 show how to send the same report to a nonlisting destination.

In order to create three tables with different titles, three PROC TABULATE steps are required. If it is not necessary to have different titles, the report can be produced with one PROC TABULATE step and three TABLE statements.

Collecting the Data

Figure 3.10 shows the survey form used to collect data.

Figure 3.10 Survey Form Used to Collect Data

Customer Questionnaire

ID#: _____

Please place a check beside all answers that apply.

Why do you buy our products?

☐Cost ☐Performance ☐Reliability ☐Sales Staff

How did you find out about our company?

☐TV/Radio ☐Internet ☐Word of Mouth

Please estimate the number of visits to each of the following locations when you bought at least one item.

_____ Store   _____Website

Thank-you!

Program

Create a format for the percentages in the first two tables. Set the default length of the format to 7 spaces. Write all values with at least one digit to the left of the decimal point and with one digit to the right of the decimal point. Place a percent sign after the digits so that the percent sign is included in the output.

```
proc format;
   picture pctfmt (default=7) low-high='009.9%';
run;
```

Write macro language statements to open the analysis data set and determine the number of nondeleted observations in the analysis data set. Do not enclose the arguments to the functions in quotes, because these functions are used with %SYSFUNC and are processed by the macro facility. Open the data set as read-only by specifying the argument "i", which stands for input mode.

```
%let dsid=%sysfunc(open(work.custresp,i));
```

Determine the number of nondeleted observations in the analysis data set.

```
%let nresps=%sysfunc(attrn(&dsid,nlobs));
```

Close the analysis data set.

```
%let rc=close(&dsid);
```

When sending the report to the LISTING destination, set the FORMDLIM option to a single blank character to suppress the default page eject that SAS writes between reports.

```
options formdlim=' ';
```

Include the number of nondeleted observations in the text of the TITLE statement. Ensure that the title text is enclosed in double quotation marks so that the macro variable resolves.

```
title "Customer Survey Results: &nresps
      Respondents";
```

```
proc tabulate data=custresp;
   title3 'Factors Influencing the Decision to
      Buy';
```

Define the check box variables in the first report as analysis variables. Include CUSTOMER, which has a value for every observation, so that it can be used as the denominator definition for the percentage calculations.

```
   var factor1-factor4 customer;
```

Place each factor as a row in the report. Calculate two columns of statistics: frequency counts of responses and percentages of the total number of respondents that the frequency counts represent.

```
   table factor1='Cost'
         factor2='Performance'
         factor3='Reliability'
         factor4='Sales Staff',
         (n='Count'*f=7.
         pctn<customer>='Percent'*f=pctfmt.);
run;
```

Produce the table that analyzes the second question, which contains three check box responses.

```
proc tabulate data=custresp;
   title 'Source of Company Name';
   var source1-source3 customer;
   table source1='TV/Radio'
         source2='Internet'
         source3='Word of Mouth',
         (n='Count'*f=7.
         pctn<customer>='Percent'*f=pctfmt.);
run;
```

Produce the table that analyzes the third question, which contains the numeric fill-in-the-blank responses.

```
proc tabulate data=custresp;
   title 'Visits Resulting in Sales';
   var website store;
   table website='Website'
         store='Store',
         (sum='Total Visits'*f=7.
         mean='Average Visits Per
            Customer'*f=8.1);
run;
```

Restore the default page eject by resetting the page delimiter to a null value.

```
options formdlim='';
```

🔍 A Closer Look

Working with SAS Functions

You can customize the presentation of information in your reports by applying SAS functions. Because these functions can be executed by macro language code, you may be able to avoid the extra processing of a DATA step or procedure. The results returned by the functions can provide text and summary information for your reports. Commonly, these features add text to titles, footnotes, and summary lines in reports. For example, you could add these types of customizations to LINE statements in a COMPUTE block in PROC REPORT.

The two macro functions, %SYSFUNC and %QSYSFUNC, and the macro statement %SYSCALL provide a means to apply functions or call routines and save the results in a macro variable. The macro variable can then be referenced in subsequent steps of the program. Many SAS functions and call routines can be used with these features.

The %QSYSFUNC function does the same task as %SYSFUNC and provides the additional feature of masking specific characters. Macro quoting and masking are beyond the scope of this book. Refer to SAS documentation (support.sas.com/v9doc) and SAS Press books (support.sas.com/saspress) for thorough discussions of these topics.

The example above used %SYSFUNC and the ATTRN function to obtain the number of nondeleted observations in the analysis data set. There are many other arguments that can be applied to ATTRN to obtain other information, as well as many other functions that you might find useful in customizing your reports.

Some of the customizations you can achieve with SAS functions include:

❑ formatting dates and times

❑ applying a format defined by PROC FORMAT to a value

❑ confirming the existence of data sets and other files

❑ obtaining information about data sets, external files, and directories

For example, you can format today's date in your title with the WORDDATE format:

```
title "Customer Survey Results as of
       %sysfunc(date(),worddate.): &nresps Respondents";
```

If the report was produced on January 10, 2005, the title would look like this:

```
Customer Survey Results as of January 10, 2005: 120
Respondents
```

Similarly, you can add these customizations to LINE statements in your PROC REPORT steps. The following example puts the date and time that the analysis data set was last modified at the end of the report.

Submit the following macro language statements before the PROC REPORT step. The macro variable MODIFIED holds the date and time of last modification of the WORK.CUSTRESP data set.

```
%let dsid=%sysfunc(open(work.custresp,i));
%let modified=%sysfunc(attrn(&dsid,modte));
%let rc=%sysfunc(close(&dsid));
```

Adding the following COMPUTE block to a PROC REPORT step lists the last modification of the data set at the end of the report.

```
compute after;
  line ' ';
  line '**********************************************';
  line "Analysis Data Set Last Modified:
         %sysfunc(putn(&modified,datetime16.))";
  line '**********************************************';
endcomp;
```

Here is an example of the text that this COMPUTE block produces.

```
* * * * * * * * * * * * * * * * * * * * * * * * * * * * * * * * * * * * * * * * * *
Analysis Data Set Last Modified: 28OCT05:10:10:24
* * * * * * * * * * * * * * * * * * * * * * * * * * * * * * * * * * * * * * * * * *
```

Remember that when you use %SYSFUNC you do not need to enclose character values in quotation marks as you do when using the functions in DATA steps.

Also, remember that you cannot nest functions within a single %SYSFUNC. You can, however, nest %SYSFUNC calls; each function must be invoked by being called by its own %SYSFUNC.

Where to Go from Here

The FORMDLIM SAS System Option. See "SAS System Options" in *SAS 9.1 Language Reference: Dictionary.*

PROC FORMAT reference, usage information, and additional examples. See "The FORMAT Procedure" in the "Procedures" section of *Base SAS 9.1 Procedures Guide.*

PROC TABULATE reference, usage information, and additional examples. See "The TABULATE Procedure" in the "Procedures" section of *Base SAS 9.1 Procedures Guide.*

SAS File Input/Output Functons. See "Functions and CALL Routines" in *SAS 9.1 Language Reference: Dictionary.*

SAS Macro Programming. In the "Understanding and Using the Macro Facility" section of *SAS 9.1 Macro Language: Reference,* see "Macro Variables" and "Using SAS Language Functions in the DATA Step and Macro Facility" in the "Interfaces with the Macro Facility" section. Also see "Macro Language Dictionary."

Working with Dates. See "Dates, Times, and Intervals" in the "SAS System Concepts" section of *SAS 9.1 Language Reference: Concepts;* the "Date and Time" category of formats described in the "Formats" section of *SAS 9.1 Language Reference: Dictionary;* and the "Date and Time" category of functions and call routines described in "Functions and Call Routines by Category" in the "Functions and Call Routines" section of *SAS 9.1 Language Reference: Dictionary.*

Working with Formats. See "Formats and Informats" in "SAS Language Elements" in the "SAS System Concepts" section of *SAS 9.1 Language Reference: Concepts,* and "Formats," in *SAS 9.1 Language Reference: Dictionary.*

Customized Reports

The reports shown in Chapters 2 and 3 used the features and options of PROC PRINT, PROC REPORT, and PROC TABULATE. Although you can add formatting features to the reports produced by these procedures, they still have a standard presentation.

This chapter presents three examples of customizing reports in styles either not available with these procedures or, in the case of PROC REPORT, available only through the use of programming statements.

❑ The first example in this chapter uses programming statements in PROC REPORT to produce a multipage listing that does not have the usual look of a detail or summary report produced by PROC REPORT.

❑ The second example shows how to use a DATA step to create a report. With SAS language programming statements, you can control placement of information on a page. This example combines the output data sets from several procedures to produce a one-page report using programming statements in a DATA step.

❑ The last example shows how you can save ODS output objects in data sets, select specific information from these data sets, and present the selected results in a report.

The three examples in this chapter send output to the default LISTING destination. The main program in Example 4.1 is written specifically to send output to the LISTING destination. The related technique for this example presents a more generic version of the program. This second program can send output to a nonlisting destination and does not rely on any ODS features.

Example 4.2 is modified in Example 6.12 to include ODS features and send output to a nonlisting destination. See Example 5.2 for another example of a DATA step program that produces a report.

See the back of this book for a list of titles related to the features of these examples, and visit the SAS Press Web site (http://support.sas.com/saspress) for current information on new and revised publications.

Several presentations at SUGI conferences show how SAS users apply report writing techniques. Recent conference proceedings that are available online provide a wealth of additional applications and examples. You can link to them through the SAS support Web site (http://support.sas.com).

Table 4.0 presents a cross-reference of the examples in this chapter to the procedures used, data sets used, and ODS enhanced versions of the examples. See Appendix A for details on the example data sets analyzed in this chapter. See Appendix B for a table that cross-references all examples in this book.

Table 4.0 Cross-Reference of Examples in Chapter 4

| Example | Report-Writing Tool Used | | | | | | ODS Enhanced Version | Data Set | Example Title |
	REPORT	TABULATE	PRINT	DATA Step	MEANS	FREQ			
4.1	X							SERVICE	Customizing a Detail Report with Individualized Page Headers
4.2				X			6.12	DEMOG	Creating a Customized Table of Descriptive Statistics
4.3	X						4.3 (output objects)	FITNESS	Customizing the Presentation of Analyses

Example 4.1   Customizing a Detail Report with Individualized Page Headers

Goal

Create a detail report that has a customized layout. Select specific information to list on each page. Customize the page and column headers by suppressing the default headings and replacing them with customized features.

Report

```
                         Supreme Tire and Auto Repair
                               Service Record

            Bert Allen
            1803 Knollton Ct.
            Bristol, NC  29345
            Ford F-150 1998

                                  Hours        Labor       Parts        Total
               Date       Description      Worked        Cost        Cost         Cost
            ----------   ---------------   ------      --------     --------     --------
            01/10/2006   replace belts       1.5        $97.50       $0.00       $97.50
            10/19/2005   oil change          0.5        $32.50      $18.00       $50.50
                                            ----       --------     -------     --------
                                             2.0       $130.00      $18.00      $148.00
                                            ----       --------     -------     --------




                   Labor cost is calculated at $65.00 per hour
                        Total cost = Labor cost + Parts cost
----------------------------------------page break----------------------------------------
                         Supreme Tire and Auto Repair
                               Service Record

            Bert Allen
            1803 Knollton Ct.
            Bristol, NC  29345
            Jeep Cherokee 2000

                                  Hours        Labor       Parts        Total
               Date       Description      Worked        Cost        Cost         Cost
            ----------   ---------------   ------      --------     --------     --------
            01/10/2006   replace brakes      2.0       $130.00      $45.00      $175.00
            02/20/2006   rotate tires        1.0        $65.00      $20.00       $85.00
                         transmission        5.5       $357.50      $50.00      $407.50
            07/01/2005   oil change          0.5        $32.50      $18.00       $50.50
                                            ----       --------     -------     --------
                                             9.0       $585.00     $133.00      $718.00
                                            ----       --------     -------     --------




                   Labor cost is calculated at $65.00 per hour
                        Total cost = Labor cost + Parts cost

----------------------------------------page break----------------------------------------
                         Supreme Tire and Auto Repair
                               Service Record

            Joe Smith
            1991 Cohansey St.
            New Ulm, NC  29545
            Ford F-150 1998
```

```
                              Hours      Labor      Parts      Total
                              Worked     Cost       Cost       Cost
       Date      Description  ------     --------   --------   --------
    ----------   -----------
    01/19/2006   oil change      0.5     $32.50     $18.00     $50.50
    02/25/2006   rotate tires    1.0     $65.00      $0.00     $65.00
                                ----     --------   --------   --------
                                 1.5     $97.50     $18.00     $115.50
                                ----     --------   -------    --------


                Labor cost is calculated at $65.00 per hour
                   Total cost = Labor cost + Parts cost
----------------------------------------page break-------------------------------------------
                         Supreme Tire and Auto Repair
                                Service Record

       Sara Jones
       202 Stargate Dr.
       Dart, NC  29445
       Chrysler Voyager 2003

                              Hours      Labor      Parts      Total
                              Worked     Cost       Cost       Cost
       Date      Description  ------     --------   --------   --------
    ----------   -----------
    12/07/2005   align frontend  1.5     $97.50     $20.00     $117.50
                 rotate tires    1.0     $65.00     $20.00     $85.00
                                ----     --------   --------   --------
                                 2.5     $162.50    $40.00     $202.50
                                ----     --------   -------    --------


                Labor cost is calculated at $65.00 per hour
                   Total cost = Labor cost + Parts cost
```

Example Features

Data Set	SERVICE
Featured Step	PROC REPORT
Featured Step Statements and Options	DEFINE statement: ANALYSIS, COMPUTED, NOPRINT, ORDER, and SUM options COMPUTE blocks BREAK AFTER statement LINE statement
Formatting Features	PROC REPORT statement: NOHEADER option PROC REPORT statement: SPACING= and WIDTH= options when sending output to the LISTING destination LINE statement: column positioning when sending output to the LISTING destination
Related Technique	OPTIONS NOBYLINE, PROC REPORT with a BY statement, and TITLE statements with #BYVAL
🔍 **A Closer Look**	Understanding the Use of ORDER and NOPRINT in PROC REPORT

Example Overview

This report shows the service records for cars brought to a car repair shop. A car can have multiple service records, and all the service records for one car are printed on one page. A heading on each page identifies the car and its owner.

Each observation in the SERVICE data set corresponds to one service record on one date for one car. A row in the body of each page of the report corresponds to one observation in SERVICE.

Some variables in the report appear in columns. Others appear only in the page heading. The columns include data set variables and computed variables.

Note that one customer has two cars and that two customers have the same car model.

Many of the features of the main example require that you send the report to a LISTING destination. Modifications to the program that would produce a similar report for a nonlisting destination are described in the Related Technique section.

This report suppresses the default placement of column headings and instead writes column headings with programming statements that are placed in a COMPUTE BEFORE block. The programming statements place the customer information in the upper left corner of the report and write the column headings in specific column positions of the report. The explicit column positioning of the column headings would not work if the report were sent to a nonlisting destination.

Program

Suppress all default column headers.

```
proc report data=service nowindows
    noheader
```

When sending the report to a LISTING destination, separate the columns with five spaces.

```
    spacing=5;
title 'Supreme Tire and Auto Repair';
title2 'Service Record';

footnote1 'Labor cost is calculated at $65.00
          per hour';
footnote2 'Total cost = Labor cost + Parts cost';
```

List the columns in the order in which they should appear in the report. Include those that appear in the report columns as well as those that appear in the customized page headers.

```
column name address city state zipcode cartype
       date workdone hours labor parts total;
```

Apply the same attributes to all variables in the COLUMN statement between the first in the list and the last in the list. Order the data based on the values of these variables, but do not print them.

```
define name--zipcode / order noprint;
```

```
                                    define cartype         / order noprint;
                                    define date            / order format=mmddyy10.;
                                    define workdone        / order;
```

Calculate the sum statistics on these two data set variables. Specify the column width when sending output to the LISTING destination.

```
                                    define hours / analysis sum format=4.1
                                                   width=4;
                                    define parts / analysis sum format=dollar8.2
                                                   width=7;
```

Define two computed variables.

```
                                    define labor / computed format=dollar8.2;
                                    define total / computed format=dollar8.2;
```

Compute values for LABOR and TOTAL in separate COMPUTE blocks. Refer to the analysis variables HOURS and PARTS by their compound names. The compound name identifies the variable and the statistic associated with it.

```
                                    compute labor;
                                       labor=hours.sum*65.00;
                                    endcomp;

                                    compute total;
                                       total=labor+parts.sum;
                                    endcomp;
```

Customize the page heading and the column headings. Execute this block every time the value of CARTYPE changes, which is before PROC REPORT writes the first row for that car.

```
                                    compute before cartype;
                                       length fulladdress $ 55;
                                       fulladdress=catx(' ',cats(city,','),state,
                                                   zipcode);
```

Write the page heading lines with column and formatted output.

```
                                    line @2 name $20.;
                                    line @2 address $20.;
                                    line @2 line @2 fulladdress $55.;
                                    line @2 cartype $21.;
                                    line ' ';
```

Write the column headings in specific locations.

```
                                    line @36 'Hours' @49 'Labor' @62 'Parts'
                                        @74 'Total';
                                    line @6 'Date'  @19 'Description' @35 'Worked'
                                        @50 'Cost' @63 'Cost' @75 'Cost';
                                    line @2 10*'-'    @17 15*'-' @35 6*'-'
                                        @46 8*'-' @59 8*'-' @71 8*'-';
                                    endcomp;
```

Create a summary line after the last row for each car. Start a new page after the summary line.

```
                                    break after cartype / summarize ol ul page;
                                    run;
```

Related Technique

The main program for this example writes page and column headings to explicit locations on a page. When you send this report to a nonlisting destination, these instructions are ignored and the formatting of the report is out of alignment.

The following program removes the explicit positioning of data in the headings of the report in the preceding example. It reinstates column headers by removing the NOHEADER option.

The TITLE statements create the page headings, and the BYVAL feature in the TITLE statements customizes these headings. If you tried to write the page headings with a COMPUTE BEFORE block and did not include the PROC REPORT NOHEADER option, PROC REPORT places the column headings before the page headings.

Figure 4.1 shows the first page of the report when sent to the RTF nonlisting destination.

Figure 4.1 First Page of Output from Related Technique Sent to the RTF Destination

The program that created the output in Figure 4.1 follows.

Sort the data set by the variables that will be included in the TITLE statements.	```
	proc sort data=service;
	  by name address city state zipcode cartype;
	run;
	``

Prevent BY lines from being printed above each BY group of the report.	``` options nobyline; ```

	``
	proc report data=service nowd;
	  title 'Supreme Tire and Auto Repair';
	  title2 'Service Record';
	``

Specify the page headings in TITLE statements and include in the title text the current values of the BY variables. When sending to a nonlisting destination, left-justify the title text.	``` title4 justify=left "#byval(name)"; title5 justify=left "#byval(address)"; title6 justify=left "#byval(city), " "#byval(state) #byval(zipcode)"; title7 justify=left "#byval(cartype)"; ```
Include a BY statement so that the data set is processed in BY groups and the BY-group values are available to be inserted into the title text.	``` by name address city state zipcode cartype; ```
Include one of the BY variables (CARTYPE) on the COLUMN statement because it's necessary for PROC REPORT to use its values to determine when to start a new page and compute summaries.	``` column cartype date workdone hours labor parts total; ```

Specify CARTYPE as an ORDER variable, even though this specification appears redundant because of the inclusion of CARTYPE on the BY statement. Do not display the values of CARTYPE, but use its values later to determine when to start a new page and compute summaries.

```
define cartype / order noprint;

define date / order format=mmddyy10. 'Date';
define workdone / order 'Description';

define hours / analysis sum format=4.1
                 'Hours/Worked';
define parts / analysis sum format=dollar8.2
                 'Parts/Cost';

define labor / computed format=dollar8.2
                 'Labor/Cost';
define total / computed format=dollar8.2
                 'Total/Cost';

compute labor;
  labor=hours.sum*65.00;
endcomp;

compute total;
  total=labor+parts.sum;
endcomp;
```

Summarize the information for each car and start the information for each car on a new page.

```
break after cartype / summarize ol ul page;
```

Instead of putting the cost information in footnotes as was done in the main program for this example, place it at the end of the body of the report.

```
compute after cartype;
  line 'Labor cost is calculated at $65.00 per hour';
  line 'Total cost = Labor cost + Parts cost';
endcomp;
run;
```

🔎 A Closer Look

Understanding the Use of ORDER and NOPRINT in PROC REPORT

Combining the ORDER and NOPRINT options in the definition of a variable in PROC REPORT provides you with a lot of flexibility for customizing a report.

❑ The ORDER option orders the rows of the report.

❑ The ORDER option also lets you place customized text at points in the report where the value of that variable changes.

❑ The NOPRINT option prevents a variable from appearing in a column. NOPRINT has no effect on the ORDER option. A variable defined with both options affects the order of the rows of the report, even though it does not appear in a column of the report.

The page heading in the main example identifies the car and its owner. This information appears before the first row of repair charges. Variables that do not appear in a column appear in the page heading.

The report is ordered by the car owner's name and within that by car for customers with more than one car with repair records.

The ORDER option on the DEFINE statements arranges the observations, while the NOPRINT option suppresses their display as columns. The values of these items, however, are still available to the step. The COMPUTE BEFORE CARTYPE block references them and writes the page heading.

Where to Go from Here

The BYLINE/NOBYLINE SAS System Options. See "SAS System Options" in *SAS 9.1 Language Reference: Dictionary*.

Inserting BY-group information in titles. See "Creating Titles that Contain BY-Group Information" in the "Fundamental Concepts in Using Base SAS Procedures" section of *Base SAS 9.1 Procedures Guide*.

PROC REPORT reference, usage information, and additional examples. See "The REPORT Procedure" in the "Procedures" section of *Base SAS 9.1 Procedures Guide*.

Example 4.2   Creating a Customized Table of Descriptive Statistics

Goal

Create a table of descriptive statistics. Obtain the statistics through use of standard SAS procedures, and then write the results in a customized style.

Report

```
                                           Client
                                          Protocol
                                         Population

                             Table  2.14

                        Baseline Demographics
         ------------------------------------------------------------
                                  Active            Placebo
         ------------------------------------------------------------
Number of Patients                 94                106

Gender
  Male                          41 (44%)          46 (43%)
  Female                        53 (56%)          60 (57%)

Age (years)
  Mean (SEM)                   52.1 (1.96)       53.9 (1.74)
  25th - 75th                  33.7 -  67.3      37.7 -  69.1
  Min - Max                    21.0 -  84.7      20.5 -  84.8
  No. Missing                       0                 0

Race
  Non-White                     37 (39%)          33 (31%)
  White                         57 (61%)          73 (69%)

Height (inches)
  Mean (SEM)                   65.4 (0.54)       65.4 (0.54)
  25th - 75th                  61.5 -  69.9      60.5 -  70.0
  Min - Max                    55.3 -  74.8      55.2 -  74.7
  No. Missing                       0                 0

Weight (lbs)
  Mean (SEM)                  188.2 (5.07)      191.1 (4.43)
  25th - 75th                 140.9 - 225.8     159.2 - 223.7
  Min - Max                   110.5 - 275.6     110.4 - 277.0
  No. Missing                       0                 0
         ------------------------------------------------------------
```

Example Features

Data Set	DEMOG
Preparatory Steps	PROC FREQ PROC MEANS with NOPRINT and NWAY options
Featured Step	DATA step
Featured Step Statements and Options	FILE statement: N= option (example uses N=PS, which is valid when sending output to the LISTING destination) PUT statement with column and formatted output when sending output to the LISTING destination
Formatting Features	FILE statement: HEADER= and NOTITLES options when sending output to the LISTING destination

A Closer Look	Creating a Format for Percentages with the PICTURE Statement in PROC FORMAT
	Computing Descriptive Statistics
	Concatenating SAS Data Sets
	Positioning the Output Line Pointer to a Specific Column by Calculating the Column Position
	Positioning the Output Line Pointer to a Specific Row by Calculating the Row Position
	Supplying Heading Information for All Pages
ODS Enhanced Version of This Example	Example 6.12
Other Examples That Use This Data Set	Example 6.12

Example Overview

This report compares the demographic data of subjects assigned to two treatment groups in a clinical trial. It mixes frequencies and statistics within the content of the report. The required structure of the table cannot be achieved with PROC TABULATE or PROC REPORT.

The FREQ and MEANS procedures summarize the data and output the results to data sets. There are six sections in the report, and the program creates an output data set from either PROC FREQ or PROC MEANS for each section. A DATA step concatenates these data sets, uses conditional processing to write rows in the report, and produces the report's headings.

Each observation in the DEMOG data set corresponds to all the measurements on one patient in one treatment group.

The sole destination of this example is intended to be the LISTING destination. The PUT statements in the DATA step write output to specific row and column positions. The same output sent to a nonlisting destination would not look properly formatted. Example 6.12 uses ODS features to construct a similar report that is sent to a nonlisting destination.

This example works with data sets produced by PROC FREQ and PROC MEANS. You can also save your output in data sets produced by ODS output objects. Example 4.3 creates a customized report from data sets produced by ODS output objects.

Program

Define an informat to use in controlling column placement of information.

```
proc format;

  invalue colplc 'Active'=45
                 'Placebo'=63;

  value racefmt  0='Non-White'
                 1='White';
  value gendrfmt 0='Male'
                 1='Female';
  value tmtdgfmt 0='Active'
                 1='Placebo';
```

Create a PICTURE format for percentages.

```
        picture percen (round)      .=' ( %)' (noedit)
                other='0009%)' (prefix='(');
run;
```

Compute the frequency counts for the first two sections of the report. Do not print the tables. Save the results for each section in its own data set.

```
proc freq data=demog;
  tables tmtdg / out=t1 noprint;
```

Save the percentage of the column frequency, the percentage of the row frequency, and the percentage of the two-way table frequency in the output data set.

```
    tables tmtdg*gender / out=t2 outpct
```

Do not print the frequency table.

```
                            noprint;
    run;
```

Compute the statistics for the third section of the report. Do not print the results. With the NWAY option, save only the statistics for the two TMTDG groups, not the overall statistics. (The NWAY option limits the output statistics to the observations with the highest _TYPE_ value.)

```
proc means data=demog noprint nway;
```

Specify the variable whose values define the categories for which to compute statistics.

```
    class tmtdg;
```

```
    var age;
```

Save the statistics in a data set. Specify the keywords of each of the statistics that should be saved and specify the variable names to assign to the statistics in the output data set.

```
    output out=t3 min=min max=max mean=mean q3=q3 q1=q1
           nmiss=nmiss stderr=stderr;
    run;
```

Compute the frequency counts for the fourth section of the report. Do not print the table. Save the results in a data set. Include the percentage of the column frequency, the percentage of the row frequency, and the percentage of the two-way table frequency in the output data set. (All three PROC FREQ TABLES statements could be submitted from one PROC FREQ step, but this example presents them separately so that the output data sets are created in the same sequence as they appear in the report.)

```
proc freq data=demog;
  tables tmtdg*race / out=t4 outpct noprint;
run;
```

Execute PROC MEANS two more times to compute statistics for the last two parts of the table. Write PROC MEANS steps that are similar to the preceding one.

```
proc means data=demog noprint nway;
   class tmtdg;
   var height;
   output out=t5 min=min max=max mean=mean q3=q3
          q1=q1 nmiss=nmiss stderr=stderr;
run;

proc means data=demog noprint;
   class tmtdg;
   var weight;
   output out=t6 min=min max=max mean=mean q3=q3
          q1=q1 nmiss=nmiss stderr=stderr;
run;
```

Process the output data sets that have already been created and do not create a new data set.

```
data _null_;
```

Send the output to an external file. Replace the text *external-file* with the name of the destination file.

```
   file 'external-file'
```

Specify that the external file contain carriage control characters.

```
      print
```

Specify the number of lines to make available to the output pointer in the current iteration of the DATA step. In this example, set that number to the value assigned to the SAS PAGESIZE option, which is represented by PS.

```
      n=ps
```

Suppress printing of the current title lines during execution of the DATA step.

```
      notitles
```

Identify a group of SAS statements by statement label that you want to execute each time SAS begins a new output page.

```
      header=reporttop;
```

Concatenate the six descriptive statistics data sets. For each data set, create a variable that indicates whether the data set contributed data to the current observation.

```
   set t1(in=in1) t2(in=in2) t3(in=in3)
       t4(in=in4) t5(in=in5) t6(in=in6);
```

Create a variable to use in conditional processing. Use INDS to track how many times the DATA step has read from the current data set.

```
   inds+1;
```

Assign a value to COL and use it later to position text under column headings.

```
   col=input(tmtdg,colplc.);
```

Execute this block when the DATA step is reading from data set T1.

Write the first row of the report when reading from data set T1.

Execute this block when processing all observations from data set T1 other than the first. Reset the value of INDS to 0 so that its value can be used on the next iteration of the DATA step when it reads from another data set for the first time. ROW is incremented by two so that the next PUT statement can write the next line of the report two lines below the first.

```
if in1 then do;

  if inds=1 then put #row
       @13 'Number of Patients' @(col+2) count;

  else do;
    put #row @(col) count;
    inds=0;
    row+2;
  end;
end;
```

Execute this block when the DATA step is reading from either data set T2 or data set T4. Because these data sets are so similar, the same lines of code process them.

Write descriptive labels when processing the first observation of either data set T2 or data set T4.

```
else if in2 or in4 then do;




  if inds=1 then do;
    if in2 then put #row @13 'Gender';
    else do;
      row+5;
      put #row @13 'Race';
    end;
    row+1;
  end;
```

Execute this block when processing observations from data set T2. Calculate the row and column positions.

```
  if in2 then put #(row+gender) @15 gender gendrfmt.
              @(col-1) count pct_row percen5.;
```

Execute this block when processing observations from data set T4.

```
  else put #(row+race) @15 race racefmt.
            @(col-1) count pct_row percen5.;
```

Reset INDS after processing the last observation contributed from T2 or T4.

```
  if inds=4 then inds=0;
end;
```

Execute this block when processing observations from data set T3, data set T5, or data set T6.

Write labelling information when processing the first observation from data set T3, data set T5, or data set T6.

```
else if in3 or in5 or in6 then do;




  if inds=1 then do;
    if in3 or in5 then row+3;
    else row+5;
    if in3 then put #row @13 'Age (years)';
    else if in5 then put #row @13 'Height (inches)';
    else put #row @13 'Weight (lbs)';
    row+1;
  end;
```

Write the rows of the report that are contributed by observations from data sets T3 and T5.

```
if in3 or in5 then put
    #row @16 'Mean (SEM)' @(col-2) mean 4.1
        @(col+3) '(' stdmean 4.2 ')'
    #(row+1) @15 '25th - 75th'
        @(col-2) q1 4.1 ' -  ' q3 4.1
    #(row+2) @16 'Min - Max'
        @(col-2) min 4.1 ' - ' max 4.1
    #(row+3) @15 'No. Missing' @(col+3) nmiss 1.;
```

Write the rows of the report that are contributed by observations from data set T6. This code is very similar to the code for writing rows while reading from T3 and T5, but subtle differences in alignment make it necessary to code these rows separately.

```
else put
    #row @16 'Mean (SEM)' @(col-3) mean 5.1
        @(col+3) '(' stdmean 4.2 ')'
    #(row+1) @15 '25th - 75th'
        @(col-3) q1 5.1 ' -  ' q3 5.1
    #(row+2) @16 'Min - Max'
        @(col-3) min 5.1 ' - ' max 5.1
    #(row+3) @15 'No. Missing' @(col+3) nmiss 1.;

if (in3 or in5) and inds=2 then inds=0;
```

When processing the last observation from T6, which is at the end of the report, write a horizontal line.

```
    if in6 and inds=2 then put #(row+4) @13 60*'-';
end;
```

Return to the top of the DATA step before executing the statements labelled by REPORTTOP.

```
return;
```

Supply heading information for all pages.

```
Reporttop:
    put #2   @67 'Client'
        #3   @65 'Protocol'
        #4   @63 'Population'
        #6   @38 'Table  2.14'
        #8   @32 'Baseline Demographics'
        #9   @13 60*'-'
        #10  @45 'Active' @62 'Placebo'
        #11  @13 60*'-';
    row=12;
    return;
run;
```

🔍 A Closer Look

Creating a Format for Percentages with the PICTURE Statement in PROC FORMAT

The PERCEN. format writes percentage values according to the templates, or pictures, in the PICTURE statement. The ROUND option rounds off values to the closest integer. If a value ends in 0.5, it is rounded up.

```
picture percen (round)  .='  ( %)' (noedit)
                other ='0009%)'
                (prefix ='(');
```

The first picture, which is for missing values, writes parentheses with a percent sign, but no number. The NOEDIT option means that the PICTURE format writes the characters between quotes exactly as they appear in the statement for the specified value or values.

For the picture for all nonmissing values, the string "0009" specifies placeholders for the formatted value. The PREFIX= option writes the open parenthesis before the first digit. The prefix character counts as one of the positions in the picture. The remaining three positions in the picture, represented by the second and the third 0 and the 9, are reserved for the percentage value. The placeholder of 0 specifies that no leading zero is written in that position. That is, if the value that is being formatted is less than 10, the left parenthesis will be put in the position of the third 0 in the picture.

Computing Descriptive Statistics

PROC MEANS provides data summarization tools that compute descriptive statistics for variables across all observations and within groups of observations. The program in this example executes three simple PROC MEANS steps. Each execution computes a few statistics on one analysis variable for groups defined by the values of one classification variable. The results are saved in output data sets.

The OUTPUT statement tells SAS to save specific statistics in an output data set. Specify each keyword for a statistic that you want to save and follow the keyword with an equal sign and the variable name that you want to assign to the statistic in the output data set. In this example, the variable names are the same as the keyword names.

The class variable TMTDG has two values, and each of the three output data sets produced by the three PROC MEANS steps has two observations, one for each value of TMTDG. The first observation in each output data set contains the statistics for the active group and the second observation contains the statistics for the placebo group.

PROC MEANS supports many variations on the form of the OUTPUT statement for computing statistics, providing variable names, and identifying specific observations. Saving these seven statistics is just a small sampling of what you can do with the OUTPUT statement in PROC MEANS. See Example 3.2 for more detail on using PROC MEANS.

Concatenating SAS Data Sets

The SET statement reads one observation on each iteration of the DATA step. It reads all the observations from the first data set, then the second, and so on, until it has read all observations from all six data sets:

```
set t1(in=in1)  t2(in=in2)  t3(in=in3)  t4(in=in4)
    t5(in=in5)  t6(in=in6);
```

The IN= data set option creates a variable that indicates whether the data set contributed to the current observation (1=true and 0=false). The values of the variables IN1 through IN6 are used in conditional processing to write different rows in the report.

Figure 4.2 identifies rows and columns in the report and shows which of the six data sets contributes to each row. Note the similar structure of the data on gender and race from data sets T2 and T4 and the similar structure of the data on age, height, and weight from data sets T3, T5, and T6. Because these sections of the report are so similar, the same code can be used to produce the rows describing GENDER and RACE, and the same code can be used to produce the rows on AGE, HEIGHT, and WEIGHT.

Figure 4.2 Identifying the Rows and Columns in the Report

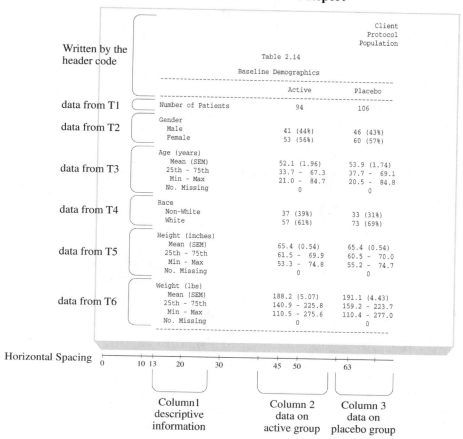

Positioning the Output Line Pointer to a Specific Column by Calculating the Column Position

This program is written to send output to the LISTING destination. Therefore, it can direct output to specific columns on the report page.

This program uses the variable COL to position the pointer when centering text under "Active" and "Placebo" in the report. The value of COL is derived by applying the informat COLPLC to the variable TMTDG.

```
proc format;
   invalue colplc 'Active'=45
                  'Placebo'=63;
```

The INPUT function reads the value of TMTDG, applies the informat COLPLC to the values of TMTDG, returns the value 45 or 63, and assigns one of these numeric values to COL.

```
col=input(tmtdg,colplc.);
```

All data written in the "Active" column is centered on column 45, and data in the "Placebo" column is centered on column 63. Many PUT statements in this program use the value of COL to correctly position text in these columns. Here are some examples:

❏ `put...@(col-1) count pct_row percen5.;`

❏ `put...@(col-2) mean 4.1`

❏ `put...@(col+3) '(' stderr 4.2 ')'`

Using this indirect method to determine where to place a value has two advantages:

❏ It puts the literal value in one location so that if you need to move that column in the report, you can make one change and yet keep the data aligned.

❏ It uses one variable value for two purposes: to place the data in the correct treatment column ("Active" or "Placebo") and to center the data under the column headings.

Positioning the Output Line Pointer to a Specific Row by Calculating the Row Position

The following lines of code write the rows on gender data when reading from data set T2 (IN2 is true) and the rows on race data when reading from T4. (Because this code is part of a larger DO group that reads only from data sets T2 or T4, the ELSE block processes data only from T4.)

```
if in2 then put ❷ #(row+gender) @15 gender gendrfmt.
                 ❶ @(col-1) count pct_row percen5.;
else put ❷ #(row+race) @15 race racefmt.
           ❶ @(col-1) count pct_row percen5.;
if inds=4 then inds=0; ❸
```

❶ The use of the variable COL to position the pointer based on the value "Active" (45) or "Placebo" (63) is discussed in the previous section.

❷ Similar to the way COL is used in conjunction with the current values of TMTDG, the values of ROW, GENDER, and RACE are used to position the pointer on the correct row based on the current value of GENDER or RACE. For example, when the observation contains data on "Male," the true value of GENDER is 0, so those values are written on the row equal to the current value of the variable ROW. When the observation contains data on "Female," the true value of GENDER is 1, so those values are written one row after the row for "Male."

❸ There are only four observations in each of the two data sets. When INDS equals 4, the DATA step reads the last observation in the data set currently being processed. It resets INDS to zero because the next observation that the DATA step processes will be from a new data set.

Supplying Heading Information for All Pages

To print headings at the top of each new page of a report:

☐ specify a label with the HEADER= option in a FILE statement

☐ place a RETURN statement before the statement label

☐ place a colon after the label

☐ place the statements that construct the heading after the statement label

☐ place a RETURN statement at the end of these statements.

Here is the code that creates the heading for this report, followed by an explanation:

```
file 'external-file' print n=ps notitles header=reporttop;  ❶

return;  ❷

reporttop:  ❸
  put #2   @67 'Client'  ❹
      #3   @65 'Protocol'
      #4   @63 'Population'
      #6   @38 'Table  2.14'
      #8   @32 'Baseline Demographics'
      #9   @13 60*'-'
      #10  @45 'Active' @62 'Placebo'
      #11  @13 60*'-';
  row=12;  ❺
  return;  ❻
run;
```

❶ The FILE statement specifies REPORTTOP as the statement label.

❷ The RETURN statement that precedes the label is necessary to prevent the statements following the label from executing with each iteration of the DATA step.

❸ The statement label is followed by a colon.

❹ The PUT statement produces the heading on this single-page report by writing data on eight lines.

❺ The assignment statement assigns a value of 12 to ROW after the heading is written. That value is used to position the next line of text in the report, which corresponds to the first line of the results.

❻ The RETURN statement signals the end of the section labeled REPORTTOP.

Where to Go from Here

Concatenating data sets. See "Combining SAS Data Sets: Basic Concepts" and "Combining SAS Data Sets: Methods" in the "Reading, Combining, and Modifying SAS Data Sets" section of *SAS 9.1 Language Reference: Concepts,* and "SET Statement" in the "Statements" section of *SAS 9.1 Language Reference: Dictionary.*

Description of how SAS processes a DATA step. See "DATA Step Processing" in the "Data Step Concepts" section of *SAS 9.1 Language Reference: Concepts.*

FILE statement syntax, usage information, and additional examples. See "FILE Statement" in the "Statements" section of *SAS 9.1 Language Reference: Dictionary.*

The IN= data set option used on the SET statement. See "SET Statement" in the "Statements" section of *SAS 9.1 Language Reference: Dictionary.*

INPUT function syntax, usage informaton, and additional examples. See "INPUT Function" in the "Functions and CALL Routines" section of *SAS 9.1 Language Reference: Concepts.*

More Examples of Writing a Report with a DATA Step. See "Writing a Report with a DATA Step" in the "DATA Step Processing" section of *SAS 9.1 Language Reference: Concepts.*

PROC FORMAT reference, usage information, and additional examples. See "The FORMAT Procedure" in *Base SAS 9.1 Procedures Guide.*

PROC FREQ reference, usage information, and additional examples. See "The FREQ Procedure" in *Base SAS 9.1 Procedures Guide.*

PROC MEANS reference, usage information, and additional examples. See "The MEANS Procedure" in *Base SAS 9.1 Procedures Guide.*

PUT statement syntax, usage information, and additional examples. See "PUT Statement," "PUT Statement, Column," "PUT Statement, Formatted," and "PUT Statement, List" in the "Statements" section of *SAS 9.1 Language Reference: Dictionary.*

SET statement syntax, usage information, and additional examples. See "SET Statement" in the "Statements" section of *SAS 9.1 Language Reference: Dictionary.*

Working with Formats. See "Formats and Informats" in "SAS Language Elements" in the "SAS System Concepts" section of *SAS 9.1 Language Reference: Concepts,* and "Formats" in *Base SAS 9.1 Language Reference: Dictionary.*

Example 4.3 Customizing the Presentation of Analyses

Goal

Analyze a data set with a statistical procedure. Save results from the analyses in data sets created from ODS output objects. Concisely summarize specific results in a report.

Report

```
                       Analysis of Fitness Data Set
              Forward Selection of Predictors of Oxygen Consumption

--------------------------------------------------------------------------------
|                                                        F      Partial  Model      |
|Step Intercept runtime   age  runpulse weight maxpulse Value Pr > F R-Square R-Square  C(p) |
|------------------------------------------------------------------------------
|  1|   82.422|  -3.310|   NS|    NS|    NS|    NS| 84.01| 0.00|   0.74|   0.74| 13.52 |
|----+--------+--------+-----+-------+------+-------+------+-----+-------+-------+-------|
|  2|   88.462|  -3.203| -0.150|   NS|    NS|    NS| 45.38| 0.00|   0.02|   0.76| 12.22 |
|----+--------+--------+-----+-------+------+-------+------+-----+-------+-------+-------|
|  3|  111.718|  -2.825| -0.256| -0.130|  NS|    NS| 38.64| 0.00|   0.05|   0.81|  6.83 |
|----+--------+--------+-----+-------+------+-------+------+-----+-------+-------+-------|
|  4|   98.148|  -2.767| -0.197| -0.348|  NS| 0.270| 33.33| 0.00|   0.03|   0.84|  4.77 |
|----+--------+--------+-----+-------+------+-------+------+-----+-------+-------+-------|
|  5|  102.204|  -2.682| -0.219| -0.373| -0.072| 0.304| 27.90| 0.00|   0.01|   0.85|  5.00 |
--------------------------------------------------------------------------------
|                     Number of Observations Read=31                      |
|                     Number of Observations Used=31                      |
|           Number of Observations with Missing Values=0                  |
|                                                                         |
|                        * NS=Not Selected                                |
--------------------------------------------------------------------------------
```

Example Features

Data Set	FITNESS
Featured Step and Statement	ODS statement PROC REPORT

Featured Step Statements and Options	ODS OUTPUT statement for saving output objects from PROC REG
	PROC REPORT
	    COMPUTE AFTER block
	    LINE statement

Additional Features	PROC TRANSPOSE Merging data sets in the DATA step PICTURE formats CALL SYMPUT and macro variables
A Closer Look	Saving Results in Data Sets Created from ODS Output Objects vs. Saving Results in Procedure Output Data Sets Designing Reports That Use Either Data Sets Created from ODS Output Objects or Procedure Output Data Sets Working with Data Sets Created from ODS Output Objects Doing More with Data Sets Created from ODS Output Objects

Example Overview

The output from an analysis can take up several pages. Features of interest to you might be in different locations of the standard output, and you might want to consolidate those results in your own presentation format. You can do this by saving in data sets the specific ODS output objects produced by the analysis. You can then use DATA steps and procedures to select the results of interest and shape the data for presentation in a style that meets your requirements.

This example saves ODS output objects produced by a PROC REG analysis. DATA steps, procedures, and macro language features process the output data sets to summarize specific results of the analysis in a concise report.

This example runs PROC REG on the SASUSER.FITNESS data set and applies the forward selection technique. Each observation in SASUSER.FITNESS contains the measurements on one study participant. The actual oxygen consumption during exercise is measured, as well as several postulated predictors of oxygen consumption. The goal is to find a model by using a forward selection technique that adequately predicts oxygen consumption.

Note that this example analyzes a data set that is provided with Base SAS and assumes that you have stored the data set in the SASUSER directory. Appendix A includes code to create the data set as well.

Program

Create data sets from four ODS output objects generated by PROC REG.

```
ods output selectionsummary=ss
           selparmest=spe
           nobs=nobs
           anova=anova;
```

Analyze the SASUSER.FITNESS data set. Apply a forward selection technique.

```
proc reg data=sasuser.fitness;
  model oxygen=age weight runtime runpulse
        rstpulse maxpulse
        / selection=forward;
quit;
```

Reshape the data set that contains the estimates so that all information for a step is in one observation rather than in multiple observations. The other ODS output objects create data sets with one observation per step. The goal is to merge the four data sets by the variable STEP and have only one observation per value of STEP.

```
proc transpose data=spe out=transpe;
  by step;
  var estimate;
  id variable;
run;
```

Merge information by the forward selection step. Save specific variables and observations needed in the final report.

```
data merged(drop=source);
  merge transpe
        anova(where=(source='Model')
        keep=fvalue probf source step)
        ss(keep=step partialrsquare modelrsquare cp);
  by step;
run;
```

Define a PICTURE format for the estimates. The text "NS" stands for "Not Selected."

```
proc format;
  picture notselected  .='NS'
          low-<0='009.999'(prefix='-')
          0-high='0009.999';
run;
```

Create macro variables from information about the observations processed by PROC REG that was saved in WORK.NOBS. Reference these macro variables later in the PROC REPORT statements that produce the footer of the report.

```
data _null_;
  set nobs;
  call symput('NOBSREAD',nobsread);
  call symput('NOBSUSED',nobsused);
  call symput('NOBSMISS',nobsmiss);
run;
```

```
proc report data=merged nowindows box;
  title 'Analysis of Fitness Data Set';
  title2 'Forward Selection of Predictors of Oxygen
          Consumption';

  column step intercept runtime age runpulse weight
         maxpulse fvalue probf partialrsquare
         modelrsquare cp;
  define step / order width=4;
  define intercept--cp / display;
```

Write at the end of the report the information that was stored in the macro variables.

```
  compute after;
    line "Number of Observations Read=&nobsread";
    line "Number of Observations Used=&nobsused";
    line "Number of Observations with Missing
          Values=&nobsmiss";
    line ' ';
    line '* NS=Not Selected';
  endcomp;
  format runtime--weight notselected.
         intercept 9.3 fvalue probf cp 6.2
         partialrsquare modelrsquare 8.2;
run;
```

🔍 **A Closer Look**

Saving Results in Data Sets Created from ODS Output Objects vs. Saving Reults in Procedure Output Data Sets

Some SAS procedures produce output data sets, whereas others do not. The report shown in Example 4.2 was created by manipulating output data sets created by statements and options available in PROC MEANS and PROC FREQ.

Procedure output data sets save components of an analysis, but not necessarily all components of an analysis can be saved in procedure output data sets. When features of the output cannot be saved in a procedure output data set, you can usually save that information in data sets created from ODS output objects.

The results in this example were saved in data sets created from ODS output objects. PROC REG does not have the output options or statements to save the step selection results that are required for the report. For example, the PROC REG OUTEST= option saves the parameter estimates for only the final model. Therefore, the only way to produce this example's report is to save the step selection results in data sets created from ODS output objects.

When writing your programs, you might need to evaluate whether to save results with procedure OUTPUT statements and options or in data sets created from ODS output objects. Review the layout of the observations in the procedure output data sets and in the data sets created from ODS output objects to determine which method makes it most efficient to process the data to meet your reporting requirements. You might even find that combining both methods works best.

Designing Reports That Use Either Data Sets Created from ODS Output Objects or Procedure Output Data Sets

You might find that it's an iterative process for you to customize a report that is based on information extracted from data sets created from ODS output objects or from data sets created from procedure statements and options. Before finalizing your report step, you will need to know the ODS output objects and procedure output data sets that your analysis procedure can produce.

Until you repeatedly use the same ODS output objects and procedure output data sets, you will probably have to submit your procedure step and examine the contents of the output data sets. Then you can write ODS statements and procedure features that save what you need. Following that, you might need to use other procedures to reshape the data sets and save specific information. These types of preparatory steps were required in the main program of this example. Finally, you can write the code for your customized report. This example used PROC REPORT, and you can use this or any other SAS reporting procedure or DATA step to produce your report.

Working with Data Sets Created from ODS Output Objects

SAS data sets are one of the several SAS and third-party formatted destinations that ODS can create. Just as you can send output objects from a procedure to a destination such as LISTING or HTML, you can send the same objects to a SAS data set.

When you want to save ODS output objects in data sets, you need to know the names of the objects that the procedure produces. Several of these names are documented in *SAS 9.1 Output Delivery System: User's Guide*. A second way to determine the names is to submit the procedure and look up the names of the output objects in the Results window. Finally, a third way you can determine them is to issue the ODS TRACE ON statement before you execute the procedure. This statement writes a trace record to the SAS log that includes the path, the label, and other information about each of the output objects. To terminate the trace record, submit ODS TRACE OFF.

The following code lists in the SAS log the output objects produced by the PROC REG step in the main program.

```
ods trace on;
proc reg data=sasuser.fitness;
   model oxygen=age weight runtime runpulse rstpulse
         maxpulse
            / selection=forward;
quit;
ods trace off;
```

The ODS TRACE ON statement writes the information to the SAS log. Figure 4.3 shows the results of the above step that includes this statement. Notice that there are four types of output objects produced by this step. There are five occurrences each of two of the output objects: ANOVA and SelParmEst. Each occurrence corresponds to one of the five steps of the forward selection analysis. PATH shows a reference to the step for those two output objects.

Figure 4.3 Results of ODS TRACE ON as Applied to This Example

```
Output Added:
-------------
Name:       NObs
Label:      Number of Observations
Template:   Stat.Reg.NObs
Path:       Reg.MODEL1.SelectionMethod.oxygen.NObs
-------------

Output Added:
-------------
Name:       ANOVA
Label:      ANOVA
Template:   Stat.REG.ANOVA
Path:       Reg.MODEL1.SelectionMethod.oxygen.Step1.ANOVA
-------------

Output Added:
-------------
Name:       SelParmEst
Label:      Parameter Estimates
Template:   Stat.REG.SelParmEst
Path:       Reg.MODEL1.SelectionMethod.oxygen.Step1.SelParmEst
-------------
```

(continued)

(continued)

```
      Output Added:
      -------------
      Name:       ANOVA
      Label:      ANOVA
      Template:   Stat.REG.ANOVA
      Path:       Reg.MODEL1.SelectionMethod.oxygen.Step2.ANOVA
      -------------

      Output Added:
      -------------
      Name:       SelParmEst
      Label:      Parameter Estimates
      Template:   Stat.REG.SelParmEst
      Path:       Reg.MODEL1.SelectionMethod.oxygen.Step2.SelParmEst
      -------------

      Output Added:
      -------------
      Name:       ANOVA
      Label:      ANOVA
      Template:   Stat.REG.ANOVA
      Path:       Reg.MODEL1.SelectionMethod.oxygen.Step3.ANOVA
      -------------

      Output Added:
      -------------
      Name:       SelParmEst
      Label:      Parameter Estimates
      Template:   Stat.REG.SelParmEst
      Path:       Reg.MODEL1.SelectionMethod.oxygen.Step3.SelParmEst
      -------------

      Output Added:
      -------------
      Name:       ANOVA
      Label:      ANOVA
      Template:   Stat.REG.ANOVA
      Path:       Reg.MODEL1.SelectionMethod.oxygen.Step4.ANOVA
      -------------

      Output Added:
      -------------
      Name:       SelParmEst
      Label:      Parameter Estimates
      Template:   Stat.REG.SelParmEst
      Path:       Reg.MODEL1.SelectionMethod.oxygen.Step4.SelParmEst
      -------------

      Output Added:
      -------------
      Name:       ANOVA
      Label:      ANOVA
      Template:   Stat.REG.ANOVA
      Path:       Reg.MODEL1.SelectionMethod.oxygen.Step5.ANOVA
      -------------
```

(continued)

(*continued*)

```
Output Added:
-------------
Name:        SelParmEst
Label:       Parameter Estimates
Template:    Stat.REG.SelParmEst
Path:        Reg.MODEL1.SelectionMethod.oxygen.Step5.SelParmEst
-------------

Output Added:
-------------
Name:        SelectionSummary
Label:       Selection Summary
Template:    Stat.REG.SelectionSummary
Path:        Reg.MODEL1.SelectionMethod.oxygen.SelectionSummary
-------------
```

The main example references the output objects by the value assigned to "Name:" in the above display. The syntax of the ODS OUTPUT statement requires that you follow the reference to your output object with an equal sign and the name you want to assign to the data set produced by the ODS output object. The example shows that you can reference multiple output objects on the ODS OUTPUT statement and produce a data set for each of those output objects.

The ANOVA and SelParmEst objects contain results from each step of the forward selection process. Five observations corresponding to the five forward selection steps are saved in each of the two data sets. The variable STEP saved in the data sets created from the ODS output objects identifies the step in the process.

There are multiple ways to reference your output object in the ODS OUTPUT statement, including the following specifications:

❑ the full path

❑ a partial path

❑ the label in quotes

❑ the name in quotes

You can create multiple copies of an object by referencing it multiple times in an ODS OUTPUT statement. For details on specifying the ODS OUTPUT statement, refer to *SAS 9.1 Output Delivery System: User's Guide* and online information.

Doing More with Data Sets Created from ODS Output Objects

If you intend to incorporate output objects in your customized reports, you might want to explore the additional features of the ODS OUTPUT statement and other features of the ODS facility. Tasks that you can accomplish when working with data sets created from ODS output objects include the following:

Saving and/or displaying specific output objects. See the ODS SELECT and ODS EXCLUDE statements. These statements control display of output objects.

Creating data sets from ODS output objects without creating a standard report. See ODS LISTING CLOSE. This statement closes the default output destination. Many procedures allow you to suppress output with a NOPRINT option, but if you do that along with an ODS OUTPUT statement, no ODS output objects are created. You must create an output object in order for its associated ODS output data set to be produced. An option such as NOPRINT suppresses the creation of ODS output objects while ODS LISTING CLOSE does not.

Creating one data set for an ODS output object from multiple executions of the same procedure and specifying the ODS OUTPUT statement once rather than before each execution of the procedure. See the PERSIST= option on the ODS OUTPUT statement. The following code creates one data set, MULTMODELS, that contains the results from both PROC REG steps. The ODS OUTPUT CLOSE statement terminates the request to save ANOVA output objects in the MULTMODELS data set. If you did not issue this statement, any subsequent executions of PROC REG or other procedures that produce an ANOVA output object would cause the ANOVA results to be added to the MULTMODELS data set.

```
ods output anova(persist=proc)=multmodels;
proc reg data=sasuser.fitness;
   model oxygen=age;
quit;
proc reg data=sasuser.fitness;
  model oxygen=runtime;
quit;
ods output close;
```

Creating multiple data sets for an output object from one execution of a procedure that is doing BY-group analyses. See the MATCH_ALL option on the ODS OUTPUT statement. The three values for GROUP in SASUSER.FITNESS cause the following code to create three data sets, one for each value of group: MULTSETS, MULTSETS1, and MULTSETS2.

```
proc sort data=sasuser.fitness out=fitsorted;
  by group;
run;

ods output anova(match_all)=multsets;

proc reg data=fitsorted;
  by group;
  model oxygen=age;
quit;
```

The MATCH_ALL option has an optional parameter that specifies the name of a macro variable that retains the names of the data sets created from the multiple output objects. This macro variable can be useful in referencing the multiple data sets in subsequent DATA steps and in saving you some typing. For example, the following code saves the data set names in the MULTSETNAMES macro variable. The DATA step concatenates the three data sets.

```
ods output anova(match_all=multsetsnames)=
                 multsets;
proc sort data=sasuser.fitness out=fitsorted;
  by group;
run;
```

```
proc reg data=fit;
  by group;
  model oxygen=age;
quit;
data combined;
  set &multsetsnames;
run;
```

Creating multiple data sets for an output object from multiple executions of the same procedure, and specifying the ODS OUTPUT statement once rather than before each execution of the procedure. See the MATCH_ALL option and the PERSIST= option on the ODS OUTPUT statement. This task combines the features of both the MATCH_ALL option and the PERSIST= options in the programs described previously in this section.

The following code creates four data sets, MULTRUN, MULTRUN1, MULTRUN2, and MULTRUN3. Each execution of PROC REG produces a data set from the ANOVA ODS output object, although only one ODS OUTPUT statement designated this instruction. As discussed previously in the section that describes the PERSIST= option, this program also requires an ODS OUTPUT CLOSE statement to terminate the request to save ANOVA output objects in a data set.

```
ods output anova (match_all persist=proc)= multrun;
proc reg data=sasuser.fitness;
  model oxygen=age;
quit;
proc reg data=sasuser.fitness;
  model oxygen=runpulse;
quit;
proc reg data=sasuser.fitness;
  model oxygen=rstpulse;
quit;
proc reg data=sasuser.fitness;
  model oxygen=maxpulse;
quit;
ods output close;
```

Where to Go from Here

MERGE statement syntax, usage information, and additional examples. See "MERGE Statement" in the "Statements" section of *SAS 9.1 Language Reference: Dictionary*.

ODS concepts. See "Output Delivery System" in "SAS Output" in the "SAS System Concepts" section of *SAS 9.1 Language Reference: Concepts,* and *SAS 9.1 Output Delivery System: User's Guide.*

ODS OUTPUT statement syntax, usage information, and additional examples. See "ODS OUTPUT Statement" in the "Dictionary of ODS Language Statements" section of *SAS 9.1 Output Delivery System: User's Guide.*

ODS TRACE statement syntax, usage information, and additional examples. See "ODS TRACE Statement" in the "Dictionary of ODS Language Statements" section of *SAS 9.1 Output Delivery System: User's Guide.*

PROC FORMAT reference, usage information, and additional examples. See "The FORMAT Procedure" in the "Procedures" section of *Base SAS 9.1 Procedures Guide.*

PROC REG reference, usage information, and additional examples. See "The REG Procedure" in *SAS/STAT 9.1 User's Guide.*

PROC TRANSPOSE reference, usage information, and additional examples. See "The TRANSPOSE Procedure" in the "Procedures" section of *Base SAS 9.1 Procedures Guide.*

SAS Macro Programming. In *SAS 9.1 Macro Language: Reference,* see "Macro Variables" in the "Understanding and Using the Macro Facility" section, "Using SAS Language Functions in the DATA Step and Macro Facility" in the "Interfaces with the Macro Facility" section, and "Macro Language Dictionary."

CHAPTER 5
Multipanel Reports

The reports in Chapters 2, 3, and 4 have an underlying structure of one panel per page. When a list or table reaches the end of the page, it does not continue to another panel on the page, but instead it continues on the next page.

This chapter presents two examples in which the underlying structure of the reports is more than one panel per page. When your reports have a narrow structure, they may look better if you can put them in multiple panels on a page.

The first example uses PROC REPORT. The second example is a customized report produced by a DATA step.

Example 5.1 uses options that function only when sending the report to the LISTING destination. Example 6.11 shows a way of creating a similar report that is sent to a nonlisting destination.

The programming statements in Example 5.2 that explicitly designate row and column positioning work best when sending the report to the LISTING destination. If you wanted to send Example 5.2 to a nonlisting destination, you could add the ODS statement option COLUMNS= as demonstrated in Example 6.11. Your DATA step would become simpler because you could write the code to output information for just one panel. ODS would handle the placement of information in the panels.

See the back of this book for a list of titles related to the features of these examples, and visit the SAS Press Web site (support.sas.com/saspress) for current information on new and revised publications.

Several presentations at SUGI conferences show how SAS users apply report-writing techniques. Recent conference proceedings that are available online provide a wealth of additional applications and examples. You can link to them through the SAS support Web site (support.sas.com).

Table 5.0 presents a cross-reference of the examples in this chapter to the procedures used, data sets used, and ODS enhanced versions of the examples. See Appendix A for details on the example data sets analyzed in this chapter. See Appendix B for a table that cross-references all examples in this book.

Table 5.0 Cross-Reference of Examples in Chapter 5

Example	Report-Writing Tool Used						ODS Enhanced Version	Data Set	Example Title
	REPORT	TABULATE	PRINT	DATA Step	MEANS	FREQ			
5.1	X						6.11	INVENTORY	Constructing a Basic Multipanel Report
5.2				X				STUDENTS	Constructing an Advanced Multipanel Report

Example 5.1   Constructing a Basic Multipanel Report

Goal

List the observations in a data set in side-by-side panels rather than in one panel.

Report

```
                          Parts Listing as of 11/15/2005

-----------------------------      -----------------------------      -----------------------------
|Part          In         |        |Part          In         |        |Part          In         |
|Number     Stock   Price |        |Number     Stock   Price |        |Number     Stock   Price |
|-------------------------|        |-------------------------|        |-------------------------|
|B01-03/0|    100|   $5.75|        |B25-04/1|     26|   $7.95|        |B49-05/2|     81|   $8.80|
|--------+--------+-------|        |--------+--------+-------|        |--------+--------+-------|
|B02-03/0|    100|   $6.60|        |B26-04/2|     31|   $7.20|        |B50-05/2|     50|   $4.15|
|--------+--------+-------|        |--------+--------+-------|        |--------+--------+-------|
|B03-03/1|     79|   $7.25|        |B27-04/2|     99|   $9.60|        |B51-05/3|     31|   $4.60|
|--------+--------+-------|        |--------+--------+-------|        |--------+--------+-------|
|B04-03/1|     37|   $7.80|        |B28-04/2|     50|   $3.95|        |B52-05/0|    100|  $13.75|
|--------+--------+-------|        |--------+--------+-------|        |--------+--------+-------|
|B05-03/1|      3|   $8.40|        |B29-04/3|     42|   $4.60|        |B53-05/0|     23|   $7.05|
|--------+--------+-------|        |--------+--------+-------|        |--------+--------+-------|
|B06-03/1|     15|   $7.95|        |B30-04/0|     87|  $11.60|        |B54-05/1|     59|   $7.10|
|--------+--------+-------|        |--------+--------+-------|        |--------+--------+-------|
|B07-03/2|     97|   $8.80|        |B31-04/0|     31|   $6.70|        |B55-05/1|     87|   $7.70|
|--------+--------+-------|        |--------+--------+-------|        |--------+--------+-------|
|B08-03/2|     24|   $4.25|        |B32-04/1|     11|   $7.10|        |B56-05/1|     22|   $7.95|
|--------+--------+-------|        |--------+--------+-------|        |--------+--------+-------|
|B09-03/3|     18|   $7.40|        |B33-04/1|      8|   $7.70|        |B57-05/1|     83|   $8.15|
|--------+--------+-------|        |--------+--------+-------|        |--------+--------+-------|
|B10-03/0|     92|   $7.10|        |B34-04/1|     14|   $8.80|        |B58-05/1|     16|   $8.45|
|--------+--------+-------|        |--------+--------+-------|        |--------+--------+-------|
|B11-03/0|     12|   $7.20|        |B35-04/1|     19|   $9.05|        |B59-05/2|     18|   $8.90|
|--------+--------+-------|        |--------+--------+-------|        |--------+--------+-------|
|B12-03/1|      9|   $7.70|        |B36-04/1|     17|   $9.60|        |B60-05/2|     29|  $10.40|
|--------+--------+-------|        |--------+--------+-------|        |--------+--------+-------|
|B13-03/1|      2|   $8.00|        |B37-04/2|     33|   $8.80|        |B61-05/2|     50|   $4.85|
|--------+--------+-------|        |--------+--------+-------|        |--------+--------+-------|
|B14-03/1|     37|   $8.80|        |B38-04/2|     51|  $11.20|        |B62-05/3|     31|   $5.25|
|--------+--------+-------|        |--------+--------+-------|        |--------+--------+-------|
|B15-03/1|     22|   $9.05|        |B39-04/2|     50|   $5.25|        |B63-06/0|    100|  $12.20|
|--------+--------+-------|        |--------+--------+-------|        |--------+--------+-------|
|B16-03/2|     15|   $9.20|        |B40-04/3|     47|   $5.50|        |B64-06/0|    100|   $7.00|
|--------+--------+-------|        |--------+--------+-------|        |--------+--------+-------|
|B17-03/2|     50|   $5.75|        |B41-05/0|     97|  $11.80|        |B65-06/1|     52|   $7.20|
|--------+--------+-------|        |--------+--------+-------|        |--------+--------+-------|
|B18-03/3|     50|   $8.00|        |B42-05/0|     13|   $6.40|        |B66-06/1|     43|   $7.45|
|--------+--------+-------|        |--------+--------+-------|        |--------+--------+-------|
|B19-04/0|    100|  $10.10|        |B43-05/1|     17|   $6.60|        |B67-06/1|     66|   $7.95|
|--------+--------+-------|        |--------+--------+-------|        |--------+--------+-------|
|B20-04/0|     33|   $5.90|        |B44-05/1|     15|   $6.80|        |B68-06/1|     69|   $8.05|
|--------+--------+-------|        |--------+--------+-------|        -----------------------------
|B21-04/1|     41|   $6.40|        |B45-05/1|      2|   $7.70|
|--------+--------+-------|        |--------+--------+-------|
|B22-04/1|      7|   $6.80|        |B46-05/1|      4|   $6.60|
|--------+--------+-------|        |--------+--------+-------|
|B23-04/1|     11|   $7.50|        |B47-05/1|     77|   $7.95|
|--------+--------+-------|        |--------+--------+-------|
|B24-04/1|     17|   $6.95|        |B48-05/2|     11|   $7.20|
-----------------------------      -----------------------------
```

Example Features

Data Set	INVENTORY
Featured Step	PROC REPORT
Featured Step Statements and Options	PROC REPORT statement: PANELS= and PSPACE= options when sending output to the LISTING destination
Formatting Features	PROC REPORT statement: BOX option when sending output to the LISTING destination
	Macro language functions
ODS Enhanced Version of This Example	Example 6.11
Other Examples That Use This Data Set	Example 6.11

Example Overview

Panels compactly present information for long, narrow reports by placing multiple rows of information side by side. Without using panels, the detail report in this example would be spread out over three pages. Using panels condenses the report to one page.

Each observation in INVENTORY corresponds to one row in one panel of the report. The three columns in each panel correspond to three variables in the INVENTORY data set.

Note that the three PROC REPORT statement options used in this example–PANELS=, PSPACE=, and BOX—are only valid when sending output to the LISTING destination. For a similar solution when sending output to a non-listing destination, see Example 6.11.

Program

```
proc report data=inventory
```

Specify the PANELS= option so that PROC REPORT creates a multipanel report. Set the value of PANELS= to 99 so that PROC REPORT fits as many panels per page as possible.

```
     panels=99
```

Specify the number of print positions between panels when sending output to the LISTING destination.

```
     pspace=5
     nowindows
```

Outline elements of the table when sending output to the LISTING destination.

```
     box;
```

Write the current date in the title.

```
title  "Parts Listing as of
       %sysfunc(date(),mmddyy10.)";

column partnmbr quantity price;

define partnmbr / 'Part Number';
define quantity / format=3. width=7 'In Stock';
define price    / format=dollar6.2 'Price';

run;
```

Where to Go from Here

PROC REPORT reference, usage information, and additional examples.
See "The REPORT Procedure" in the "Procedures" section of *Base SAS 9.1
Procedures Guide.*

SAS file input/output functions. See "Functions and CALL Routines" in *SAS
9.1 Language Reference: Dictionary.*

SAS macro programming. In the "Understanding and Using the Macro
Facility" section of *SAS 9.1 Macro Language: Reference,* see "Macro Variables"
and "Using SAS Language Functions in the DATA Step and Macro Facility" in
the "Interfaces with the Macro Facility" section. Also see "Macro Language
Dictionary."

Example 5.2   Constructing an Advanced Multipanel Report

Goal

Group data and list the observations within each group in multiple panels per
page.

Report

```
                                                                              1
                        Biology Division Upperclass List

     *********Biochemistry***********        Williams, Mary.........5666...JR
     Adams, Cynthia.........5167...JR         Young, Sandra..........5830...JR
     Adams, Kimberly........5066...SR         ******Students in Department: 14
     Anderson, Nancy........5842...SR
     Bailey, Kimberly.......5923...SR         ***********Ecology*************
     Baker, Cynthia.........5034...SR         Adams, Susan...........5186...SR
     Bell, Michelle.........5448...SR         Allen, Mark............5760...JR
     Campbell, Angela.......5759...JR         Anderson, Michelle.....5590...JR
     Campbell, Karen........5578...SR         Clark, Jason...........5195...JR
     Ford, Laura............5814...JR         Flores, Helen..........5255...SR
     Gonzalez, Cynthia......5861...JR         Graham, Elizabeth......5226...SR
     Hamilton, Emma.........5548...SR         Gray, Ashley...........5193...JR
     Harris, Donna..........5121...SR         Gray, Mark.............5386...JR
     Howard, Ruth...........5580...JR         Griffin, Sandra........5804...SR
     Jackson, Emily.........5874...SR         Harrison, Richard......5713...JR
     Jordan, Betty..........5518...SR         Jackson, Lisa..........5608...JR
     Kelly, Cynthia.........5581...SR         Jackson, Ronald........5092...SR
     King, Linda............5225...JR         Johnson, Linda.........5725...JR
     Morris, Kimberly.......5738...JR         Marshall, Emily........5903...SR
     Nelson, Angela.........5923...SR         Morris, Barbara........5748...JR
     Perry, Donna...........5964...SR         Parker, Susan..........5562...JR
     Peterson, Michelle.....5694...SR         Patterson, Emma........5108...SR
     Price, Elizabeth.......5565...JR         Powell, Donald.........5624...SR
     Roberts, Linda.........5701...SR         Ross, Daniel...........5095...JR
     Rogers, Cynthia........5859...JR         Sanders, William.......5480...SR
     Rogers, Ruth...........5879...JR         Turner, Betty..........5178...JR
     Russell, Sarah.........5266...JR         White, Nicholas........5197...SR
     Sanchez, Dorothy.......5314...SR         Young, Timothy.........5866...JR
     Simmons, Shirley.......5968...JR         ******Students in Department: 23
     Thomas, Dorothy........5379...JR
     Walker, Sharon.........5399...JR         *********Microbiology***********
     Watson, Deborah........5212...JR         Campbell, Elizabeth....5316...SR
     Watson, Maria..........5744...JR         Cooper, Betty..........5303...JR
     Wood, Margaret.........5847...SR         Cox, Kimberly..........5030...JR
     Woods, Angela..........5625...SR         Diaz, Betty............5177...SR
     Wright, Kimberly.......5145...JR         Diaz, Sarah............5683...SR
     ******Students in Department: 35         Freeman, Barbara.......5351...JR
                                              Gibson, Donna..........5424...SR
     **********Biophysics***********          Hayes, Patricia........5777...JR
     Adams, Donna...........5224...JR         Henderson, Ruth........5628...SR
     Brooks, Shirley........5720...SR         Hernandez, Maria.......5409...JR
     Cox, Maria.............5944...JR         Hill, Donna............5107...JR
     Garcia, Lisa...........5272...SR         Jackson, Betty.........5152...SR
     Gomez, Elizabeth.......5295...SR         Jenkins, Barbara.......5217...SR
     James, Emma............5145...SR         Jordan, Dorothy........5732...JR
     Kelly, Mary............5314...JR         Long, Lisa.............5586...JR
     Lee, Lisa..............5787...JR         Morgan, Donna..........5291...SR
     Miller, Donna..........5543...SR         Myers, Helen...........5147...SR
     Mitchell, Margaret.....5331...SR         Nelson, Betty..........5609...SR
     Perez, Linda...........5729...SR         Perez, Michelle........5579...JR
     Sanders, Barbara.......5048...JR         Ramirez, Emma..........5631...SR

------------------------------page break---------------------------------------
```

```
                    Biology Division Upperclass List                          2

   Scott, Kimberly........5439...JR        James, Robert..........5419...SR
   Simmons, Ruth..........5193...SR        Long, Edward...........5078...JR
   Thompson, Abigail......5383...JR        Patterson, Kenneth.....5504...SR
   Thompson, Laura........5464...JR        Reed, George...........5145...JR
   Wallace, Ruth..........5345...SR        Rivera, Jeffrey........5283...SR
   Ward, Michelle.........5961...JR        Ross, Jacob............5886...SR
   West, Susan............5756...JR        Sanders, Kenneth.......5967...JR
   Young, Jessica.........5547...SR        Scott, Jose............5918...JR
   ******Students in Department: 28        Smith, Daniel..........5299...SR
                                           Smith, Jason...........5408...JR
   *********Neurobiology**********          Taylor, Joshua.........5192...SR
   Bailey, Anthony........5428...SR        Taylor, Joshua.........5958...SR
   Butler, Nicholas.......5307...JR        Wallace, Jose..........5880...JR
   Coleman, Paul..........5577...JR        Ward, Christopher......5968...JR
   Cook, Christopher......5188...SR        Watson, Steven.........5972...JR
   Ellis, Christopher.....5369...SR        ******Students in Department: 23
   Flores, Jason..........5229...JR
   Gomez, Joshua..........5020...SR
   Graham, John...........5833...JR
   Hayes, Michael.........5320...SR
   Lopez, Joseph..........5494...JR
   Reynolds, Paul.........5808...SR
   Rodriguez, Kenneth.....5787...JR
   Simmons, Edward........5293...SR
   ******Students in Department: 13

   ********Plant Sciences**********
   Baker, Kenneth.........5948...SR
   Butler, Joshua.........5780...SR
   Freeman, Jacob.........5458...SR
   Graham, Timothy........5188...JR
   Gray, Ethan............5387...SR
   Hamilton, Brian........5571...JR
   Harrison, Kevin........5212...JR
   Martin, Ethan..........5249...JR
   Ortiz, Thomas..........5620...JR
   Patterson, Brian.......5611...JR
   Ramirez, John..........5167...SR
   Ross, Paul.............5756...SR
   Turner, Timothy........5890...JR
   ******Students in Department: 13

   *****Zoology and Behavior*******
   Bennett, Matthew.......5509...SR
   Cole, Gary.............5793...JR
   Coleman, Jeffrey.......5431...JR
   Ford, Brian............5475...JR
   Ford, Kenneth..........5489...SR
   Gonzalez, Timothy......5864...SR
   Gray, Mark.............5670...SR
   Hughes, Daniel.........5725...SR
```

Example Features

Data Set	STUDENTS
Featured Step	DATA step
Featured Step Statements and Options	SAS language statements to create a report FILE PRINT statement: N= option (example uses N=PS) when sending output to the LISTING destination BY statement $VARYING format

Example Overview

This report shows groups of information of varying lengths printed in two panels per page. It groups biology student information by department and lists the name, telephone extension, and class year of each of the students. Following each department section, the report lists the total number of students in the department.

The example directs output to specific row and column locations and works best when sending output to the LISTING destination. Output sent to a nonlisting destination by this program might not look properly formatted.

Each observation in STUDENTS corresponds to the information for one student.

Program

Group the data by department and alphabetize the names within each department.

```
proc sort data=students;
  by department fullname;
run;
```

Set linesize and pagesize options to correspond to the layout of the report.

```
options ls=80 ps=56;
```

Do not create a data set and instead just process the observations in data set STUDENTS.

```
title 'Biology Division Upperclass List';
data _null_;
  set students;
```

Initialize variables that will retain the same values across all observations.

```
  retain panel row colptr nstudents colpos1 colpos2;

  retain dots '................................';
  retain stars '********************************';

  length deptstr $ 32 namedots 20;
```

Define the starting column number for each of the two panels on the page.

```
  array colpos{2} colpos1-colpos2 (5,45);
```

Direct the report to the default print destination.

```
  file print
```

Specify the number of lines per page that are available to the output pointer. Set that value to the value assigned to the PAGESIZE option so that the pointer can be directed to any line on the report page.

```
    n=ps;
```

Process the data in groups defined by the values of the BY variable.

```
  by department;
```

Execute this block when the current observation is the first one in a department.

```
  if first.department then do;
```

When processing the first observation in the data set, initialize the positioning of the report to panel 1 and row 3.

```
   if _n_=1 then do;
     panel=1;
     row=3;
   end;
```

Do not start a new department beyond row 50 of the report.

```
if row gt 50 then do;
```

Move to panel 2.

```
  if panel=1 then panel=2;
```

When in panel 2, start a new page in panel 1.

```
  else do;
    put _page_;
    panel=1;
  end;
```

Position the pointer to the row where the first row of student information should be printed in the panel.

```
  row=3;
end;
```

Initialize the variable that tallies the number of students per department.

```
nstudents=0;
```

Based on the current panel, determine the starting position for a student's data.

```
colptr=colpos{panel};
```

Center the department name within the string of asterisks.

```
deptl=length(department);
deptstr=stars;
if deptl lt 32 then
    substr(deptstr,(32-deptl)/2,deptl)=department;
else deptstr=department;
```

Write out the department heading to the row defined by the value of ROW starting in the column defined by the value of COLPTR.

```
put #row @colptr deptstr;
row+1;
end;
```

Pad the student's name with periods to the column that lists the telephone extension.

```
namel=length(fullname);
ndots=23-namel;
namedots=substr(dots,1,ndots);
```

Write out the student's information to the row defined by the value of the variable ROW, starting in the column position defined by the value of COLPTR. Use only the number of columns equal to the length of the current value of FULLNAME when writing out FULLNAME.

```
put #row @colptr fullname $varying. namel
```

With +(-1), move the column pointer back one column to eliminate the default space between unformatted output written by the PUT statement.

```
    namedots +(-1) extension +(-1) '...' class;
```

Increment the row counter.

```
row+1;
```

Increment the variable that retains the number of students per department.

```
nstudents+1;
```

Execute this block when the current observation is the last one in a department.

```
if last.department then do;
  put #row @colptr '******Students in Department: '
      nstudents;
  row+1;
  put #row;
  row+1;
end;
```

After writing each student's information and, if appropriate, the department heading and footer, determine if the current row is at the end of a panel. If it is, move to the top of the next panel.

```
if row gt 53 then do;
  if panel=1 then panel=2;
  else do;
    put _page_;
    panel=1;
  end;
  colptr=colpos{panel};
  row=3;
end;

run;
```

Where to Go from Here

FILE statement syntax, usage information, and additional examples. See "FILE Statement" in the "Statements" section of *SAS 9.1 Language Reference: Dictionary.*

More examples of writing a report with a DATA step. See "Writing a Report with a DATA Step" in the "DATA Step Processing" section of *SAS 9.1 Language Reference: Dictionary.*

PUT statement syntax, usage information, and additional examples. See "PUT Statement," "PUT Statement, Column," "PUT Statement, Formatted," and "PUT Statement, List" in the "Statements" section of *SAS 9.1 Language Reference: Dictionary.*

Enhancing Reports with ODS

Once you understand how to program your reports, you can explore enhancing and modifying the output by adding ODS features. The previous examples in this book sent output to the LISTING destination and did not require ODS formatting features. (Example 4.3 created data sets from ODS output objects, but did not format the report using ODS features.)

The LISTING destination is the traditional monospace SAS output, and it is the default destination when you start your SAS session. Even though the examples previous to this chapter did not explicitly invoke ODS, they did use ODS to send output to the default LISTING destination.

This chapter takes advantage of ODS features to format the output produced by several of the examples in the previous chapters and to send the output from these examples to nonlisting destinations. Most examples send output to the RTF destination, with a few sent to the HTML destination. When you specify an ODS destination, you tell SAS to produce specific types of output.

Unless the example explicitly references a style, the example uses the style definition that is specified in the SAS registry subkey associated with the destination. For example, the default definition for the RTF destination is STYLES.RTF, which is found in SASHELP.TMPLMST.

Understanding ODS Destinations

The destinations that ODS supports can be grouped into two categories: SAS formatted and third-party formatted.

A *SAS formatted destination* is one that produces output that is controlled and interpreted by SAS. The SAS LISTING destination is a SAS formatted destination, as are the ODS output objects processed in Example 4.3.

A *third-party formatted destination* is one that enables you to apply styles and markup languages and to print to physical printers using page description languages. Examples of third-party formatted destinations are HTML and PDF.

Table 6.0a lists the ODS destination categories, the destinations that each category includes, and the formatted output that results from each destination.

Table 6.0a ODS Categories and Destinations

Category	Destination	Results
SAS Formatted	DOCUMENT	ODS document
	LISTING	SAS output listing
	OUTPUT	SAS data set
Third-Party Formatted	HTML	HTML file for online viewing
	MARKUP	Markup language tagsets (HTML output can also be produced by this destination designation.)
	PRINTER	Printable output in one of three different formats: PCL, PDF, or PS (PostScript)
	RTF	Output written in Rich Text Format for use with Microsoft Word

Understanding SAS Formatted Destinations

SAS formatted destinations create SAS entities such as a SAS data set, a SAS output listing, or an ODS document. The three SAS formatted destinations are

DOCUMENT destination

The DOCUMENT destination provides a GUI interface so that you can restructure, navigate, and replay your data in different ways and send your data to different destinations without rerunning your analysis. The output is kept in its original internal representation.

LISTING destination

The LISTING destination produces the traditional SAS monospace output.

OUTPUT destination

The OUTPUT destination produces SAS output data sets that save components of your analysis. Virtually all output from SAS procedures can be saved in output data sets.

Understanding Third-Party Formatted Destinations

Third-party formatted destinations enable you to apply styles to the output objects that are used by applications other than SAS. For example, these destinations support attributes such as "font" and "color." The three third-party formatted destinations are

HTML destination

The HTML destination produces HTML output for online viewing. HTML output can also be produced with the MARKUP destination.

MARKUP destination

The MARKUP destination produces SAS output that is formatted using one of many different markup languages, including XML and HTML. The output type is determined by the tagset you specify. You can use a tagset that SAS supplies, or you can create your own with PROC TEMPLATE.

PRINTER destination

The PRINTER destination can produce two types of output:

- ❑ printing to physical printers such as Windows printers under Windows or PostScript printers on other operating systems

- ❑ producing portable PostScript, PCL, and PDF files

The output from the PRINTER destination is intended to be the final form of the output. The PRINTER destination contains page description language that describes precise positions of text and other elements of the report.

RTF destination

The RTF (Rich Text Format) destination produces output for Microsoft Word. Other applications might be able to read the RTF files, but their appearance in those applications might not be as expected.

References

The examples in this chapter are based on earlier examples in this book. See the earlier examples for discussions of their non-ODS features.

The main reference for the material in this chapter is the *SAS 9.1 Output Delivery System: User's Guide*. For updates to the reference and new developments in ODS, see online resources at support.sas.com.

The PRINT, REPORT, and TABULATE procedures have options to specify ODS style attributes. For additional information on these procedures and the syntax to specify ODS style attributes, see:

❏ "The PRINT Procedure" in the "Procedures" section of *Base SAS 9.1 Procedures Guide*

❏ "The REPORT Procedure" in the "Procedures" section of *Base SAS 9.1 Procedures Guide*

❏ "The TABULATE Procedure" in the "Procedures" section of *Base SAS 9.1 Procedures Guide*

See the back of this book for a list of titles related to the features of these examples, and visit the SAS Press Web site (support.sas.com/saspress) for current information on new and revised publications.

Several presentations at SUGI conferences show how SAS users apply report-writing techniques. Recent conference proceedings that are available online provide a wealth of additional applications and examples. You can link to them through the SAS support Web site (support.sas.com).

Table 6.0b presents a cross-reference of the examples in this chapter to the examples from which they were derived. It includes the procedures and data sets used. See Appendix A for details on the example data sets analyzed in this chapter. See Appendix B for a table that cross-references all examples in this book.

Table 6.0b Cross-Reference of Examples in Chapter 6

Example	REPORT	TABULATE	PRINT	DATA Step	TEMPLATE	Data Set	Chapter 6 Example Title	Derived from Example(s)
		Report-Writing Tool Used						
6.1	X					HOUSING	Customizing a PROC REPORT Detail Report	2.2
6.2	X					CARSALES	Customizing a PROC REPORT Summary Report	3.8
6.3		X				JOBCLASS	Customizing a PROC TABULATE Report	3.5
6.4	X,RT*					LIPIDS	Adding "Traffic Lighting" to a Report Created by PROC REPORT	2.7
6.5		X				BREAD	Adding "Traffic Lighting" to a Report Created by PROC TABULATE	3.2 Related Technique
6.6	X					CARSALES	Including Images in a Report Created by PROC REPORT	3.8, 6.2
6.7		X				JOBCLASS	Including Images in a Report Created by PROC TABULATE	3.5, 6.3
6.8		X				LIPIDS	Presenting Graphics and Tables in the Same Report	3.3
6.9	RT*	X				LIPIDS	Placing Hyperlinks in a Report	3.3
6.10			X			POWERUSE	Customizing the Appearance of a Detail Report Created by PROC PRINT	2.4 Related Technique
6.11	X					INVENTORY	Customizing a Multipanel Report Created by PROC REPORT	5.1
6.12				X	X	DEMOG	Customizing the Appearance of a Report Produced by a DATA Step	4.2
6.13		X				CUSTRESP	Condensing a Multipage, Multitable Report to One Page and Customizing the Output	3.10
6.14		X			X	CUSTRESP	Defining a Reusable Generic Style	3.10, 6.13
6.15				X	X	BREAD	Organizing Results into Tables Using ODS	3.2

* Note that "RT" stands for Related Technique.

Example 6.1   Customizing a PROC REPORT Detail Report

Goal

Customize the appearance of the report produced in Example 2.2 by modifying style attributes with ODS. Send the output to a nonlisting destination.

Report

SAS Output

Listing of Local Residential Properties
Price Range $200,000 to $350,000
Listed by Zone

Residential Zone	Listing Price	House Style	Address	Bedrooms	Bathrooms	Square Feet	Age
East Lake	$329,900	ranch	8122 Maude Steward Rd.	3	3.0	2,400	2
	$281,900	split	6424 Old Jenks Rd.	3	1.5	1,225	18
	$260,000	split	4341 Rock Quarry	3	1.0	1,010	28
	$207,900	ranch	6509 Orchard Knoll	3	2.0	1,526	6
Ensley	$260,000	townhouse	409 Galashiels	2	1.5	1,280	4
Inside Beltline	$343,000	capecod	100 Cumberland Green	3	2.5	1,650	0
	$284,000	townhouse	765 Crabtree Crossing	3	2.0	1,471	1
	$279,950	split	101 Meadowglade Ln.	3	2.0	2,004	0
	$279,900	townhouse	108 Chattle Close	3	2.5	2,080	4
	$259,900	townhouse	216 Concannon Ct.	2	1.5	1,040	9
	$249,900	townhouse	1239 Donaldson Ct.	2	1.5	1,150	15
Mountain Brook	$200,000	duplex	108 South Elm St.	3	1.0	1,569	73

SAS Output

North Ridge	$344,500	bungalow	6008 Brass Lantern Ct.	3	2.5	2,416	6
	$314,900	colonial	4000 Skipjack Ct.	3	2.5	2,750	0
	$285,000	split	2414 Van Dyke	3	1.0	1,245	36
	$282,900	split	500 E. Millbrook Rd.	3	1.5	1,329	23
	$200,000	split	6324 Lakeland, Lake Park	3	2.0	1,662	12
Roebuck	$323,500	split	110 Skylark Way	3	2.0	1,976	10
	$286,900	split	5617 Laurel Crest Dr.	3	1.5	1,441	28
	$271,000	townhouse	8 Stonevillage	2	2.0	1,276	6
Southside	$202,000	townhouse	154 Montrose	2	2.0	1,595	6
Westend	$278,900	split	Rt.5 Yarbororugh Rd.	2	1.0	960	2
	$217,800	split	603 Greentree Dr.	3	2.0	1,533	5

Listing Produced on Dec 10, 2005

Example Features

Data Set	HOUSING
Report Example	Example 2.2
Featured Step	PROC REPORT
Featured Step Statements and Options	PROC REPORT statement ODS options: STYLE(HEADER)=, and STYLE(REPORT)= DEFINE statement ODS options: STYLE(COLUMN)= and STYLE(HEADER)
Output Destination of Example	HTML
🔎 **A Closer Look**	Understanding PROC REPORT ODS Options Placing STYLE= Options in a PROC REPORT Step
Other Examples That Use This Data Set	Examples 2.1 and 2.2

Example Overview

The report in Example 2.2 lists selected observations in the HOUSING data set in a specific order. When sending the report to a destination other than the LISTING destination, you can further customize the report by changing style attributes in specific locations of the report.

This example sends the same report to an HTML destination. The program overrides some of the style attributes in the current style definition in three locations in the report: the overall report, the heading, and specific columns.

Program

Do not send results to the LISTING destination.

```
ods listing close;
```

Send subsequent results to the HTML destination and save the results in a file.

```
ods html file='c:\reports\example22.html';

proc report data=housing nowindows split='/'
```

Override existing style attributes in specific locations of the report. Apply style changes to the overall report. Insert rules between the rows in the table produced by PROC REPORT. Do not put any space between the cells. (This suppresses the appearance of background color between the cells if the background color is different from the cell border color.)

```
        style(report)={rules=rows cellspacing=0}
```

Italicize all column headings in the report.

```
        style(header)={font_style=italic};

title 'Listing of Local Residential Properties';
title2 'Price Range $200,000 to $350,000';
title3 'Listed by Zone';

footnote "Listing Produced on
        %sysfunc(today(),worddate12.)";

where price between 200000 and 350000;

column zone price type address bedr bath sqfeet age;

define  zone    / order format=$zonefmt15. width=15
                  'Residential/Zone'
```

Write all values in the ZONE column in bold.

```
                  style(column)={font_weight=bold};
define  price   / order descending format=dollar10.
                  width=10 'Listing/Price';

define  type    / display format=$9.'House/Style';

define  address / format=$25. width=25 'Address'
```

Left justify the heading for the ADDRESS column.

```
                  style(header)={just=left};
```

Center the contents of the BEDR and BATH columns.

```
define  bedr    / format=2. width=8 'Bedrooms'
                  style(column)={just=center};
define  bath    / format=3.1 width=9 'Bathrooms'
                  style(column)={just=center};
define  sqfeet  / format=comma6. width=6
                  'Square/Feet';
```

```
                                    define  age     / format=3. 'Age';

                              run;
```

Terminate sending output to the   `ods html close;`
HTML destination.

Send subsequent output to the   `ods listing;`
LISTING destination.

 **A Closer Look**

Understanding PROC REPORT ODS Options

PROC REPORT ignores options such as line spacing and underlining when instructed to send your report to a nonlisting destination. Conversely, the style attributes that you modify for a nonlisting destination are ignored if instead you send the output to the LISTING destination.

The PROC REPORT statement options HEADLINE and SPACING= were removed from Example 2.2 because of their application only to the LISTING destination.

This example's program also does not include the BREAK AFTER statement because its only function is to skip a line between zones. PROC REPORT ignores the SKIP option when sending the output to a nonlisting destination. If you still want a space between zones in such a report, you could write a COMPUTE AFTER block and a LINE statement similar to the one that follows:

```
compute after zone;
  line ' ';
endcomp;
```

The following PROC REPORT statement options are ignored when you send your report to a nonlisting destination:

```
    BOX         COLWIDTH=    FORMCHAR=    HEADLINE     HEADSKIP

    LINESIZE=   PANELS=      PSPACE=      SPACING=
```

The following options on the BREAK and RBREAK statements are ignored when you send your report to a nonlisting destination:

```
    DOL         OL           UL           DUL          SKIP
```

Placing STYLE= Options in a PROC REPORT Step

When you send your PROC REPORT report to a nonlisting destination, you can take advantage of the formatting capabilities of the destination by customizing style elements in the report. You can do this either by using STYLE= options in PROC REPORT or by defining a style and referencing it on the ODS destination statement.

Modifying style attributes in a PROC REPORT step makes changes only to the report in which the modifications are applied. If you want to modify the output the same way repeatedly, you might find it more efficient to define and save a style rather than to code the same style attributes every time you execute a report. Examples 6.12, 6.14 and 6.15 define styles and table definitions for that purpose.

The remainder of this section discusses how to use STYLE= options in PROC REPORT. The syntax of the STYLE= option is

```
STYLE<(location(s))>=<style-element-name>
      <[style-attribute-specification(s)]
```

Table 6.1a lists the report locations where style elements can be modified with the STYLE= option. It also lists the statements where the STYLE= option can be placed.

Table 6.1a Locations in PROC REPORT Where Style Elements Can Be Modified with the STYLE= Option

Location	Option Specification	Statements Where STYLE= Option Can Be Included
Column cells	STYLE(COLUMN)	PROC REPORT DEFINE
Column header	STYLE(HEADER)	PROC REPORT DEFINE
Entire report	STYLE(REPORT)	PROC REPORT
Lines generated by summaries	STYLE(SUMMARY)	PROC REPORT BREAK RBREAK
Lines written by LINE statements in COMPUTE blocks	STYLE(LINES)	PROC REPORT COMPUTE
Cells identified by a CALL DEFINE statement	STYLE(CALLDEF)	PROC REPORT CALL DEFINE

Each statement has a default location and style element as shown in Table 6.1b. For example, if you omit the location on a STYLE= option placed on a DEFINE statement and specify an attribute for the style element "font_style," both the data and header for the column are modified according to the attribute assigned to "font_style."

Table 6.1b Locations and Default Style Elements for Each Statement in PROC REPORT

Statement	Valid Location Values	Default Location Value	Default Style Element
PROC REPORT	REPORT, COLUMN, HEADER, SUMMARY, LINES, CALLDEF	REPORT	Table
BREAK	SUMMARY, LINES	SUMMARY	Data Emphasis
CALL DEFINE	CALLDEF	CALLDEF	Data
COMPUTE	LINES	LINES	NoteContent
DEFINE	COLUMN, HEADER	COLUMN and HEADER	COLUMN: Data HEADER: Header
RBREAK	SUMMARY, LINES	SUMMARY	Data Emphasis

Unless you modify an attribute with a STYLE= option, PROC REPORT uses the style element attributes in the style definition that are in effect at the time PROC REPORT executes. This will be your system's default style definition unless you specify a different style on the ODS statement that processes the output from PROC REPORT.

The STYLE= options that you code on your PROC REPORT statement affect all associated locations in the report. STYLE= options placed on specific statements override the same named style element attributes placed on the PROC REPORT statement. For example, STYLE= options that you place on a DEFINE statement override the attributes specified on the PROC REPORT statement for the column that the DEFINE statement defines.

Example 6.2   Customizing a PROC REPORT Summary Report

Goal

Customize the appearance of the report produced in Example 3.8 by modifying style attributes with ODS. Replace features specific to the LISTING destination with those compatible with ODS nonlisting destinations. Send the output to a nonlisting destination.

Report

Quality Motor Company				
Sales Representative	Quarter	Cars Sold by Quarter	Total Sales by Quarter	Average Sale
Johnson	1st	6	$204,000.00	$34,000.00
	2nd	10	$336,000.00	$33,600.00
	3rd	7	$255,000.00	$36,428.57
	4th	10	$407,000.00	$40,700.00
Sales Totals for Johnson		33	$1,202,000.00	$36,424.24
Best Quarter for Johnson: 4th				
Langlois-Peele	1st	6	$217,000.00	$36,166.67
	2nd	20	$935,000.00	$46,750.00
	3rd	10	$358,000.00	$35,800.00
	4th	13	$667,000.00	$51,307.69
Sales Totals for Langlois-Peele		49	$2,177,000.00	$44,428.57
Best Quarter for Langlois-Peele: 2nd				
Annual Totals		82	$3,379,000.00	$41,207.32

Example Features

Data Set	CARSALES
Report Example	Example 3.8
Featured Step	PROC REPORT
Featured Step Statements and Options	PROC REPORT statement ODS options: STYLE(LINES)= and STYLE(SUMMARY)= DEFINE statement ODS option: STYLE(COLUMN)=
Output Destination of Example	RTF
A Closer Look	Comparing Example 3.8 and Example 6.2
Other Examples That Use This Data Set	Examples 3.8 and 6.6

Example Overview

When you write a report program, you might need to consider the destination of the output. Some statements and options apply only to specific destinations. This example illustrates how you can change Example 3.8 to send it to a nonlisting destination instead of the LISTING destination.

The report in Example 3.8 summarized sales information by quarter for two car sales representatives and identified each sales representative's best quarter. It also presented an annual sales summary for each sales representative and for both sales representatives combined.

Program

```
proc format;
   value mnthfmt 1-3 = '1st'
                 4-6 = '2nd'
                 7-9 = '3rd'
               10-12 = '4th';
run;
```

Do not send results to the LISTING destination.

```
ods listing close;
```

Send subsequent results to the RTF destination and save the results in a file.

```
ods rtf file='c:\reports\example38.rtf';
```

```
proc report data=carsales nowindows
```

Override current style element attributes in specific locations of the report. Write the summary lines in bold.

```
            style(summary)={font_weight=bold}
```

Italicize the output produced by LINE statements and write them in bold. Center the output.

```
            style(lines)={font_weight=bold
                          font_style=italic
                          just=center};
   title 'Quality Motor Company';
   column name month numsold amtsold avgsales
          maxsales;
   define name     / group width=25
                     'Sales/Representative'
```

Write all values in the NAME column in bold.

```
                     style(column)={font_weight=bold};
   define month    / group width=8 'Quarter' center
                     format=mnthfmt. width=8;

   define numsold  / analysis sum
                     'Cars Sold/by/Quarter'
                     format=2. width=9;
   define amtsold  / analysis sum
                     'Total Sales/by/Quarter'
                     format=dollar13.2;

   define avgsales / computed 'Average/Sale'
                     format=dollar13.2;

   define maxsales / computed noprint;
```

```
compute before name;
  bigsales=0;
  bigqtr=50;
endcomp;

compute avgsales;
   avgsales = amtsold.sum / numsold.sum;
endcomp;

compute maxsales;
  if _break_=' ' and bigsales lt amtsold.sum then
    do;
       bigsales=amtsold.sum;
       bigqtr=month;
  end;
endcomp;
```

Summarize each sales representative's information and write the sales representative's totals at the end of the person's quarterly sales results.

```
break after name / summarize;
```

Replace the default summary line value for NAME and write a customized line after the sales representative's totals.

```
compute after name;
```

Define a character variable that will contain the contents of the customized summary line.

```
  length fullline $ 50;
```

Concatenate the elements of the customized line and assign the results to a character variable.

```
  fullline=catx(' ','Best Quarter for',
            cats(name,':'),
            put(bigqtr,mnthfmt.));
```

Assign a value to NAME for display in the NAME cell associated with the summary lines produced by the BREAK AFTER NAME statement.

```
  name=catx(' ','Sales Totals for ',name);
```

Write the customized summary line. Be sure to specify a format for FULLLINE, because the LINE statement requires a format for items such as data set variables, computed variables, and statistics.

```
  line fullline $50.;
endcomp;
```

Summarize both sales representatives' information and write the totals at the end of the report.

```
rbreak after / summarize;
```

Assign a value to NAME for display in the NAME cell associated with the report summary line produced by the RBREAK AFTER statement.

```
compute after;
  name='Annual Totals';
endcomp;
run;
```

Terminate sending output to the RTF destination.

```
ods rtf close;
```

**Send subsequent output to the
LISTING destination.**

```
ods listing;
```

 **A Closer Look**

Comparing Example 3.8 and Example 6.2

The differences in the COMPUTE blocks, BREAK statement, and RBREAK statement between Example 3.8 and Example 6.2 result from the requirements of the output destinations of the two reports. The report in Example 3.8 was sent to the LISTING destination, whereas the report in Example 6.2 was sent to a nonlisting destination.

With no other programming changes, Example 3.8 sent to the RTF destination appears as shown in Figure 6.2.

Figure 6.2 Example 3.8 Output Sent to the RTF Destination

Quality Motor Company

Sales Representative	Quarter	Cars Sold by Quarter	Total Sales by Quarter	Average Sales
Johnson	1st	6	$204,000.00	$34,000.00
	2nd	10	$336,000.00	$33,600.00
	3rd	7	$255,000.00	$36,428.57
	4th	10	$407,000.00	$40,700.00

Sales totals for Johnson   33 $1,202,000.00 $36,424.24
Best Quarter for Johnson: 4th

Langlois-Peele	1st	6	$217,000.00	$36,166.67
	2nd	20	$935,000.00	$46,750.00
	3rd	10	$358,000.00	$35,800.00
	4th	13	$667,000.00	$51,307.69

Sales totals for Langlois-Peele   49 $2,177,000.00 $44,428.57
Best Quarter for Langlois-Peele: 2nd

Annual totals   82 $3,379,000.00 $41,207.32

The results of the LINE statements that write the separator lines do not look appropriate in this example. The COMPUTE AFTER NAME block in Example 3.8 writes values starting in specific columns. The report sent to the RTF destination was written with a style that used a proportional font, so attempts to position the values in specific columns do not work.

Table 6.2 compares the COMPUTE blocks between the two examples.

Table 6.2 Comparing the COMPUTE Blocks between Examples 3.8 and 6.2

Example 3.8	Example 6.2

<pre>compute before name;
  bigsales=0;
  bigqtr=50;
  line @6 70*'=';
endcomp;
 	
compute avgsales;
   avgsales = amtsold.sum / numsold.sum;
endcomp;
 	
compute maxsales;
  if _break_=' ' and bigsales lt
     amtsold.sum then do;
      bigsales=amtsold.sum;
      bigqtr=month;
  end;
endcomp;
 	
compute after name;
  length fullline $ 50;
  fullline=catx(' ','Best Quarter for',
            cats(name,':'),
            put(bigqtr,mnthfmt.));
 	
  line @6 70*'=';
  line @6 'Sales Totals for ' name $14.
      @42 numsold.sum 3.
      @45 amtsold.sum dollar15.2
      @60 avgsales dollar15.2;
 	
  line @6 fullline $50.;
 	
  line @6 70*'=';
  line ' ';
endcomp;
 	
compute after;
  line @6 70*'=';
  line @6 'Annual Totals '
      @41 numsold.sum 4.
      @45 amtsold.sum dollar15.2
      @60 avgsales dollar15.2;
  line @6 70*'=';
  line ' ';
endcomp;</pre>
	<pre>compute before name;
	  bigsales=0;
	  bigqtr=50; ❶
	endcomp;
	
	compute avgsales;
	   avgsales = amtsold.sum / numsold.sum;
	endcomp;
	
	compute maxsales;
	  if _break_=' ' and bigsales lt
	     amtsold.sum then do;
	      bigsales=amtsold.sum;
	      bigqtr=month;
	  end;
	endcomp;
	
	break after name / summarize; ❷
	
	compute after name;
	  length fullline $ 50;
	  fullline=catx(' ','Best Quarter for',
	            cats(name,':'),
	            put(bigqtr,mnthfmt.));
	
	  name=catx(' ', ❸
	         'Sales Totals for ',name);
	                          ❹
	  line fullline $50.;
	
	endcomp;
	
	rbreak after / summarize; ❺
	
	compute after; ❻
	  name='Annual Totals';
	endcomp;</pre>

❶ Remove the LINE statement from the COMPUTE BEFORE NAME block.

❷ Replace the first two LINE statements in the COMPUTE AFTER NAME block with the BREAK AFTER NAME statement.

❸ Assign a value to NAME for display in the NAME cell associated with the summary lines produced by the BREAK AFTER NAME statement.

❹ Remove the explicit column specifications on the LINE statements. Keep only the LINE statement that writes out the "Best Quarter for...." Remove the LINE statements that write the separator lines and the blank line.

❺ Remove all LINE statements from the COMPUTE AFTER block. Replace the LINE statements with the RBREAK AFTER statement.

❻ Assign a value to NAME for display in the NAME cell associated with the report summary line produced by the RBREAK AFTER statement.

Example 6.3 Customizing a PROC TABULATE Report

Customize the appearance of the report produced in Example 3.5 by modifying style attributes with ODS. Send the output to a nonlisting destination.

Report

	Region											
Job Class	*North*				*South*				*East*			
	Female		Male		Female		Male		Female		Male	
	Count	%	Count	%	Count	%	Count	%	Count	%	Count	%
Technical	7	50.0	7	50.0	3	75.0	1	25.0	5	50.0	5	50.0
Manager/Supervisor	7	58.3	5	41.7	6	100.0	0	0	7	50.0	7	50.0
Clerical	7	70.0	3	30.0	2	28.6	5	71.4	4	66.7	2	33.3
Administrative	0	0	6	100.0	6	54.5	5	45.5	5	62.5	3	37.5
All Employees	21	50.0	21	50.0	17	60.7	11	39.3	21	55.3	17	44.7

Regional Gender Distribution among Job Classes

	Region				All Regions Combined			
Job Class	*West*							
	Female		Male		Female		Male	
	Count	%	Count	%	Count	%	Count	%
Technical	1	16.7	5	83.3	16	47.1	18	52.9
Manager/Supervisor	0	0	3	100.0	20	57.1	15	42.9
Clerical	1	20.0	4	80.0	14	50.0	14	50.0
Administrative	0	0	1	100.0	11	42.3	15	57.7
All Employees	2	13.3	13	86.7	61	49.6	62	50.4

Example Features

Data Set	JOBCLASS
Report Example	Example 3.5
Featured Step	PROC TABULATE
Featured Step Statements and Options	ODS STYLE= options placed on these statements: PROC TABULATE CLASS CLASSLEV TABLE, including BOX= option KEYWORD
Output Destination of Example	RTF
🔍 **A Closer Look**	Placing STYLE= Options in a PROC TABULATE Step
Other Examples That Use This Data Set	Examples 3.4, 3.5, 3.6, and 6.7

Example Overview

The report in Example 3.5 summarizes the observations in JOBCLASS by region, occupation, and gender. This example customizes the output by sending it to a nonlisting destination and assigning attributes to style elements.

This example specifies attributes in several components of the report: data cells, class-level headings, variable name headings, keyword headings, and the box cell text.

The PROC TABULATE options NOSEPS and RTS= which do not apply in a nonlisting destination, are removed from the step.

Program

Do not send results to the LISTING destination.

```
ods listing close;
```

Send subsequent results to the RTF destination and save the results in a file.

```
ods rtf file='c:\reports\example35.rtf';

proc tabulate data=jobclass
              format=5.

              style={background=white};
```

Apply style changes to the data cells. Set the background color of the data cells.

```
title 'Regional Gender Distribution';
title2 'among Job Classes';
```

Do not apply any style changes to the heading of OCCUPAT since its specification in the TABLE statement suppresses the heading.

```
class occupat;
```

Set the background color of the cells containing the heading for GENDER.

```
class gender / style={background=white};
```

Set the background color of the cells containing the heading for REGION. Italicize the heading.

```
class region / style={background=white
               font_style=italic};
```

Set the background color of the cells containing the values of REGION. Italicize the values of REGION.

```
classlev region / style={background=white
                  font_style=italic };
```

Set the background color of the cells containing the values of GENDER and OCCUPAT.

```
classlev gender occupat /
  style={background=white};

table occupat=' '
```

Write the row containing the summary in very light gray.

```
    all='All
        Employees'*{style={background=grayee}},
(region='Region'
all='All Regions Combined')*
gender=' '*
(n='Count'
```

Override the background color of the data cells containing the percentages by setting the color to very light gray.

```
pctn<gender>='%'*f=7.1*{style={background=
                               grayee}}) /
nocontinued
misstext='0'
```

Specify style element attributes for the text placed in the PROC TABULATE box in the upper left corner of the table. Set the background color of the box and italicize the text.

```
box={label="Job Class"
     style={background=grayee font_style=italic}};
```

Set the background color of the cells containing the PCTN keyword heading.

```
keyword pctn / style={background=grayee};
```

Set the background color of the cells containing the ALL keyword heading. Italicize the heading.

```
keyword all / style={background=grayee
                     font_style=italic};
```

Set the background color of the cells containing the N keyword heading.

```
keyword n / style={background=grayaa};

    format gender gendfmt. occupat occupfmt.
           region regfmt.;
run;
```

Terminate sending output to the RTF destination.

```
ods rtf close;
```

Send subsequent output to the LISTING destination.

```
ods listing;
```

🔍 A Closer Look

Placing STYLE= Options in a PROC TABULATE Step

When you send your PROC TABULATE report to a nonlisting destination, you can take advantage of the formatting capabilities of the destination by customizing style elements in the report. You can do this either by using the STYLE= option in the PROC TABULATE step or by defining a style and referencing it on the ODS destination statement.

Modifying style attributes in a PROC TABULATE step makes changes only to the report in which the modifications are applied. If you want to modify the output the same way repeatedly, you might find it more efficient to define and save a style rather than to code the same style attributes every time you execute a report. Examples 6.12, 6.14 and 6.15 define styles and table definitions for that purpose.

The remainder of this section discusses how to use the STYLE= option in PROC TABULATE. The syntax of the STYLE= option is

```
STYLE=<style-element-name|PARENT>
[style-attribute-name=style-attribute-value<...
 style-attribute-name=style-attribute-value>]
```

Table 6.3 lists the statements where you can add the STYLE= option in PROC TABULATE and the report elements that the STYLE= option can modify. The program above defines style attributes on all of the statements listed in Table 6.3 except for VAR and the MISSTEXT= option on the TABLE statement.

In PROC TABULATE, you do not specify a report location in your STYLE= option specification as you do in PROC REPORT and PROC PRINT. PROC TABULATE determines the location by the statement with which the STYLE= option is associated.

Table 6.3 PROC TABULATE Statements Where the STYLE= Option Can Be Placed and the Report Elements That the Option Affects

Place STYLE= option on this statement...	To affect this part of the report....
PROC TABULATE	Data cells
CLASS	Class variable name headings
CLASSLEV	Class level value headings
VAR	Analysis variable name headings
KEYWORD	Keyword headings
TABLE	Table borders, rules, and other parts that are not specified elsewhere
TABLE statement, BOX= option	Text in the upper left box of the report
TABLE statement, MISSTEXT= option	Text for missing values in data cells

Note that you can have multiple CLASS, CLASSLEV, and KEYWORD statements. You can group similar style attributes on one statement.

You can also control attributes of specific rows and columns, such as the summaries in this example, by nesting the STYLE= option below the location. Sometimes this is referred to as "traffic lighting." Examples 6.4 and 6.5 show how to do this. Example 6.4 uses PROC REPORT, and Example 6.5 uses PROC TABULATE. The remaining examples in this chapter each show various ways of customizing specific style attributes, some down to the cell level.

Example 6.4   Adding "Traffic Lighting" to a Report Created by PROC REPORT

Goal

Customize the appearance of the report produced in Example 2.7 by modifying style attributes with ODS. Use "traffic lighting" to draw attention to specific results by changing the color of rows depending upon the value of a cell in the row. Send the output to a nonlisting destination.

Report

		Pre Program Results		Post Program Results				
Gender	Study ID	Chol	HDL	Chol	HDL	Chol/HDL Pre	Chol/HDL Post	Chol/HDL Change
Females	1001	156	48	150	50	3.3	3.0	Minimal Change
	1002	151	50	139	54	3.0	2.6	Improved
	1003	165	51	149	51	3.2	2.9	Minimal Change
	1004	158	51	143	53	3.1	2.7	Improved
	1009	187	71	174	69	2.6	2.5	Minimal Change
	1010	161	64	155	66	2.5	2.3	Minimal Change
	1011	164	72	149	73	2.3	2.0	Improved
	1012	160	66	168	61	2.4	2.8	Worsened
	1024	196	61	186	62	3.2	3.0	Minimal Change
	1025	216	51	171	54	4.2	3.2	Improved
	1026	195	60	195	60	3.3	3.3	Minimal Change
Males	1005	296	47	272	51	6.3	5.3	Improved
	1006	155	31	152	33	5.0	4.6	Minimal Change
	1007	250	55	231	60	4.5	3.9	Improved
	1008	264	43	195	44	6.1	4.4	Improved
	1013	183	51	192	49	3.6	3.9	Minimal Change
	1014	256	43	235	43	6.0	5.5	Minimal Change
	1015	235	43	216	44	5.5	4.9	Improved
	1016	238	36	207	36	6.6	5.8	Improved
	1017	215	50	205	52	4.3	3.9	Minimal Change
	1018	190	31	164	32	6.1	5.1	Improved
	1019	168	52	172	44	3.2	3.9	Worsened
	1020	219	57	207	58	3.8	3.6	Minimal Change
	1021	203	28	169	28	7.3	6.0	Improved
	1022	215	51	205	52	4.2	3.9	Minimal Change
	1023	222	32	210	32	6.9	6.6	Minimal Change

Exercise Program Results

Example Features

Data Set	LIPIDS
Report Example	Example 2.7
Featured Step	PROC REPORT
Featured Step Statements and Options	PROC REPORT statement ODS option: STYLE(HEADER)= DEFINE statement ODS option: STYLE= CALL DEFINE statement within COMPUTE blocks
Output Destination of Example	RTF
Related Technique	Using PROC FORMAT and PROC REPORT to assign colors as value labels
🔍 A Closer Look	Setting Style Attributes with the CALL DEFINE Statement in PROC REPORT
Other Examples That Use This Data Set	Examples 2.7, 3.3, and 6.8

Example Overview

The report in Example 2.7 lists the results of lipid tests on the subjects in a clinical study. The study evaluates the ratio of cholesterol to HDL before and after the subjects participated in an exercise program. Example 2.7 computed the ratios and determined the proportional change in the ratios. The proportional change results were classified into three groups: "Improved," "Minimal Change," and "Worsened."

This example colors the background of each study participant's row based on the change in the cholesterol-to-HDL ratio. It also modifies the background color of the headings and the font weight of two columns.

This example does not include the features in Example 2.7 that apply only to the LISTING destination. The BREAK AFTER GENDER / SKIP statement was removed, as was the WIDTH= option on the DEFINE statement for RESULTS.

Program

```
proc format;
  value ratio low-<-.1='Improved'
              -.1-.1  ='Minimal Change'
              .1<-high='Worsened';
  value $gender 'M'='Males'
                'F'='Females';
run;
```

Do not send results to the LISTING destination.

```
ods listing close;
```

Send subsequent results to the RTF destination and save the results in a file.

```
ods rtf file='c:\reports\example27.rtf';
```

<table>
<tr><td>

Set the background color of the headings.

</td><td>

```
proc report data=lipids nowindows split='$'

                    style(header)={background=grayee};
```

</td></tr>
<tr><td></td><td>

```
  title 'Exercise Program Results';

  column gender studyid testperiod,(chol hdl)
         ratiopre ratiopost results;
```

</td></tr>
<tr><td>

Write the data cells in the next two columns in bold.

</td><td>

```
  define gender / group 'Gender' format=$gender.
                  style={font_weight=bold};
  define studyid / group 'Study ID'
                   style={font_weight=bold};
```

</td></tr>
<tr><td></td><td>

```
  define time    / across descending ' ';
  define testperiod / across order=data ' ' center
                      format=$results.;
```

</td></tr>
<tr><td></td><td>

```
  define chol / display 'Chol';
  define hdl / display 'HDL';
```

</td></tr>
<tr><td></td><td>

```
  define ratiopre  / computed format=5.1 'Chol/HDL Pre'
                     center;
  define ratiopost / computed format=5.1
                     'Chol/HDL Post' center;
```

</td></tr>
<tr><td>

Format the values of this column. Omit the WIDTH= option that is in Example 2.7, since it has no effect when sending output to a nonlisting destination.

</td><td>

```
  define results   / computed format=ratio.
                     'Chol/HDL Change' left
```

</td></tr>
<tr><td>

Write the formatted values of RESULTS in bold.

</td><td>

```
                    style={font_weight=bold};
```

</td></tr>
<tr><td>

Omit the BREAK AFTER statement that is in Example 2.7, since its only function was to skip a line between genders. The SKIP option has no effect when sending output to a nonlisting destination.

</td><td>

```
compute ratiopre;
  ratiopre=_c3_/_c4_;
endcomp;
compute ratiopost;
  ratiopost=_c5_/_c6_;
endcomp;

compute results;
  results=(ratiopost-ratiopre)/ratiopre;
```

</td></tr>
<tr><td>

Compare the proportional change between the before and after results. Set the background color of each row based on the proportional change.

</td><td>

```
  if results <-.1 then call
    define(_ROW_,'style','style={background=white}');
  else if -.1 le results le .1 then call
    define(_ROW_,'style','style={background=graydd}');
  else if results gt .1 then call
    define(_ROW_,'style','style={background=grayaa}');
endcomp;
run;
```

</td></tr>
<tr><td>

Terminate sending output to the RTF destination.

</td><td>

```
ods rtf close;
```

</td></tr>
<tr><td>

Send subsequent output to the LISTING destination.

</td><td>

```
ods listing;
```

</td></tr>
</table>

Related Technique

The preceding program changes the background color of entire rows. The program described in this section sets the background color of specific cells by applying a format to the values of the computed variable RESULTS. Its output is shown in Figure 6.4.

A color is assigned to each of the three ranges defined by the format COLORRES. This format is assigned to the background style of the computed variable RESULTS on the DEFINE RESULTS statement.

The CALL DEFINE statements that are in the preceding example are removed from the following program, since the goal of this new program is not to highlight rows, but rather to highlight cells.

Figure 6.4 Output from PROC REPORT That Sets the Background Color of Specific Cells of the Report

		Pre		Post				
		Results		Results				
		Chol	HDL	Chol	HDL			
Gender	Study ID	Test	Test	Test	Test	Chol/HDL Pre	Chol/HDL Post	Chol/HDL Change
Females	**1001**	156	48	150	50	3.3	3.0	Minimal Change
	1002	151	50	139	54	3.0	2.6	Improved
	1003	165	51	149	51	3.2	2.9	Minimal Change
	1004	158	51	143	53	3.1	2.7	Improved
	1009	187	71	174	69	2.6	2.5	Minimal Change
	1010	161	64	155	66	2.5	2.3	Minimal Change
	1011	164	72	149	73	2.3	2.0	Improved
	1012	160	66	168	61	2.4	2.8	Worsened
	1024	196	61	186	62	3.2	3.0	Minimal Change
	1025	216	51	171	54	4.2	3.2	Improved
	1026	195	60	195	60	3.3	3.3	Minimal Change
Males	**1005**	296	47	272	51	6.3	5.3	Improved
	1006	155	31	152	33	5.0	4.6	Minimal Change
	1007	250	55	231	60	4.5	3.9	Improved
	1008	264	43	195	44	6.1	4.4	Improved
	1013	183	51	192	49	3.6	3.9	Minimal Change
	1014	256	43	235	43	6.0	5.5	Minimal Change
	1015	235	43	216	44	5.5	4.9	Improved
	1016	238	36	207	36	6.6	5.8	Improved
	1017	215	50	205	52	4.3	3.9	Minimal Change
	1018	190	31	164	32	6.1	5.1	Improved
	1019	168	52	172	44	3.2	3.9	Worsened
	1020	219	57	207	58	3.8	3.6	Minimal Change
	1021	203	28	169	28	7.3	6.0	Improved
	1022	215	51	205	52	4.2	3.9	Minimal Change
	1023	222	32	210	32	6.9	6.6	Minimal Change

Exercise Program Results

The program that produced the output in Figure 6.4 follows.

```
ods listing close;
ods rtf file='c:\reports\example26b.rtf';

proc format;
  value ratio low-<-.1='Improved'
               -.1-.1  ='Minimal Change'
               .1<-high='Worsened';
  value $gender 'M'='Males'
                 'F'='Females';
  value colorres low-<-.1='white'
                  -.1-.1  ='graydd'
                  .1<-high='grayaa';
run;

proc report data=lipids split='$'
            style(header)={background=grayee};

  title 'Exercise Program Results';

  column gender studyid
         testperiod,(chol hdl)
         ratiopre ratiopost results;

  define gender / group 'Gender' format=$gender.
                  style={font_weight=bold};
  define studyid / group 'Study ID'
                  style={font_weight=bold};

  define testperiod / across order=data ' ' center
                     format=$results.;
  define chol / display 'Chol' width=5;
  define hdl / display 'HDL' width=5;
  define ratiopre  / computed format=5.1 'Chol/HDL Pre'
                    center;
  define ratiopost / computed format=5.1 'Chol/HDL
                    Post'
                    center;

  define results    / computed format=ratio.
                    'Chol/HDL Change'
                    left style={background=colorres.};

  compute ratiopre;
    ratiopre=_c3_/_c4_;
  endcomp;
  compute ratiopost;
    ratiopost=_c5_/_c6_;
  endcomp;
  compute results;
    results=(ratiopost-ratiopre)/ratiopre;
  endcomp;
run;

ods rtf close;
ods listing;
```

Define a format to associate with the RESULTS computed variable. Set the value labels to colors. Enclose the value labels in quotation marks.

Set the background color of the cells using the COLORRES format.

🔍 A Closer Look

Setting Style Attributes with the CALL DEFINE Statement in PROC REPORT

The CALL DEFINE statement in PROC REPORT is inserted in a COMPUTE block. You can use CALL DEFINE to set style attributes for a specific column or for all columns of the current row that the COMPUTE block is processing.

The syntax of the CALL DEFINE statement is

```
CALL DEFINE(column-id|_ROW_, attribute-name, value);
```

The first argument to CALL DEFINE designates where to apply the style attribute. It can be written as a reference either to a column or to the automatic variable _ROW_.

When you want to reference a column, you can specify the COLUMN-ID argument in one of several ways:

- ❑ an explicit column reference such as 'STUDYID' or '_C1_'.

- ❑ a character expression that resolves to the column name.

- ❑ a numeric expression that resolves to the column number .

- ❑ a numeric literal that resolves to the column number.

- ❑ the automatic variable _COL_ . The automatic variable _COL_ identifies the column that contains the report item to which the COMPUTE block is attached.

When you specify the first argument as the automatic variable _ROW_, you indicate that ODS should apply the style attributes to the entire row currently being processed.

The main example references _ROW_ in the COMPUTE RESULTS block. Therefore, the style changes specified in the CALL DEFINE statements are applied to the entire row.

The COMPUTE block for RESULTS executes for each row in the report. It evaluates the current value of RESULTS and then executes the CALL DEFINE statement based on the current value of RESULTS.

There are many possible values for the second argument to CALL DEFINE, the ATTRIBUTE-NAME. These include items such as highlighting and blinking for the location identified by the COLUMN-ID as well as setting style attributes. The example above specifies STYLE as the ATTRIBUTE-NAME. This tells PROC REPORT that the CALL DEFINE statement will modify ODS style elements.

The third argument, VALUE, sets the value for ATTRIBUTE-NAME. Enclose the argument in quotation marks. Values for this argument depend on the ATTRIBUTE-NAME. When specifying STYLE as the ATTRIBUTE-NAME, you can enclose style element attributes in brackets following the STYLE= keyword as shown in the main example.

The CALL DEFINE statement also allows you to place hyperlinks in a cell of your report. To do this, specify the ATTRIBUTE-NAME as 'URL' and specify the VALUE as the hyperlink. Example 6.9 shows how to place hyperlinks in elements of your reports.

```
compute studyid;
  urllink=put(studyid,4.) || '.html';
  call define('studyid','url',urllink);
endcomp;
```

Example 6.5 Adding "Traffic Lighting" to a Report Created by PROC TABULATE

Goal

Customize the appearance of the report produced in the related technique of Example 3.2 by modifying style attributes with ODS. Use "traffic lighting" to draw attention to specific results in the report by setting style elements to specific colors. Send the output to a nonlisting destination.

Report

<table>
<tr><td colspan="11">Nutritional Information about Breads Available in the Region
Values Per Bread Slice, Calories in kcal, Fiber in Grams</td></tr>
<tr><td></td><td></td><td colspan="4">Calories per Slice</td><td colspan="4">Dietary Fiber(g) per Slice</td></tr>
<tr><td></td><td></td><td>N</td><td>Mean</td><td>Min</td><td>Max</td><td>N</td><td>Mean</td><td>Min</td><td>Max</td></tr>
<tr><td>Source</td><td>Brand</td><td></td><td></td><td></td><td></td><td></td><td></td><td></td><td></td></tr>
<tr><td>Bakery</td><td>Aunt Sal Bakes</td><td>10</td><td>91.3</td><td>74.0</td><td>105.0</td><td>10</td><td>1.8</td><td>0.5</td><td>3.9</td></tr>
<tr><td></td><td>Demeter</td><td>15</td><td>96.7</td><td>71.0</td><td>111.0</td><td>15</td><td>2.3</td><td>0.5</td><td>4.2</td></tr>
<tr><td></td><td>Downtown Bakers</td><td>10</td><td>96.9</td><td>82.0</td><td>138.0</td><td>10</td><td>2.4</td><td>1.0</td><td>4.3</td></tr>
<tr><td></td><td>Pain du Prairie</td><td>13</td><td>86.6</td><td>74.0</td><td>108.0</td><td>13</td><td>1.9</td><td>0.3</td><td>4.4</td></tr>
<tr><td>Grocery</td><td>BBB Brands</td><td>5</td><td>81.8</td><td>65.0</td><td>90.0</td><td>5</td><td>1.8</td><td>1.2</td><td>2.6</td></tr>
<tr><td></td><td>Choice 123</td><td>6</td><td>80.7</td><td>71.0</td><td>92.0</td><td>6</td><td>1.5</td><td>0.5</td><td>2.3</td></tr>
<tr><td></td><td>Fabulous Breads</td><td>15</td><td>82.8</td><td>71.0</td><td>97.0</td><td>15</td><td>1.8</td><td>0.0</td><td>3.2</td></tr>
<tr><td></td><td>Five Chimneys</td><td>10</td><td>86.6</td><td>75.0</td><td>98.0</td><td>10</td><td>2.6</td><td>1.2</td><td>3.8</td></tr>
<tr><td></td><td>Gaia's Hearth</td><td>11</td><td>89.0</td><td>77.0</td><td>101.0</td><td>11</td><td>1.8</td><td>0.0</td><td>3.6</td></tr>
<tr><td></td><td>Mill City Bakers</td><td>9</td><td>85.3</td><td>66.0</td><td>112.0</td><td>9</td><td>1.9</td><td>0.5</td><td>3.1</td></tr>
<tr><td></td><td>Owasco Ovens</td><td>12</td><td>83.3</td><td>72.0</td><td>92.0</td><td>12</td><td>2.2</td><td>0.8</td><td>4.8</td></tr>
<tr><td></td><td>RiseNShine Bread</td><td>8</td><td>81.9</td><td>56.0</td><td>100.0</td><td>8</td><td>1.7</td><td>0.9</td><td>3.1</td></tr>
</table>

Example Features

Data Set	BREAD
Report Example	Example 3.2 Related Technique
Featured Steps	PROC FORMAT PROC TABULATE

Featured Step Statements and Options	PROC FORMAT
	   Assigning colors to value labels
	ODS STYLE= options placed on these PROC TABULATE statements:
	   CLASS
	   CLASSLEV
	   TABLE, including BOX= option
	   KEYWORD

Output Destination of Example	RTF
Other Examples That Use This Data Set	Examples 3.2 and 6.15

Example Overview

The report in the Related Technique section of Example 3.2 shows descriptive statistics for several combinations of classifications in the BREAD data set. This example presents only the table produced by the last request in the TABLE statement. The last table request computes descriptive statistics on calories and dietary fiber for the categories defined by the combination of the values of SOURCE and BRAND.

The report in this example visually identifies the means above and below specific values by setting the background color of the cell. Formats created by PROC FORMAT associate ranges of values to colors. A format is defined for ranges of calorie values, and a format is defined for ranges of dietary fiber values. The program applies each format to the mean statistic of the specific analysis variable by setting the background style element attribute to the format name.

Program

Define formats that associate ranges of values to colors.

```
proc format;
```

Define a format to associate with the CALORIES analysis variable. Do not change the middle range's color from the default color.

```
value colorcal low-85='graycc'
               95-high='grayee';
```

Define a format to associate with the DIETARY_FIBER analysis variable. Do not change the middle range's color from the default color.

```
value colorfib low-1.8='grayee'
               2-high='graycc';
run;
```

Do not send results to the LISTING destination.

```
ods listing close;
```

Send subsequent results to the RTF destination and save the results in a file.	`ods rtf file='c:\reports\example32.rtf';`

	`proc tabulate data=bread;`
	`   title 'Nutritional Information about Breads Available`
	`         in the Region';`
	`   title2 'Values Per Bread Slice, Calories in kcal,`
	`          Fiber in Grams';`

Set the background color of the cells containing the headings for SOURCE and BRAND.	`class source brand / style={background=grayee};`
Set the background color of the cells containing the levels of SOURCE and BRAND.	`classlev source brand / style={background=white};`

Set the background color of the cells containing the headings for CALORIES and DIETARY_FIBER.	`var calories dietary_fiber /`
	`        style={background=grayee};`
	`table source*brand,`
	`     calories*(n*f=3.`

Set the background color of the cells containing the means of CALORIES to the colors defined in the COLORCAL format.	`    (mean*{style={background=colorcal.}}`
	`    min max)*f=7.1)`
	`     dietary_fiber*(n*f=3.`

Set the background color of the cells containing the means of DIETARY_FIBER to the colors defined in the COLORFIB format.	`    (mean*{style={background=colorfib.}}` `    min max)*f=7.1) /`
Set the background color of the PROC TABULATE upper left corner box.	`    / box={style={background=white}}` `    rts=30;`
Set the background color of the N, MEAN, MIN, and MAX keyword headings.	`  keyword n mean min max / style={background=white};` `run;`
Terminate sending output to the RTF destination.	`ods rtf close;`
Send subsequent output to the LISTING destination.	`ods listing;`

Example 6.6   Including Images in a Report Created by PROC REPORT

Goal

Add images to the report produced in Example 6.2. Send the output to a non-listing destination.

Report

Sales Representative	Quarter	Cars Sold by Quarter	Total Sales by Quarter	Average Sale
Johnson	1st	6	$204,000.00	$34,000.00
	2nd	10	$336,000.00	$33,600.00
	3rd	7	$255,000.00	$36,428.57
	4th	10	$407,000.00	$40,700.00
Sales Totals for Johnson		*33*	*$1,202,000.00*	*$36,424.24*
Best Quarter for Johnson: 4th				
Langlois-Peele	1st	6	$217,000.00	$36,166.67
	2nd	20	$935,000.00	$46,750.00
	3rd	10	$358,000.00	$35,800.00
	4th	13	$667,000.00	$51,307.69
Sales Totals for Langlois-Peele		*49*	*$2,177,000.00*	*$44,428.57*
Best Quarter for Langlois-Peele: 2nd				
Annual Totals		*82*	*$3,379,000.00*	*$41,207.32*

Keep Selling!

Example Features

Data Set	CARSALES
Report Example	Example 6.2, which was based on Example 3.8
Featured Step	PROC REPORT
Featured Step Statements and Options	PROC REPORT statement ODS options: STYLE(LINES)=, STYLE(SUMMARY)=, and STYLE (REPORT)= with PREIMAGE style attribute DEFINE statement ODS options: STYLE(COLUMN)= COMPUTE BEFORE _PAGE_ block, ODS STYLE= option: PREIMAGE style attribute COMPUTE AFTER _PAGE_ block, ODS STYLE= option: POSTMAGE style attribute
Output Destination of Example	RTF
Other Examples That Use This Data Set	Examples 3.8 and 6.2

The program in this example modifies the report presented in Example 6.2. It adds two images at the beginning of the report and one at the end.

You can include images in your report at specific locations by adding style attributes that reference images. The images in this example are saved in JPEG files.

Program

Clear any existing titles and footnotes. The display of title and footnote information will be handled by the COMPUTE BEFORE _PAGE_ and COMPUTE AFTER _PAGE_ blocks in PROC REPORT.

```
title;
footnote;
```

Define the MNTHFMT format as in Example 3.8.

```
proc format;
   value mnthfmt 1-3 = '1st'
                 4-6 = '2nd'
                 7-9 = '3rd'
                 10-12 = '4th';
run;
```

Do not send results to the LISTING destination.

```
ods listing close;
```

Send subsequent results to the RTF destination and save the results in a file.

```
ods rtf file='c:\reports\example38a.rtf';
```

Lengthen the variable NAME so that the summary line label can be completely inserted into NAME.

```
data carsales;
  length name $ 50;
  set carsales;
run;
```

Maintain the same style element attributes for SUMMARY and LINES as in Example 6.2.

Place an image before the table. Identify the path and name of the image file.

Maintain the same code from the COLUMN statement through the COMPUTE AFTER block as in Example 6.2.

```
proc report data=carsales nowindows
             style(summary)={font_weight=bold}
             style(lines)={font_weight=bold
                           font_style=italic
                           just=center}

             style(report)=
                 {preimage='c:\reports\vroomsales.jpg'};

column name month numsold amtsold avgsales maxsales;

define name      / group 'Sales/Representative'
                   style(column)={font_weight=bold};
define month     / group 'Quarter' center
                   format=mnthfmt.;

define numsold   / analysis sum 'Cars Sold/by/Quarter'
                   format=2.;
define amtsold   / analysis sum
                   'Total Sales/by/Quarter'
                   format=dollar13.2;

define avgsales / computed 'Average/Sale'
                   format=dollar13.2;

define maxsales / computed noprint;


compute before name;
  bigsales=0;
  bigqtr=50;
endcomp;

compute avgsales;
   avgsales = amtsold.sum / numsold.sum;
endcomp;

compute maxsales;
  if _break_=' ' and bigsales lt amtsold.sum then do;
    bigsales=amtsold.sum;
    bigqtr=month;
  end;
endcomp;

break after name / summarize;

compute after name;
  length fullline $ 50;
  fullline=catx(' ','Best Quarter for',
              cats(name,':'),
              put(bigqtr,mnthfmt.));

  name=catx(' ','Sales Totals for ',name);

  line fullline $50.;
endcomp;

rbreak after / summarize;

compute after;
  name='Annual Totals';
endcomp;
```

| **Insert an image in the space between the titles and the column headings, which is referenced with the keyword _PAGE_.** | ```
compute before _page_ /
          style={preimage='c:\reports\qmc.jpg'};
``` |
| **Include the LINE statement even though it writes only a space, because without a LINE statement, the preimage would not be displayed.** | ```
   line ' ';
endcomp;
``` |
| **Insert an image in the space between the last row of the report and the end of the report, which is referenced with the keyword _PAGE_.** | ```
compute after _page_ /
          style={postimage='c:\reports\keepselling.jpg'};
``` |
| **Include the LINE statement even though it writes a space, because without a LINE statement, the postimage would not be displayed.** | ```
   line ' ';
endcomp;
run;
``` |
| **Terminate sending output to the RTF destination.** | ```
ods rtf close;
``` |
| **Send subsequent output to the LISTING destination.** | ```
ods listing;
``` |

Example 6.7   Including Images in a Report Created by PROC TABULATE

Goal

Add images to the report produced in Example 6.3 and send the output to a non-listing destination.

Report

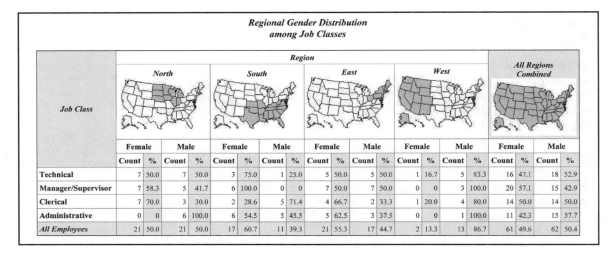

Example Features

Data Set	JOBCLASS
Report Example	Example 6.3, which was based on Example 3.5
Featured Steps and Statement	PROC FORMAT PROC TABULATE ODS statement

Featured Step Statements and Options	PROC FORMAT
	   Assigning pictures as value labels
	ODS statement: ESCAPECHAR= option
	Inline formatting
	ODS STYLE= options placed on these statements:
	    PROC TABULATE
	    CLASS
	    CLASSLEV
	    TABLE, including BOX= option
	    KEYWORD

Formatting Features	OPTIONS ORIENTATION=
Output Destination of Example	RTF
Other Examples That Use This Data Set	Examples 3.4, 3.5, 3.6, and 6.3

Example Overview

The reports in Examples 3.5 and 6.3 summarize the observations in JOBCLASS by region, occupation, and gender. When sending the report to a nonlisting destination, you can further customize the report by changing the attributes of style elements for specific features of the report.

The program in this example adds images to the report in Example 6.3. It places an image in the heading cell for each value of the variable REGION and in the heading cell for the summary column.

You can include images in your report at specific locations by adding style attributes that reference images. This example employs two different methods of including images in the report.

The images for each region are placed by applying a format that associates an image with each region. Inline formatting places the image in the summary column.

The images in this example are saved in JPEG files.

Examples 6.9 and 6.12 also include inline formatting specifications. Example 6.12 includes a discussion on how to use inline formatting.

Program

Do not send results to the LISTING destination.

```
ods listing close;
```

Specify the character that indicates to ODS that what follows the character are style attributes and formatting instructions. Select a character that you know is not part of a character value in your data.

```
ods escapechar='^';
```

Output the report in the landscape orientation. Be sure to place this option specification before the ODS statement that opens the nonlisting destination.

```
options orientation=landscape;
```

Send subsequent results to the RTF destination and save the results in a file.

```
ods rtf file='c:\reports\example35b.rtf';

proc format;
```

Define formats for GENDER, OCCUPATION, and REGION as in Example 3.5.

```
value gendfmt 1='Female'
               2='Male';
value occupfmt 1='Technical'
               2='Manager/Supervisor'
               3='Clerical'
               4='Administrative';
value regfmt 1='North'
             2='South'
             3='East'
             4='West';
```

Define a format to associate the unformatted values of OCCUPAT with an image.

```
value regjpg 1='c:\reports\north.jpg'
             2='c:\reports\south.jpg'
             3='c:\reports\east.jpg'
             4='c:\reports\west.jpg';
run;
```

Maintain the same code as in Example 6.3 unless otherwise indicated.

```
proc tabulate data=jobclass
              format=5.
              noseps
              style={background=white};
title 'Regional Gender Distribution';
title2 'among Job Classes';

class occupat;
class gender / style={background=white};
class region / style={font_style=italic
              background=white};
classlev region / style={background=white
              font_style=italic


              postimage=regjpg.};
classlev gender occupat / style={background=white};

table occupat=' '
      all='All Employees'*{style={background=grayee}},
      (region='Region'

      all="^S={postimage='c:\reports\allstates.jpg'
```

Associate an image with each value of REGION through the format REGJPG. Place the images after the text values of REGION.

Set style attributes that affect the summary column heading.
Precede the specification with the escape character. Insert an image after the heading for the summary column.

Set the background color for the heading in the summary column.
This instruction placed on the TABLE statement overrides the setting specified in the KEYWORD ALL statement that follows.

```
background=white}All Regions Combined")*
gender=' '*
(n='Count'
pctn<gender>='%'*f=7.1*{style=
                        {background=grayee}})/
    nocontinued
    misstext='0'
    box={label="Job Class"
    style={background=grayee font_style=italic}};
```

Set attributes for the cells containing the PCTN, ALL, and N keyword headings.

```
keyword pctn / style={background=grayee};
keyword all / style={background=grayee
                     font_style=italic};
keyword n / style={background=white};
```

Format the values of REGION with the REGFMT. format as in Example 3.5.

```
format gender gendfmt. occupat occupfmt.
       region regfmt.;
run;
```

Terminate sending output to the RTF destination.	`ods rtf close;`
Set the orientation of subsequent output to portrait.	`options orientation=portrait;`
Send subsequent output to the LISTING destination.	`ods listing;`

Example 6.8   Presenting Graphics and Tables in the Same Report

Goal

Describe data visually in graphs and numerically in tables in the same report. Add graphs to the report in Example 3.3. Send the output to a nonlisting destination.

Report

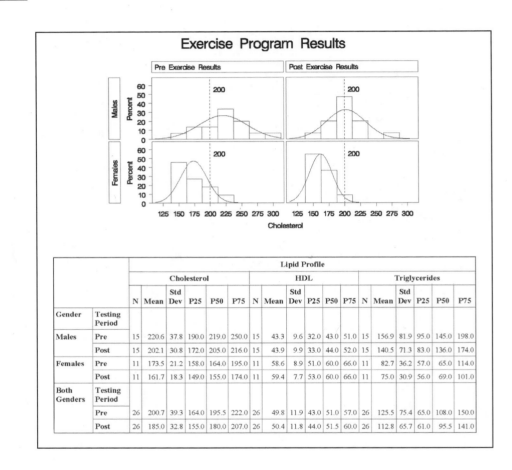

		Lipid Profile															
		Cholesterol					HDL					Triglycerides					
		N	Mean	Std Dev	P25	P50	P75	N	Mean	Std Dev	P25	P50	P75	N	Mean	Std Dev	P25	P50	P75
Gender	Testing Period																	
Males	Pre	15	220.6	37.8	190.0	219.0	250.0	15	43.3	9.6	32.0	43.0	51.0	15	156.9	81.9	95.0	145.0	198.0
	Post	15	202.1	30.8	172.0	205.0	216.0	15	43.9	9.9	33.0	44.0	52.0	15	140.5	71.3	83.0	136.0	174.0
Females	Pre	11	173.5	21.2	158.0	164.0	195.0	11	58.6	8.9	51.0	60.0	66.0	11	82.7	36.2	57.0	65.0	114.0
	Post	11	161.7	18.3	149.0	155.0	174.0	11	59.4	7.7	53.0	60.0	66.0	11	75.0	30.9	56.0	69.0	101.0
Both Genders	Testing Period																	
	Pre	26	200.7	39.3	164.0	195.5	222.0	26	49.8	11.9	43.0	51.0	57.0	26	125.5	75.4	65.0	108.0	150.0
	Post	26	185.0	32.8	155.0	180.0	207.0	26	50.4	11.8	44.0	51.5	60.0	26	112.8	65.7	61.0	95.5	141.0

Example Features

Data Set	LIPIDS
Report Example	Example 3.3
Featured Steps and Statement	PROC UNIVARIATE PROC TABULATE ODS statement

Featured Step Statements and Options	ODS statement: STARTPAGE= option
	
	PROC UNIVARIATE
	    PROC UNIVARIATE statement: NOPRINT option
	    CLASS statement: (ORDER=) option
	    HISTOGRAM statement
	    HISTOGRAM statement: NORMAL(NOPRINT COLOR=), FONT=, HREF=,
	        MIDPOINTS=, and HREFLABELS= options
	ODS STYLE= options placed on these PROC TABULATE statements:
	    CLASS
	    CLASSLEV
	    KEYWORD
	    TABLE, including BOX= option
	    VAR

Output Destination of Example	RTF
🔍 A Closer Look	Summarizing Data in Graphs
Other Examples That Use This Data Set	Examples 2.7, 3.3, 6.4, and 6.9

Example Overview

Example 3.3 statistically summarizes the three lipid measurements in the LIPIDS data set. It presents the descriptive statistics for the categories defined by testing period and for those defined by the combination of testing period and gender.

This example includes histograms of the cholesterol measurements for the categories defined by testing period and gender, as well as the table of statistics. The graphs are placed before the table and are generated by PROC UNIVARIATE.

Style attributes for the background are added to components of the PROC TABULATE table.

The ODS option STARTPAGE=NO causes the table to follow the graphs on the same page. Example 6.13 also uses the STARTPAGE= option on the ODS statement and includes a discussion of its usage.

The RTF file created by this program contains the histograms and the table of statistics. The four histograms are treated as one picture in the RTF file, and the title specified on the TITLE statement is included in the picture, not in the RTF header.

Program

Do not send results to the LISTING destination.	`ods listing close;`
Send subsequent results to the RTF destination and save the results in a file.	`ods rtf file='c:\reports\example33b.rtf'`
Suppress the automatic insertion of new pages at the start of each procedure.	`        startpage=no;`

```
proc format;
```

Define this format with a blank space before the text "Males" so that when the data is ordered by the formatted value, the results for males display before those for females.	`  value $gender 'M'=' Males'` `                'F'='Females';`

```
      value $prepost 'Pre'='Pre Exercise Results'
                     'Post'='Post Exercise Results';
run;

title 'Exercise Program Results';
proc univariate data=lipids
```

Suppress all tables of descriptive statistics.	`              noprint;`
Group the data into categories defined by the value of the two CLASS variables. Order the results for GENDER by its formatted values.	`  class gender (order=formatted)`
Order the results for TESTPERIOD by the order of its values in the data set. This will put the values for the "PRE" testing period ahead of the values for the "POST" testing period, because the first observation in the data set contains data for the "PRE" testing period. If you have reordered the observations in the LIPIDS data set, you might need to modify this option or define a format for testing period that is similar to the $GENDER format, with a blank space preceding the text "Pre Exercise Results".	`          testperiod (order=data);`
Specify the analysis variable.	`  var chol;` `  label chol='Cholesterol';`

Create a histogram for each combination of the CLASS variables and specify characteristics of the graphs.	`histogram /`
Superimpose a normal density curve on each histogram. Suppress the tables that summarize the fitted curves. Specify the color of the normal density curve.	`normal(noprint color=black)`
Specify the font for reference lines and axis labels.	`font=swiss`
Specify the midpoints of the histogram intervals.	`midpoints=125 to 300 by 25`
Display a horizontal reference line at 200 and label the line.	`href=200 hreflabels='200';`

```
      format gender $gender. testperiod $prepost.;
    run;

    proc tabulate data=lipids;
      class gender testperiod / descending
```

Set the background color of the class variable name headings.	`style={background=white};`
Set the background color of the class-level value headings.	`classlev gender testperiod /` `style={background=white};`
Set the background color of the analysis variable name headings.	`var chol hdl tri / style={background=white};`

```
      table (gender='Gender'
          all='Both Genders')*testperiod='Testing
                                        Period',
          all='Lipid Profile'*(chol='Cholesterol'
          hdl='HDL' tri='Triglycerides')*
          (n*f=3. (mean std='Std Dev' p25 p50 p75)*f=5.1)

          / nocontinued
```

Set the background color of the box in the upper left corner of the table.	`box={style={background=white}};`

```
      keyword all n mean std p25 p50 p75
```

Set the background color of the keyword headings.	`/ style={background=white};`

```
      format gender $gender.;
    run;
```

Terminate sending output to the RTF destination.	`ods rtf close;`

Send subsequent output to the LISTING destination.   `ods listing;`

🔍 A Closer Look

Summarizing Data in Graphs

The examples in this book concentrate on producing text-based tables. Some images are included in the text reports in this chapter, but only this example includes a programmatically derived graphical report.

A picture can be invaluable in conveying results. When you combine both pictures and text in a report, you can help your audience better understand your results.

This example applies some of the graphing capabilities of PROC UNIVARIATE. SAS/GRAPH provides the tools and foundation for producing many types of graphical reports. Other SAS products also include procedures that display your data in a graphical format.

While plotting data is beyond the scope of this book, do not ignore this topic. The reference for presenting data graphically is *SAS/GRAPH 9.1 Reference*. SAS Press has several titles related to this topic. See the back of this book for a list of titles related to the features of this example, and visit the SAS Press Web site (support.sas.com/saspress) for current information on new and revised publications.

Several presentations at SUGI conferences show how SAS users have applied SAS graphical procedures. Recent conference proceedings that are available online through the SAS Web site provide a wealth of additional applications and examples to get you started in this form of report writing. You can link to them through the SAS support Web site (support.sas.com).

Example 6.9   Placing Hyperlinks in a Report

Goal

Add hyperlinks to elements of a report so that the reader can access additional information related to the report by selecting a hyperlink.

Report

Exercise Program Results																				
									Lipid Profile											
Exercise and Lipids Study		Cholesterol						HDL						Triglycerides						
		N	Mean	Std Dev	P25	P50	P75	N	Mean	Std Dev	P25	P50	P75	N	Mean	Std Dev	P25	P50	P75
Gender	Testing Period																		
Males	Pre	15	220.6	37.8	190.0	219.0	250.0	15	43.3	9.6	32.0	43.0	51.0	15	156.9	81.9	95.0	145.0	198.0
	Post	15	202.1	30.8	172.0	205.0	216.0	15	43.9	9.9	33.0	44.0	52.0	15	140.5	71.3	83.0	136.0	174.0
Females	Pre	11	173.5	21.2	158.0	164.0	195.0	11	58.6	8.9	51.0	60.0	66.0	11	82.7	36.2	57.0	65.0	114.0
	Post	11	161.7	18.3	149.0	155.0	174.0	11	59.4	7.7	53.0	60.0	66.0	11	75.0	30.9	56.0	69.0	101.0
Both Genders	Testing Period																		
	Pre	26	200.7	39.3	164.0	195.5	222.0	26	49.8	11.9	43.0	51.0	57.0	26	125.5	75.4	65.0	108.0	150.0
	Post	26	185.0	32.8	155.0	180.0	207.0	26	50.4	11.8	44.0	51.5	60.0	26	112.8	65.7	61.0	95.5	141.0

After the reader selects the "Exercise and Lipids Study" hyperlink in the upper left box of the report, the window in Figure 6.9a is presented.

Figure 6.9a The Window Displayed after Selecting the Hyperlink in the Upper Left Box of the Report

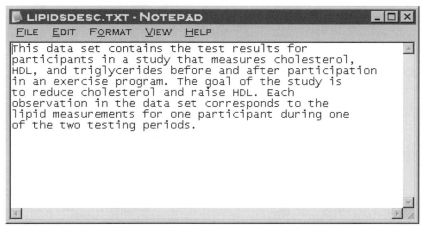

After the reader selects the hyperlink associated with the "Males" class-level heading, the window in Figure 6.9b is presented.

**Figure 6.9b The Window Displayed after Selecting the Hyperlink
Associated with the "Males" Class-Level Heading**

| | MICROSOFT EXCEL · LIPIDS.XLS | | | | | | | |

	A	B	C	D	E	F	G	H
1	**Males**		Pre			Post		
2	Study ID	Chol	HDL	TRI	Chol	HDL	Tri	
3	1005	296	47	129	272	51	116	
4	1006	155	31	145	152	33	136	
5	1007	250	55	149	231	60	141	
6	1008	264	43	55	195	44	47	
7	1013	183	51	182	192	49	170	
8	1014	256	43	100	235	43	83	
9	1015	235	43	151	216	44	141	
10	1016	238	36	198	207	36	174	
11	1017	215	50	68	205	52	59	
12	1018	190	31	252	164	32	249	
13	1019	168	52	95	172	44	90	
14	1020	219	57	78	207	58	63	
15	1021	203	28	301	169	28	232	
16	1022	215	51	325	205	52	285	
17	1023	222	32	125	210	32	122	
18	**Mean**	220.6	43.33333	156.8667	202.1333	43.86667	140.5333	

After the reader selects the hyperlink associated with the "Females" class-level
heading, the window in Figure 6.9c is presented.

**Figure 6.9c The Window Displayed after Selecting the Hyperlink
Associated with the "Females" Class Level Heading**

| | MICROSOFT EXCEL · LIPIDS.XLS | | | | | | | |

	A	B	C	D	E	F	G	H
1	**Females**		Pre			Post		
2	Study ID	Chol	HDL	TRI	Chol	HDL	Tri	
3	1001	156	48	134	150	50	127	
4	1002	151	50	102	139	54	81	
5	1003	165	51	114	149	51	101	
6	1004	158	51	150	143	53	124	
7	1009	187	71	57	174	69	72	
8	1010	161	64	50	155	66	43	
9	1011	164	72	43	149	73	32	
10	1012	160	66	65	168	61	56	
11	1024	196	61	70	186	62	69	
12	1025	216	51	64	171	54	59	
13	1026	195	60	61	195	60	61	
14	**Mean**	173.5455	58.63636	82.72727	161.7273	59.36364	75	

After the reader selects the hyperlink associated with the "Both Genders" summary heading, the window in Figure 6.9d is displayed.

Figure 6.9d The Window Displayed after Selecting the Hyperlink Associated with the "Both Genders" Summary Heading

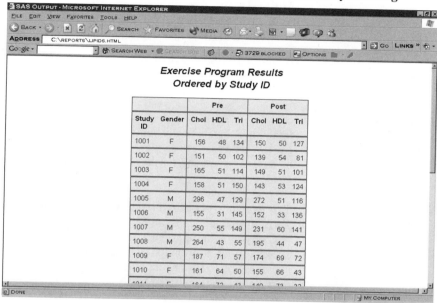

Example Features

Data Set	LIPIDS
Report Example	Example 3.3
Featured Steps and Statement	PROC FORMAT PROC TABULATE ODS statement

Featured Step Statements and Options	ODS statement: ESCAPECHAR= option
	PROC FORMAT
	    Assigning style options that associate hyperlinks to value labels
	Inline formatting
	ODS STYLE= options that associate hyperlinks with text in the report placed on these PROC TABULATE statements:
	    TABLE
	    BOX= option on the TABLE statement

Output Destination of Example	RTF
Related Technique	PROC REPORT

Related Technique Features	PROC REPORT statement ODS option: STYLE(HEADERS)
	CALL DEFINE statement ODS option: URL attribute
	COMPUTE block
	COMPUTE AFTER block
	Inline formatting
	Specifying a heading that spans multiple columns
Other Examples That Use This Data Set	Examples 2.7, 3.3, 6.4, and 6.8

Example Overview

Example 3.3 statistically summarizes the three lipid measurements in the LIPIDS data set. It presents the descriptive statistics for the categories defined by testing period and for those defined by the combination of testing period and gender.

This example produces a report similar to the one produced by the PROC TABULATE step in Example 3.3. It illustrates how you can add hyperlinks to the body of your reports. Hyperlinks can provide your readers with a means to access further information associated with your report. The hyperlinks in this example link to files containing descriptive and detailed information about the data that was summarized.

Four hyperlinks are placed in the body of the report in these locations:

❑ the upper left box of the table

❑ the class-level heading for males

❑ the class-level heading for females

❑ the summary-level heading for both genders

The URL attribute is added to the style formatting instruction in the $GENDER format definition and to the STYLE option in two places on the TABLE statement in the PROC TABULATE step. The value assigned to a URL attribute is the name of the file that opens when the reader selects the hyperlink.

This example specifies links to three kinds of files: a Microsoft Excel workbook, an HTML file, and a text file. The references to the Microsoft Excel workbook point to specific cells in specific sheets in the workbook.

A hyperlink to a Microsoft Excel workbook can be written in one of two ways:

❑ a hyperlink to the workbook (e.g., url='c:\reports\lipids.xls')

❑ a hyperlink to a specific worksheet and cell in the workbook (e.g., url='c:\reports\lipids.xls#Males!A1')

The user-defined format uses ODS inline formatting and relies on the assignment of an ODS escape character before any application of the format. See example 6.12 for a discussion of inline formatting.

Program

Do not send results to the LISTING destination.

```
ods listing close;
```

Specify the character that indicates to ODS that what follows the character are style attributes and formatting instructions. Select a character that you know is not part of a character value in your data.

```
ods escapechar='^';
```

Send subsequent results to the RTF destination and save the results in a file.

```
ods rtf file='c:\reports\example33c.rtf';
```

Associate a hyperlink with each value label. Precede the value label text with a formatting instruction. Start the formatting instruction with the escape character. Indicate that this is a style instruction. Conclude the style instruction with the hyperlink assigned to the URL attribute.

```
proc format;
   value $gender 'M'=
       "^S={url='c:\reports\lipids.xls#Males!A1'}Males"
                 'F'=
   "^S={url='c:\reports\lipids.xls#Females!A1'}Females";

run;
proc tabulate data=lipids;
   title 'Exercise Program Results';
   class gender testperiod / descending
                             style={background=white};
   classlev gender testperiod /
                  style={background=white};
   var chol hdl tri / style={background=white};
   table (gender='Gender'
```

Set the background color of the cells containing the headings for the class variables, the headings for the analysis variables, and the cells containing the class level values.

Associate a hyperlink with the descriptive text assigned to the ALL keyword.

```
all="^S={url='c:\reports\lipids.html'}Both Genders")*
```

```
         testperiod='Testing Period',
         all='Lipid Profile'*
         (chol='Cholesterol' hdl='HDL'
         tri='Triglycerides')*
         (n*f=3.
         (mean std='Std Dev' p25 p50 p75)*f=5.1)
         / box={label='Exercise and Lipids Study'
          style={url='c:\reports\lipidsdesc.txt'
              background=white}}
```

Associate a hyperlink with the descriptive text placed in the upper left corner of the report and set the background color of the box.

Set the background color of the cells containing the headings for the keywords.

```
      nocontinued;
   keyword all n mean std p25 p50 p75
           / style={background=white};

   format gender $gender.;
run;
```

| Terminate sending output to the RTF destination. | `ods rtf close;` |
| Send subsequent output to the LISTING destination. | `ods listing;` |

Related Technique

You can also adapt the related technique in Example 3.3 to include hyperlinks to additional information. The following program uses the same PROC REPORT program with the addition of code that assigns hyperlinks to elements of the report and that formats some elements of the report. Figure 6.9e presents the output from this program.

Figure 6.9e Output from the PROC REPORT Related Technique that Includes Hyperlinks

Exercise Program Results

Exercise and Lipids Study		Cholesterol						HDL					
Gender	Testing Period	N	Mean	Std Dev	P25	P50	P75	N	Mean	Std Dev	P25	P50	P75
Males	Pre	15	220.6	37.8	190.0	219.0	250.0	15	43.3	9.6	32.0	43.0	51.0
	Post	15	202.1	30.8	172.0	205.0	216.0	15	43.9	9.9	33.0	44.0	52.0
Females	Pre	11	173.5	21.2	158.0	164.0	195.0	11	58.6	8.9	51.0	60.0	66.0
	Post	11	161.7	18.3	149.0	155.0	174.0	11	59.4	7.7	53.0	60.0	66.0
View Data for Both Genders													

Exercise and Lipids Study		Triglycerides					
Gender	Testing Period	N	Mean	Std Dev	P25	P50	P75
Males	Pre	15	156.9	81.9	95.0	145.0	198.0
	Post	15	140.5	71.3	83.0	136.0	174.0
Females	Pre	11	82.7	36.2	57.0	65.0	114.0
	Post	11	75.0	30.9	56.0	69.0	101.0
View Data for Both Genders							

Four hyperlinks are placed in the body of the report in these locations:

❑ the upper left box of the table

❑ the class-level heading for males

❑ the class-level heading for females

❑ the summary line below the table

This related technique adds a text string above the GENDER and TESTPERIOD columns and associates a hyperlink with the text string.

The program includes a COMPUTE AFTER block that adds a summary line at the end of the report and associates a hyperlink with this summary text.

Instead of associating hyperlinks with the value labels of the $GENDER format as in the PROC TABULATE step in the preceding program, this program uses a CALL DEFINE statement in a COMPUTE block for the variable GENDER. The CALL DEFINE statement can place hyperlinks in cells of your report. The attribute name provided to the CALL DEFINE statement for this purpose is URL.

The same four windows that were displayed by the hyperlinks in the PROC TABULATE step and shown at the beginning of this example are also displayed when their respective hyperlinks are selected from the report produced by PROC REPORT.

The program that produced the output in Figure 6.9e follows.

Do not send results to the LISTING destination.

```
ods listing close;
```

Specify the character that indicates to ODS that what follows the character are style attributes and formatting instructions. Select a character that you know is not part of a character value in your data.

```
ods escapechar='^';
```

Send subsequent results to the RTF destination and save the results in a file.

```
ods rtf file='c:\reports\example33c.rtf';

proc format;
  value $gender 'M'='Males'
                'F'='Females';
run;

proc report data=lipids nowindows box
            style(headers)={background=white};
```

Set the background color of the headings.

Define a heading that spans the GENDER and TESTPERIOD columns. Associate a hyperlink with the heading. Precede the heading text with a formatting instruction. Start the formatting instruction with the escape character. Indicate that this is a style instruction. Conclude the style instruction with the hyperlink assigned to the URL attribute.

```
  title 'Exercise Program Results';
  column
      ("^S={url='c:\reports\lipidsdesc.txt'}Exercise
        and Lipids Study" gender testperiod)
```

```
                                          chol,(n mean std p25 p50 p75)
                                          hdl,(n mean std p25 p50 p75)
                                          tri,(n mean std p25 p50 p75);

                               define gender / group format=$gender. left id
                                                 descending 'Gender';
                               define testperiod / group left id descending
                                                 'Testing Period';
                               define chol / 'Cholesterol';
                               define hdl / 'HDL';
                               define tri / 'Triglycerides';
                               define n / format=4. 'N';
                               define mean / format=5.1 'Mean';
                               define std / format=5.1 'Std Dev';
                               define p25 / format=5.1 'P25';
                               define p50 / format=5.1 'P50';
                               define p75 / format=5.1 'P75';
```

Define a COMPUTE block for the variable GENDER.

```
                               compute gender;
```

Define a new variable to hold the pathname of the hyperlinked file whose values will be supplied to the CALL DEFINE statement. Specify a different file for each of the two values of GENDER.

```
                                 if gender='M' then
                                       urllink="c:\reports\lipids.xls#Males!A1";
                                 else if gender='F' then
                                       urllink="c:\reports\lipids.xls#Females!A1";
```

Associate a hyperlink with each class-level heading of GENDER.

```
                                   call define('gender','url',urllink);
                               endcomp;
```

Define a COMPUTE block that executes at the end of the report.

```
                               compute after;
```

Place a line of text at the end of the report. Associate a hyperlink with this concluding text.

```
                                 line "^S={url='c:\reports\lipids.html'}View Data for
                                    Both Genders";
                                 endcomp;
                               run;
```

Terminate sending output to the RTF destination.

```
                               ods rtf close;
```

Send subsequent output to the LISTING destination.

```
                               ods listing;
```

Example 6.10   Customizing the Appearance of a Detail Report Created by PROC PRINT

Goal

Customize the appearance of the report produced in the related technique of Example 2.4. Use "traffic lighting" to draw attention to specific results in the report by setting style elements to specific colors. Send the output to a nonlisting destination.

Report

Regional Energy
Quarterly Use by Residential and Commercial Customers

	Service	January	February	March	April	May	June
Commercial	Area Lights	6,526	11,999	17,533	10,221	17,218	8,857
	Flood Lights	10,911	12,648	15,502	9,120	8,624	18,338
	General Service	1,203	641	728	1,039	1,156	782
	Off Peak	15,062	15,635	9,509	11,717	11,456	12,461
	Other Service	1,390	1,672	1,638	1,282	1,654	1,915
	Space Heating	111	85	121	109	125	103
	Water Heating	160	168	130	187	101	101
Commercial		35,363	42,848	45,161	33,675	40,334	42,557
Residential	Area Lights	118	116	91	92	95	137
	Flood Lights	96	89	75	87	75	82
	General Service	22,281	21,505	22,556	22,784	25,977	25,371
	Off Peak	1,152	1,362	698	1,047	534	1,492
	Other Service	286	238	109	33	158	465
	Space Heating	8,280	10,984	10,111	13,234	13,723	11,072
	Water Heating	9,589	10,625	14,160	18,130	8,592	7,654
Residential		41,802	44,919	47,800	55,407	49,154	46,273
		77,165	87,767	92,961	89,082	89,488	88,830

Example Features

Data Set	POWERUSE
Report Example	Related Technique in Example 2.4
Featured Steps	PROC FORMAT PROC PRINT

Featured Step Statements and Options	PROC FORMAT
	  Setting colors as value labels
	ODS STYLE= options placed on these PROC PRINT statements:
	    PROC PRINT statement for components DATA, HEADER, OBS,
	      OBSHEADER, TABLE, and TOTAL
	    ID
	    VAR

Output Destination of Example	HTML
🔍 A Closer Look	Placing STYLE= Options in a PROC PRINT Step
Other Examples That Use This Data Set	Examples 2.4, 2.5, and 2.6

Example Overview

PROC PRINT produced the report in the Related Technique of Example 2.4. It listed the power usage by type, service, and month for the first two quarters of a year and summed power usage by type and overall.

This example sends a PROC PRINT report to a nonlisting destination. It illustrates how to assign attributes to style elements in several locations of the report. Additionally, it sets the background color of the cells of the SERVICE variable based on the values of the variable. It does this by defining a format that associates colors to values. Within the PROC PRINT step, the background attribute of the variable is set to the format name. Formatting in this manner presents a visual way to group similar values of a variable.

Program

```
proc format;
```

Define formats for TYPE and SERVICE as in Example 2.4.

```
   value $type     'res'='Residential'
                   'com'='Commercial';
   value $service  'gen'='General Service'
                   'wtr'='Water Heating'
                   'op' ='Off Peak'
                   'spc'='Space Heating'
                   'fld'='Flood Lights'
                   'area'='Area Lights'
                   'oth'='Other Service';
```

Define a format to group the *formatted* values of SERVICE to colors.

```
   value $colorserv 'Area Lights',
                    'Flood Lights'='grayee'
                    'General Service',
                     Other Service'='graydd'
                    'Off Peak'='graycc'
                    'Space Heating',
                     Water Heating'='graybb';
run;
```

Do not send results to the LISTING destination.	```ods listing close;```
Send subsequent results to the HTML destination and save the results in a file.	```ods html file='c:\reports\example23.html';```

```
title 'Regional Energy';
title2 'Quarterly Use by Residential and Commercial
    Customers';
proc sort data=poweruse out=sorted;
    by type service;
run;
```

Assign style attributes to several locations in the report.	```proc print data=sorted label```
Set the background color of the data cells.	```style(data)={background=white}```
Apply style changes to the column headings. Set the background color and the font.	```style(header)={background=white``` ``` font_face='Times'}```
Set the background color of the OBS column (In this example, that's the same as the ID column).	```style(obs)={background=white}```
Set the background color of the heading for the OBS column.	```style(obsheader)={background=white}```

Apply style changes to the SUM line. Set the background color of the rows and specify the font. Italicize the text.	```style(total)= {background=white```
	``` font_face='Times'```
	``` font_style=italic}```

Apply style changes to the structural part of the PROC PRINT table. Set the color between the lines outlining the cells. Set the color of the borders of the table.	```style(table)={background=black``` ``` bordercolor=black};```

Apply style changes to the ID column, which in this example is the same as the OBS column. Set the font and italicize the text.	```id type / style={font_face='Times'```
	``` font_style=italic};```
	```by type;```

Apply style changes to the SERVICE column. Set the background color of the cells according to the formatted values of SERVICE. Italicize the text, write the text in bold, and set the font.	```var service / style={background=$colorserv.```
	``` font_style=italic```
	``` font_weight=bold```
	``` font_face='Times'};```

	```var jan feb mar apr may jun;``` ```sum jan feb mar apr may jun;```

```
                    label type='00'x
                          service='Service'
                          jan='January'
                          feb='February'
                          mar='March'
                          apr='April'
                          may='May'
                          jun='June';
```

Format the variables as in
Example 2.4.

```
          format type $type. service $service.
                 jan--jun comma6.;
      run;
```

Terminate sending output to the
HTML destination.

```
      ods html close;
```

Send subsequent output to the
LISTING destination.

```
      ods listing;
```

 **A Closer Look**

Placing STYLE= Options in a PROC PRINT Step

When you send your PROC PRINT report to a nonlisting destination, you can
take advantage of the formatting capabilities of the destination by customizing
style elements in the report. You can do this either by using the STYLE= option
in PROC PRINT or by defining a style and referencing it on the ODS
destination statement.

Modifying style attributes in a PROC PRINT step makes changes only to the
report in which the modifications are applied. If you want to modify the output
the same way repeatedly, you might find it more efficient to define and save a
style rather than to code the same style attributes every time you execute a
report. Examples 6.12, 6.14 and 6.15 define styles and table definitions for that
purpose.

The remainder of this section discusses how to use the STYLE= option in PROC
PRINT. The syntax of the STYLE= option is

```
      STYLE<(location(s))>=<style-element-name>
           <[style-attribute-specification(s)]
```

You can add the STYLE= option to the following PROC PRINT statements:

❑ PROC PRINT

❑ ID

❑ SUM

❑ VAR

A PROC PRINT report can be divided into components whose style attributes
can be modified. You can add options to the PROC PRINT statement to modify
style attributes in several report locations, as listed in Table 6.10.

Table 6.10 Locations That Can Be Modified in a PROC PRINT Report Using STYLE= Options

Location	Report Location Modified	Can also be specified for individual items on this statement
BYLABEL	The label for the BY variable on the line containing the SUM totals	None
DATA	The data cells for all columns	ID SUM VAR
GRANDTOTAL	The SUM line containing the grand totals for the whole report	SUM
HEADER	All column headings	ID SUM VAR
N	N= line	None
OBS	The data in the OBS column	None
OBSHEADER	The header of the OBS column	None
TABLE	The structural part of the report (e.g. border widths, space between cells)	None
TOTAL	The SUM line containing totals for each BY group	SUM

The PROC PRINT, ID, SUM, and VAR statements each have default locations. For the PROC PRINT, ID, and VAR statements, the default locations are DATA and HEADER. For the SUM statement, the default locations are DATA, HEADER, and TOTAL.

For example, if you omit the location on a STYLE= option placed on a VAR statement and specify an attribute for the style element "font_style," both the data cells and headings for the variables on the VAR statement are modified according to the attribute assigned to "font_style."

The preceding example sets attributes for style elements on the PROC PRINT statement for the following report locations: DATA, HEADER, OBS, OBSHEADER, TABLE, and TOTAL. It also sets attributes on the ID and VAR statements. The ID TYPE statement causes TYPE to become the OBS column. Therefore, you can assign attributes for TYPE either in the ID statement or on the PROC PRINT statement STYLE= options for the locations OBS and OBSHEADER.

Example 6.11   Customizing a Multipanel Report Created by PROC REPORT

Goal

Revise the program in Example 5.1 that lists the observations in a data set in side-by-side panels so that it can be sent to a nonlisting destination using ODS.

Report

Parts Listing as of November 15, 2005

Part Number	In Stock	Price	Part Number	In Stock	Price	Part Number	In Stock	Price
B01-03/0	100	$5.75	B33-04/1	8	$7.70	B65-06/1	52	$7.20
B02-03/0	100	$6.60	B34-04/1	14	$8.80	B66-06/1	43	$7.45
B03-03/1	79	$7.25	B35-04/1	19	$9.05	B67-06/1	66	$7.95
B04-03/1	37	$7.80	B36-04/1	17	$9.60	B68-06/1	69	$8.05
B05-03/1	3	$8.40	B37-04/2	33	$8.80			
B06-03/1	15	$7.95	B38-04/2	51	$11.20			
B07-03/2	97	$8.80	B39-04/2	50	$5.25			
B08-03/2	24	$4.25	B40-04/3	47	$5.50			
B09-03/3	18	$7.40	B41-05/0	97	$11.80			
B10-03/0	92	$7.10	B42-05/0	13	$6.40			
B11-03/0	12	$7.20	B43-05/1	17	$6.60			
B12-03/1	9	$7.70	B44-05/1	15	$6.80			
B13-03/1	2	$8.00	B45-05/1	2	$7.70			
B14-03/1	37	$8.80	B46-05/1	4	$6.60			
B15-03/1	22	$9.05	B47-05/1	77	$7.95			
B16-03/2	15	$9.20	B48-05/2	11	$7.20			
B17-03/2	50	$5.75	B49-05/2	81	$8.80			
B18-03/3	50	$8.00	B50-05/2	50	$4.15			
B19-04/0	100	$10.10	B51-05/3	31	$4.60			
B20-04/0	33	$5.90	B52-05/0	100	$13.75			
B21-04/1	41	$6.40	B53-05/0	23	$7.05			
B22-04/1	7	$6.80	B54-05/1	59	$7.10			
B23-04/1	11	$7.50	B55-05/1	87	$7.70			
B24-04/1	17	$6.95	B56-05/1	22	$7.95			
B25-04/1	26	$7.95	B57-05/1	83	$8.15			
B26-04/2	31	$7.20	B58-05/1	16	$8.45			
B27-04/2	99	$9.60	B59-05/2	18	$8.90			
B28-04/2	50	$3.95	B60-05/2	29	$10.40			
B29-04/3	42	$4.60	B61-05/2	50	$4.85			
B30-04/0	87	$11.60	B62-05/3	31	$5.25			
B31-04/0	31	$6.70	B63-06/0	100	$12.20			
B32-04/1	11	$7.10	B64-06/0	100	$7.00			

Example Features

Data Set	INVENTORY
Report Example	Example 5.1
Featured Step and Statement	PROC REPORT ODS statement
Featured Step Statements and Options	ODS statement: COLUMNS= option (SAS 9 only) PROC REPORT statement ODS option: STYLE(COLUMN)
Additional Features	Macro language functions
Output Destination of Example	RTF
Other Examples That Use This Data Set	Example 5.1

Example Overview

Example 5.1 created a multipanel report by using the PANELS= option of PROC REPORT. This option is available only when sending the report to the LISTING destination.

A way to create a similar multipanel report that can be sent to a nonlisting destination is to remove the PANELS= option from PROC REPORT and add the COLUMNS= option to the ODS statement that specifies the destination of the report. This example creates a multipanel report of the INVENTORY data set by specifying the COLUMNS= option on the ODS statement.

Example 5.1 set the PANELS= option to 99. This tells PROC REPORT to fit as many panels per page as possible. The COLUMNS= option requires that you specify exactly the number of panels to place per page. You might need to experiment with different values for COLUMNS= to determine the best layout of your report.

The COLUMNS= option does not work when sending output to the LISTING destination. Adding it to the ODS LISTING statement generates an error.

Program

```
options pageno=1;
```

Do not send results to the LISTING destination.

```
ods listing close;
```

Send subsequent results to the RTF destination and save the results in a file.

```
ods rtf file='c:\reports\example51.rtf'
```

Specify the number of columns per page.

```
columns=3;
```

```
proc report data=inventory nowindows box
```

Specify the font size of all column cells.

```
                              style(column)={font_size=12pt};
```

Place the current date in the title.

```
   title "Parts Listing as of
          %sysfunc(date(),worddate.)";

   column partnmbr quantity price;

   define partnmbr / 'Part Number';
   define quantity / format=3. 'In Stock';
   define price    / format=dollar6.2 'Price';

run;
```

Terminate sending output to the RTF destination.

```
ods rtf close;
```

Send subsequent output to the LISTING destination.

```
ods listing;
```

Example 6.12   Customizing the Appearance of a Report Produced by a DATA Step

Goal

Customize the appearance of the report produced in Example 4.2 by modifying style attributes with ODS. Send the output to a nonlisting destination.

Report

Client
Protocol
Population

Table 2.14

Baseline Demographics

	Active	Placebo
Number of Patients	94	106
Gender		
Male	41 (21%)	46 (23%)
Female	53 (27%)	60 (30%)
Age (years)		
Mean (SEM)	52.1 (1.96)	53.9 (1.74)
25th - 75th	33.7 - 67.3	37.7 - 69.1
Min - Max	21.0 - 84.7	20.5 - 84.8
No. Missing	0	0
Race		
Non-White	37 (19%)	33 (17%)
White	57 (29%)	73 (37%)
Height (inches)		
Mean (SEM)	65.4 (0.54)	65.4 (0.54)
25th - 75th	61.5 - 69.9	60.5 - 70.0
Min - Max	55.3 - 74.8	55.2 - 74.7
No. Missing	0	0
Weight (lbs)		
Mean (SEM)	188.2 (5.07)	191.1 (4.43)
25th - 75th	140.9 - 225.8	159.2 - 223.7
Min - Max	110.5 - 275.6	110.4 - 277.0
No. Missing	0	0

Example Features

Data Set	DEMOG
Report Example	Example 4.2
Preparatory Steps	PROC FREQ PROC MEANS PROC SORT PROC TRANSPOSE DATA steps
Featured Steps and Statement	PROC TEMPLATE DATA step ODS statement
Featured Step Statements and Options	PROC TEMPLATE statements: 　DEFINE COLUMN 　DEFINE HEADER 　DEFINE TABLE 　STYLE= 　COLUMN 　HEADER= 　TEXT DATA step: FILE PRINT ODS statement ODS ESCAPECHAR= Inline formatting
Additional Features	DATA step programming
Output Destination of Example	RTF
🔍 A Closer Look	Comparing DATA Steps That Send and Do Not Send Output to ODS Learning More about ODS Inline Formatting
Other Examples That Use This Data Set	Example 4.2

Example Overview

The report in Example 4.2 presents statistics in a customized format that cannot be produced easily by a SAS procedure. The program in Example 4.2 uses a DATA step to write the summary statistics produced by PROC FREQ and PROC MEANS, which were saved in several output data sets.

Example 4.2 is a tabular summary report. It has titles and three columns. The first column lists the demographic categories. The second and third columns contain the statistics for the two groups, "Active" and "Placebo," for each of the categories.

The report in this example takes advantage of the tabular structure of the Example 4.2 report and adds ODS features to the program to send the report to a nonlisting destination.

This program uses the same summary statistics data sets that PROC FREQ and PROC MEANS created in Example 4.2. Rather than processing the data sets in the DATA step as in Example 4.2, this program combines the summary statistic data sets into one data set. It sorts and restructures the observations in this new data set to fit the three-column format of the report. The primary purpose of the DATA _NULL_ step in this example is to send the three-column report to the output destination. The DATA step does minimal processing of the observations.

The FILE statement in the DATA step directs SAS to use a table definition to construct the report. A PROC TEMPLATE step before the DATA step creates the table definition. This table definition is saved in a template store and can be reused. The table definition defines three columns and some of the style attributes of these columns. The PROC TEMPLATE step also defines some of the style attributes of the headers in the table.

The FILE statement and the PUT statements in the DATA step communicate instructions to ODS. The FILE statement includes options that are specific to sending data to an ODS destination. The PUT statements write to the columns of the report and have a different syntax than in Example 4.2.

Specific formatting instructions for the titles and demographic categories are embedded in text strings. Instructions are preceded by a symbol defined with the ODS ESCAPECHAR= statement. This symbol followed by an "S" triggers ODS to intrepret the information that follows as instructions to set style attributes for the text that follows.

Program

```
/* Execute the PROC FORMAT, PROC FREQ, and PROC MEANS */
/* steps in Example 4.2 before executing the following*/
```

Concatenate the summary statistics data sets in the order they will be presented in the report.

```
data all;
```

Create variables that indicate the origin of the current observation.

```
set t1(in=in1) t2(in=in2) t3(in=in3) t4(in=in4)
    t5(in=in5) t6(in=in6);
```

Define two character variables to hold the results and categories.

```
length text $ 25 factor $ 50;
```

Define SECTION to track the demographic category. Define ROW to track placement within the section. Place the category text in the variable FACTOR. Save the formatted statistics results in the variable TEXT. Define the contents of section 1, the counts by treatment group.

```
if in1 then do;
  section=1;
  row=1;
  factor='Number of Patients';
  text=put(count,4.);
  output;
end;
```

Define the contents of section 2, the counts by gender and treatment group.

```
else if in2 then do;
  section=2;
  if gender=0 then do;
    row=1;
    factor='Male';
```

```
                              end;
                            else if gender=1 then do;
                              row=2;
                              factor='Female';
                            end;
                            text=catx(' ', put(count,4.),
                                 cats('(',put(percent,3.),'%',')'));
                            output;
                          end;
```

Define the contents of section 4, the counts by race and gender.

```
                          else if in4 then do;
                            section=4;
                            if race=0 then do;
                              row=1;
                              factor='Non-White';
                            end;
                            else if race=1 then do;
                              row=2;
                              factor='White';
                            end;
                            text=catx(' ', put(count,4.),
                                 cats('(',put(percent,3.),'%',')'));
                            output;
                          end;
```

Define the contents of sections 3, 5, and 6, the statistics for age, height, and weight by treatment group.

```
                          else if in3 or in5 or in6 then do;
                            if in3 then section=3;
                            else if in5 then section=5;
                            else if in6 then section=6;
```

Specify the label and contents for the row with the means and standard errors.

```
                            factor='Mean (SEM)';
                            text=catx(' ', put(mean,5.1),
                                 cats('(',put(stderr,5.2),')'));
                            row=1;
                            output;
```

Specify the label and contents for the row with the interquartile range.

```
                            factor='25th - 75th';
                            text=catx(' ',put(q1,5.1),'-',put(q3,5.1));
                            row=2;
                            output;
```

Specify the label and contents for the row with the range.

```
                            factor='Min - Max';
                            text=catx(' ',put(min,5.1),'-',put(max,5.1));
                            row=3;
                            output;
```

Specify the label and contents for the row with the number of missing values.

```
                            factor='No. Missing';
                            text=put(nmiss,2.);
                            row=4;
                            output;
                          end;
                        run;
```

Arrange the observations in the order they should appear in the report.

```
                     proc sort data=all;
                       by section row factor;
                     run;
```

Type   Col1   Col 2

Reshape the ALL data set so that each observation in ALL2 now corresponds to a row in the report. Keep FACTOR with the transposed observation by including it on the BY statement.

```
                     proc transpose data=all out=all2;
                       by section row factor;
```

Create a variable for each treatment group and assign the name of each variable the corresponding value of TMTDG, which is ACTIVE or PLACEBO.	`id tmtdg;`
Assign the values of TEXT to the corresponding variable ACTIVE or PLACEBO.	`var text;` `run;`
Specify the character that indicates to ODS that what follows the character are style attributes and formatting instructions. Select a character that you know will not be part of a character value in your data.	`ods escapechar='^';`

Define titles and format them. Change the default style of italic to roman by setting the style with the escape character and S= specification.	`title  justify=right '^S={font_style=roman}Client';`
	`title2 justify=right '^S={font_style=roman}Protocol';`
	`title3 justify=right '^S={font_style=roman}Population';`
	`title5 '^S={font_style=roman}Table 2.14';`
	`title7 '^S={font_style=roman}Baseline Demographics';`

Define style attributes of components of the report and define the layout of the report. Save this in the SASUSER library. This step has to be executed only once because the information is permanently saved in the SASUSER library.	`proc template;`
Define and save a heading that will be used in rendering the ACTIVE and PLACEBO columns of the report.	`define header sasuser.statscol;`
Do not specify a background color of the header.	`  style={background=_undef_};` `end;`
Define a table definition that will be used in rendering the report.	`define table sasuser.demog;`
Remove rules and the frame from the table layout.	`  style={rules=none frame=void};`
Specify three columns in the table that will later be associated with the variables in the analysis data set.	`column a b c;`
Specify characteristics of column a.	`define column a;`

Specify the characteristics of the heading for column a. Do not specify a background color and suppress the column heading.

```
      define header notext;
         style={background=_undef_};
         text ' ';
      end;
```

Specify the heading definition for column a, which is the heading defined previous to this statement.

```
      header=notext;
   end;
```

Specify characteristics of column b.

```
   define column b;
```

Center the contents of column b.

```
      just=center;
```

Specify the header definition for column b, which is defined above.

```
      header=sasuser.statscol;
   end;
```

Specify the characteristics of column c.

```
   define column c;
```

Center the contents of column c.

```
      just=center;
```

Specify the header definition for column c, which is defined above.

```
      header=sasuser.statscol;
    end;
  end;
run;
```

Do not send results to the LISTING destination.

```
ods listing close;
```

Send subsequent results to the RTF destination and save the results in a file.

```
ods rtf file='c:\reports\example42.rtf';
```

```
data _null_;
  set all2;
```

Send the report to the ODS destination. Lay out the report according to the template SASUSER.DEMOG.

```
  file print ods=(template='sasuser.demog'
```

Specify the correspondence between the columns in the SASUSER.DEMOG table definition and the variables in the analysis data set.

```
                 columns=(a=factor b=active
                          c=placebo));
```

Add formatting features at the beginning of each demographic section.

```
  if row=1 then do;
```

Write the value of FACTOR ("Number of Patients") in the first section in bold.

```
    if section=1 then
       factor=cats("^S={font_weight=bold}" ,factor);
    else if section=2 then
```

Skip a line between sections.

```
       put /
```

Write specific text in bold in the cell corresponding to the first column and first row in each of the sections two through six.

```
         @1 "^S={font_weight=bold}Gender";
   else if section=3 then
      put / @1 '^S={font_weight=bold}Age (years)';
   else if section=4 then
      put / @1 '^S={font_weight=bold}Race';
   else if section=5 then
      put / @1 '^S={font_weight=bold}Height (inches)';
   else if section=6 then
      put / @1 '^S={font_weight=bold}Weight (lbs)';
   end;
```

Write the observation's data to the report using the template specified on the FILE PRINT statement. Place the values of FACTOR in column 1, the values of ACTIVE in column 2, and the values of PLACEBO in column 3. These associations were made above in the FILE PRINT statement.

```
  put _ods_;
run;
```

Terminate sending output to the RTF destination.

```
ods rtf close;
```

Send subsequent output to the LISTING destination.

```
ods listing;
```

 **A Closer Look**

Comparing DATA Steps That Send and Do Not Send Output to ODS
The DATA step in this program uses FILE and PUT statements to create the report. Example 4.2 also uses FILE and PUT statements to create its report. However, the syntax of these two statements in Example 4.2 is different from that in this example.

The program in Example 4.2 directs the placement of information on the page by computing and designating column and row positions. The PUT statement uses line control pointers and column control pointers to move a pointer to a specific byte location on a page.

The column pointers in this example's program, however, do not explicitly direct output to a column character location. The direction is instead to an *entire* column. "Column" means something different when using ODS in the DATA step:

❑ When you specify FILE PRINT, an "@3" moves the line pointer to byte location 3.

❑ When you specify FILE PRINT ODS, an "@3" moves the line pointer to what ODS considers the third column of data in the tabular layout of the report.

The FILE statement with the ODS option and ODS suboptions controls different features than the FILE PRINT statement does. It tells SAS to bind the data component of your report to a table definition (template). In this example, this results in an RTF report whose basic structure is controlled by the SASUSER.DEMOG table definition.

The suboptions on the FILE PRINT ODS statement specify the table definition, and they associate variable names in the data set to columns in the table definition.

Since the likely reason you're using ODS in a DATA step is because you need to prepare a highly formatted report, it would not be sensible to point to specific column and row locations as in Example 4.2. The software that manages your output destination would do a better job at positioning your data. For example, when you use a proportional font such as Times Roman, characters have different widths. Directing output to a specific byte location would cause strange looking results, with some characters surrounded by excess space and others running into other characters. The output in the "A Closer Look" section of Example 6.2 illustrates what happens when you try to explicitly position data when using a proportional font.

Learning More about ODS Inline Formatting

This example shows how you can insert formatting instructions within text strings. These instructions temporarily override existing instructions that are provided by the template.

To use ODS inline formatting, first submit the ODS ESCAPECHAR= statement to define an escape character that SAS will interpret as a trigger for inline formatting. Be sure that the character you pick will not be in your text. This example specified the caret (^).

Once the escape character has been defined, you can insert formatting instructions in your report. Following the escape character is the type of instruction, an equal sign, and the instructions enclosed in brackets. This example specified style-type instructions, and style is represented as "S." The instructions remain in effect until the end of the text string, unless another instruction is encountered in the same text string.

If you want to revert to the original style of the text string after applying an inline formatting instruction, you can terminate the instruction as shown in the following TITLE statement. The text "Baseline Demographics" is printed with font size of 22 pt, whereas the remaining text in the title is printed in the font size that was in effect before the 22 pt attribute specification.

```
title '^S={font_size=22pt}Baseline Demographics^S={}
        (collected at initial visit)';
```

The syntax of the style attribute specifications is similar to that for style attributes in table definitions, PROC PRINT, PROC REPORT, and PROC TABULATE. For further examples of specifying style attributes, look at the other examples in this chapter, all of which use one of these four processes. For more detailed information, see *SAS 9.1 Output Delivery System: User's Guide* and *Base SAS 9.1 Procedures Guide* (support.sas.com/v9doc).

There are additional instruction types that can be specified to do actions such as starting new lines, wrapping lines, and so on. Please refer to the SAS online documentation for this information (support.sas.com/v9doc).

Example 6.13 Condensing a Multipage, Multitable Report to One Page and Customizing the Output

Goal

Send the report produced in Example 3.10, which consists of several tables produced by separate procedure steps, to a nonlisting destination. Keep all the tables on one page and customize the output by adding ODS style attributes to the PROC TABULATE step.

Report

Customer Survey Results: 120 Respondents

Factors Influencing the Decision to Buy	Count	Percent
Cost	87	72.5%
Performance	62	51.6%
Reliability	30	25.0%
Sales Staff	120	100.0%

Source of Company Name	Count	Percent
TV/Radio	92	76.6%
Internet	69	57.5%
Word of Mouth	26	21.6%

Visits Resulting in Sales	Total Visits	Average Visits Per Customer
Website	279	2.3
Store	327	2.7

Example Features

Data Set	CUSTRESP
Report Example	Example 3.10
Featured Step and Statement	PROC TABULATE ODS statement

Featured Step Statements and Options	ODS statement: STARTPAGE= option ODS STYLE= options placed on the BOX= option on the PROC TABULATE TABLE statement
Additional Features	Macro programming SAS file input/output functions
Output Destination of Example	RTF
🔍 **A Closer Look**	Adding Titles When Using ODS STARTPAGE=NO
Other Examples That Use This Data Set	Examples 3.10 and 6.13

Example Overview

The three tables in this report show a survey of customers of a business where products can be purchased either in a store or online. The report in Example 3.10 on which this example is based shows the three tables on one page. A separate PROC TABULATE step produced each of the tables.

Since the tables were small, it made sense to combine them on one page. The program in Example 3.10 suppressed the automatic page break between each procedure by setting the SAS option FORMDLIM to a single blank character. This option controls only output sent to the LISTING destination.

This example's report is similar to the one in Example 3.10. The text of the titles placed above each table in Example 3.10 is now found in each of the boxes of the PROC TABULATE report. Since the goal is to send the report to a non-listing destination, the FORMDLIM option cannot be used to suppress the automatic page break between the output from each PROC TABULATE step. This example instead suppresses page breaks between the steps by using the ODS statement option STARTPAGE=NO.

Note that the STARTPAGE= option does not apply to the HTML destination.

This example also adds style attributes to the text in the upper left box of each table. It sets the font size and the cell width of the box. Setting the cell width of the box also applies the same width to the rest of the cells in the column below the box.

Program

Do not send results to the LISTING destination.

```
ods listing close;
```

Send subsequent results to the RTF destination and save the results in a file.

```
ods rtf file='c:\reports\example310.rtf'
```

Suppress the automatic insertion of new pages at the start of each procedure.

```
    startpage=no;
```

```
proc format;
  picture pctfmt (default=7) low-high='009.9%';
run;
```

```
%let dsid=%sysfunc(open(work.custresp,i));
%let nresps=%sysfunc(attrn(&dsid,nlobs));
%let rc=close(&dsid);

title "Customer Survey Results: &nresps Respondents";

proc tabulate data=custresp;
  var factor1-factor4 customer;
  table factor1='Cost'
        factor2='Performance'
        factor3='Reliability'
        factor4='Sales Staff',
        (n='Count'*f=7.
         pctn<customer>='Percent'*f=pctfmt.)
```

Place the TITLE3 text from the first step in Example 3.10 in the box of the table.

Modify attributes of the text in the box. Set the font size and the width of the box cell, which also sets the rest of the cells in the column to the same width.

```
    / box={label='Factors Influencing the Decision to
                  Buy'


             style={font_size=12pt cellwidth=2in}} ;
run;


proc tabulate data=custresp;
  var source1-source3 customer;
  table source1='TV/Radio'
        source2='Internet'
        source3='Word of Mouth',
        (n='Count'*f=7.
         pctn<customer>='Percent'*f=pctfmt.)

    / box={label='Source of Company Name'
```

Place the TITLE3 text from the second step in Example 3.10 in the box of the table.

Modify attributes of the text in the box. Set the font size and the width of the box cell, which also sets the rest of the cells in the column to the same width.

```
             style={font_size=12pt cellwidth=2in}};
run;


proc tabulate data=custresp;
  var website store;
  table website='Website'
        store='Store',
        (sum='Total Visits'*f=7.
         mean='Average Visits Per Customer'*f=8.1)

    / box={label='Visits Resulting in Sales'
```

Place the TITLE3 text from the second step in Example 3.10 in the box of the table.

Modify style attributes of the text in the box. Set the font size and the width of the box cell, which also sets the rest of the cells in the column to the same width.

```
             style={font_size=12pt cellwidth=2in}};
run;
```

Terminate sending output to the RTF destination.

```
ods rtf close;
```

Send subsequent output to the LISTING destination.

```
ods listing;
```

🔍 A Closer Look

Adding Titles When Using ODS STARTPAGE=NO

When you set the ODS statement option STARTPAGE=NO, your report contains only the first set of titles and footnotes and suppresses the rest until the ODS destination is closed or the option value is changed.

The program in Example 3.10 defined a title for each of the PROC TABULATE steps. SAS would ignore the TITLE statements for the second and third steps if you kept them in this example. Therefore, to send such a report to a nonlisting destination, a way to include the specific table title text must be found. This example shows an easy way to accomplish this by using the BOX= option of PROC TABULATE.

Here are three other ways of including title text in such a situation:

❑ Define a table definition for each table with PROC TEMPLATE and put the TITLE on the TEXT statement that's specific to the table.

❑ Add the PRETEXT= style attribute to the STYLE= option on the TABLE statement. For this application, this method can be cumbersome. The text specified as PRETEXT is formatted with the document font, which by default does not look like a title. If you change the document font, then the contents of parts of your table also change, unless you specify additional style attributes for your table. Further, SAS 9.1 does not allow inline formatting of the PRETEXT= text with the ODS ESCAPECHAR= technique.

❑ Add the TEXT= option to an ODS statement preceding each table and apply inline formatting with the ODS ESCAPECHAR= to the text. The default spacing between the text and table, however, is not optimal, and further customization may be required.

Example 6.14   Defining a Reusable Generic Style

Goal

Define a style that will be used repeatedly. Apply this style to a report. Add additional style attributes specific to this report. Send the report to a nonlisting destination.

Report

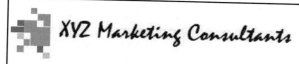

XYZ Marketing Consultants

Customer Survey Results for *Great Electronics Everyday*
120 Respondents

Factors Influencing the Decision to Buy	Count	Percent
Cost	87	72.5%
Performance	62	51.6%
Reliability	30	25.0%
Sales Staff	120	100.0%

Source of Company Name	Count	Percent
TV/Radio	92	76.6%
Internet	69	57.5%
Word of Mouth	26	21.6%

Visits Resulting in Sales	Total Visits	Average Visits Per Customer
Website	279	2.3
Store	327	2.7

Report Prepared February 3, 2005
83872 West Lake Road Townville, CA 99999
http://www.xyzmarketingconsultants.com   (999)555-5555

Example Features

Data Set	CUSTRESP
Report Example	Examples 3.10 and 6.13
Featured Steps and Statement	PROC TEMPLATE PROC TABULATE ODS statement
Featured Step Statements and Options	PROC TEMPLATE DEFINE STYLE, PARENT=, REPLACE, and STYLE statements Inline formatting ODS statement: ESCAPECHAR=, STARTPAGE=, and STYLE= options ODS STYLE= options placed on the PROC TABULATE TABLE statement, including the BOX= option
Additional Features	Macro programming SAS file input/output functions
Output Destination of Example	RTF
A Closer Look	Learning More about ODS Styles
Other Examples That Use This Data Set	Examples 3.10 and 6.13

Example Overview

The three tables in this report present a survey of the customers of a business where products can be purchased either in a store or online. The report presents the three tables on one page, and a separate PROC TABULATE step produces each of the tables. This report is similar to those in Examples 3.10 and 6.13.

As in Example 6.13, this report is also sent to a nonlisting destination. It sets the ODS statement option STARTPAGE=NO to keep all the tables on one page.

This example modifies the report presented in Example 6.13 by applying a style defined by PROC TEMPLATE, by applying inline formatting with ODS ESCAPECHAR=, and by setting specific style attributes on the TABLE statement in each of the PROC TABULATE steps.

One of the goals of this example is to define a style that can be reused by other programs when you want to render the output from those programs the same way. This program starts by defining a style with PROC TEMPLATE that controls the major aspects of a report. It includes setting attributes for the title font, footnote font, margins, and rule lines in the tables.

The program also adds information to the title and footnote statements through simple macro programming statements.

Program

	```proc template;```
Define a style and designate its storage location.	```define style marketing / store=sasuser.templat;```
Inherit all the styles from STYLES.PRINTER.	```parent=styles.printer;```
Modify several of the font settings defined in STYLES.PRINTER. Change TitleFont2, TitleFont, headingFont, and docFont. Keep the settings for the rest the same as in STYLES.PRINTER.	```replace fonts```

```
        / 'TitleFont2' = ("Times Roman",12pt,Bold)
          'TitleFont' = ("Times Roman",14pt,Bold)
          'StrongFont' = ("Times Roman",10pt,Bold)
          'EmphasisFont' = ("Times Roman",10pt,Italic)
          'FixedEmphasisFont' = ("Courier",9pt,Italic)
          'FixedStrongFont' = ("Courier",9pt,Bold)
          'FixedHeadingFont' = ("Courier",9pt,Bold)
          'BatchFixedFont' = ("SAS Monospace,
                              Courier",6.7pt)
          'FixedFont' = ("Courier",9pt)
          'headingEmphasisFont' = ("Times Roman",
                                   11pt,Bold Italic)
          'headingFont' = ("Times Roman",12pt,Bold)
          'docFont' = ("Times Roman",12pt);
```

Modify the background color of the headers (bgH). Keep the other colors the same as in STYLES.PRINTER.	```replace color_list```

```
        / "Change background to undefined"
          'link' = blue
          'bgH' = _undef_
          'fg' = black
          'bg' = _undef_;
```

Change all margin settings of the document.	```replace Body from Document```

```
            "Change margins"
        / bottommargin = 1in
          topmargin = 1in
          rightmargin = 1in
          leftmargin = 1in;
```

Assign a different font to the footer than the TitleFont used in STYLES.PRINTER.	```style SystemFooter from TitlesAndFooters```

```
            "Controls system title text."
        / font = Fonts('EmphasisFont');
```

Place only row rules in the tables.	```style table from table```

```
        / rules=rows;
    end;
run;
```

Suppress the date and page number.	```options nodate nonumber;```
Do not send results to the LISTING destination.	```ods listing close;```
Send subsequent results to the RTF destination and save the results in a file.	```ods rtf file='c:\reports\example310b.rtf'```
Apply a style to the RTF output.	```style=marketing```

Suppress the automatic insertion of new pages at the start of each procedure.

```
                        startpage=no;
proc format;
  picture pctfmt (default=7) low-high='009.9%';
run;

%let dsid=%sysfunc(open(work.custresp,i));
%let nresps=%sysfunc(attrn(&dsid,nlobs));
%let rc=close(&dsid);
```

Define a macro variable whose value will be inserted in the title.

```
%let companyname=Great Electronics Everyday;
```

Define a macro variable that equals the formatted value of today's date.

```
%let today=%sysfunc(date(),worddate.);
```

Specify the character that indicates to ODS that what follows the character are style attributes and formatting instructions. Select a character that you know will not be a character value in your data.

```
ods escapechar='^';
```

Insert an image in the first title line.

```
title '^S={preimage="c:\reports\xyz.jpg"}';

title2 "Customer Survey Results for
```

Italicize the value of the macro variable COMPANYNAME.

```
        ^S={font_style=italic}&companyname";

title3 "&nresps Respondents";
```

Insert today's date in the first footnote line.

```
footnote "Report Prepared &today";
footnote2 "83872 West Lake Road  Townville, CA  99999";
footnote3 "www.xyzmarketingconsultants.com
           (999)555-5555";

proc tabulate data=custresp;
  var factor1-factor4 customer;
  table factor1='Cost'
        factor2='Performance'
        factor3='Reliability'
        factor4='Sales Staff',
        (n='Count'*f=7.
        pctn<customer>='Percent'*f=pctfmt.)
      / box={label='Factors Influencing the Decision
              to Buy'
            style={font_size=12pt cellwidth=2in}};
  run;

proc tabulate data=custresp;
  var source1-source3 customer;
  table source1='TV/Radio'
        source2='Internet'
        source3='Word of Mouth',
        (n='Count'*f=7.
        pctn<customer>='Percent'*f=pctfmt.)
      / box={label='Source of Company Name'
            style={font_size=12pt cellwidth=2in}};
  run;
```

```
proc tabulate data=custresp;
  var website store;
  table website='Website'
        store='Store',
        (sum='Total Visits'*f=7.
        mean='Average Visits Per Customer'*f=8.1)
      / box={label='Visits Resulting in Sales'
        style={font_size=12pt cellwidth=2in}};
run;
```

Terminate sending output to the RTF destination.

```
ods rtf close;
```

Send subsequent output to the LISTING destination.

```
ods listing close;
```

A Closer Look

Learning More about ODS Styles

A discussion of defining styles is beyond the scope of this book. The purpose of this example is to show you that it's possible to design a style that you can define once and reuse so that your reports have a uniform appearance.

There are many ways to achieve the look of this report. Some of the attributes defined in the MARKETING style could have been done with inline formatting or with STYLE= options in PROC TABULATE. The opposite is also true. For example, you could modify the SystemTitle style that is inherited from STYLES.PRINTER to place the image, which is the company logo, ahead of the title.

(NOTE: This example did not include this feature because it has three title statements. Putting the image in the SystemTitle style would insert the logo ahead of each of the three TITLE statements. Again, there are additional ways around this problem, but discussion of these is beyond the scope of this book.)

When you intend to use the same attributes over and over for style elements in your report, it might be more efficient to design and save your own style. For attributes that you infrequently need to modify, it is more efficient to add the attributes to your PROC steps or to use inline formatting.

Example 6.15   Organizing Results into Tables Using ODS

Goal

Organize into tables selected analyses saved in the output data set created by Example 3.2. Send the results to a nonlisting destination.

Report

Nutritional Information about Breads Available in the Region
Values Per Bread Slice, Calories in kcal, Fiber in Grams

Results Overall			
Lowest Calories	**kcal**	**Highest Fiber**	**grams**
RiseNShine Bread White Sandwich	56	Owasco Ovens Whole Wheat Bran	4.8
BBB Brands White Sandwich	65	Pain du Prairie Whole Wheat Bran	4.4
Mill City Bakers White Sandwich	66	Downtown Bakers Whole Wheat Bran	4.3

Results by Source				
Source	**Lowest Calories**	**kcal**	**Highest Fiber**	**grams**
Bakery	Demeter White Sourdough	71	Pain du Prairie Whole Wheat Bran	4.4
	Demeter White Sandwich	73	Downtown Bakers Whole Wheat Bran	4.3
	Pain du Prairie White Sourdough	74	Demeter Rye Pumpernickel	4.2
Grocery	RiseNShine Bread White Sandwich	56	Owasco Ovens Whole Wheat Bran	4.8
	BBB Brands White Sandwich	65	Owasco Ovens Whole Wheat 100% Whole Wheat	4
	Mill City Bakers White Sandwich	66	Five Chimneys Whole Wheat Bran	3.8

Results by Type				
Type	**Lowest Calories**	**kcal**	**Highest Fiber**	**grams**
Specialty	Demeter White	71	Owasco Ovens Whole Wheat	4.8
	Owasco Ovens Whole Wheat	72	Pain du Prairie Whole Wheat	4.4
	Fabulous Breads Whole Wheat	74	Downtown Bakers Whole Wheat	4.3
Sandwich	RiseNShine Bread White	56	Aunt Sal Bakes Multigrain	3.9
	BBB Brands White	65	Demeter Oatmeal	3.9
	Mill City Bakers White	66	Gaia's Hearth Oatmeal	3.5

Nutritional Information about Breads Available in the Region
Values Per Bread Slice, Calories in kcal, Fiber in Grams

Results by Source and Brand					
Source	**Brand**	**Lowest Calories**	**kcal**	**Highest Fiber**	**grams**
Bakery	Aunt Sal Bakes	White Sourdough Whole Wheat Nutty Rye Sandwich	74 81 81	Multigrain Sandwich Rye Pumpernickel Whole Wheat Sandwich	3.9 3.5 2.4
Bakery	Demeter	White Sourdough White Sandwich Rye Sandwich	71 73 94	Rye Pumpernickel Whole Wheat Bran Oatmeal Sandwich	4.2 3.9 3.9
Bakery	Downtown Bakers	Rye Sandwich White Sourdough Whole Wheat Bran	82 82 85	Whole Wheat Bran Whole Wheat Sandwich Rye Pumpernickel	4.3 3 3
Bakery	Pain du Prairie	White Sourdough Whole Wheat Bran Whole Wheat Sandwich	74 76 80	Whole Wheat Bran Whole Wheat Sandwich Whole Wheat Organic	4.4 2.9 2.8
Grocery	BBB Brands	White Sandwich Rye Sandwich Rye Pumpernickel	65 82 84	Whole Wheat Sandwich Rye Pumpernickel Rye Sandwich	2.6 2 1.5
Grocery	Choice 123	White Sandwich White Sandwich Multigrain Sandwich	71 71 76	Multigrain Seven Grain Multigrain Sandwich Whole Wheat Sandwich	2.3 2 1.8
Grocery	Fabulous Breads	White Sandwich Whole Wheat 100% Whole Wheat White Sourdough	71 74 77	Multigrain Eight Grain Whole Wheat Sandwich Rye Pumpernickel	3.2 3.1 3.1
Grocery	Five Chimneys	White Sourdough Rye Sandwich White Raisin Cinnamon	75 77 82	Whole Wheat Bran Rye Pumpernickel Oatmeal Sandwich	3.8 3.5 3.3
Grocery	Gaia's Hearth	White Sourdough Whole Wheat 100% Whole Wheat Multigrain High Protein	77 80 81	Rye Pumpernickel Oatmeal Sandwich Whole Wheat Sandwich	3.6 3.5 2.3
Grocery	Mill City Bakers	White Sandwich Rye Sandwich Multigrain Sandwich	66 71 77	Multigrain Soy Multigrain Sandwich Whole Wheat Sandwich	3.1 2.9 2.6
Grocery	Owasco Ovens	Whole Wheat 100% Whole Wheat Whole Wheat Sandwich Whole Wheat Bran	72 75 79	Whole Wheat Bran Whole Wheat 100% Whole Wheat Rye Pumpernickel	4.8 4 2.9
Grocery	RiseNShine Bread	White Sandwich White Honey Multigrain Sandwich	56 74 76	Multigrain Six Grain Whole Wheat Sandwich White Honey	3.1 2 1.7

Example Features

Data Set	BREADSTATS
Report Example	Output data set created by Example 3.2
Featured Steps and Statement	PROC TEMPLATE DATA step ODS statement

Featured Step Statements and Options	PROC TEMPLATE
	   DEFINE TABLE statement
	Statements within table definition:
	   COLUMN
	   DEFINE
	   DYNAMIC
	   GENERIC=
	   HEADER=
	   MVAR
	   Style attributes
	ODS statement: STARTPAGE= option
	DATA step: FILE PRINT ODS= statement

Output Destination of Example	RTF
🔍 **A Closer Look**	Doing More with ODS
Other Examples That Use This Data Set	Examples 3.2 and 6.5

Example Overview

The program in Example 3.2 summarized nutritional data for a sample of bread products. Its goal was to identify products with the lowest calories and highest dietary fiber in several categories. The results of analyses of specific combinations of the four classification variables were saved in an output data set.

A simple PROC PRINT of the output data set created by Example 3.2 would adequately display the results. Figure 3.2b presents such a listing. This example, however, selects specific analyses from the output data set and presents them in a customized tabular format using ODS and DATA steps.

The DATA steps select observations from the output data set based on the variable _TYPE_ that PROC MEANS adds to the output data set. The variable _TYPE_ identifies the analysis classification to which the observation belongs. Each classification is assigned a number.

The report in this example shows one table with overall statistics, two tables with one classification variable, and one table with two classification variables. A separate DATA step creates each of the four tables.

PROC TEMPLATE creates one table definition that each of the DATA steps references. The table definition specifies columns for the most complex of the four analyses, which is the one with the two classification variables. The other three tables each reference the same definition, but only use the necessary number of classification columns found in the specific analysis.

The ODS STARTPAGE=NO statement keeps the three simplest tables on one page. The final table, the one with the two classification variables, is on its own page. The ODS STARTPAGE=NOW statement forces the fourth table to a new page.

Program

Run PROC TEMPLATE to create a table definition for the output from this report.

```
proc template;
```

Begin the table definition and assign it the name "categories."

```
define table categories;
```

Name a macro variable that the table definition will reference.

```
mvar titleone;
```

Define a symbol whose value will be assigned when the DATA step executes.

```
dynamic categoryheader;
```

Specify the columns in the order they should appear in the tables. Enclose the column symbols in parentheses so that the results within a symbol are listed in rows rather than columns. In this example, there are three results for the minimum calories and three results for the maximum fiber. If the symbols were not enclosed in parentheses, the values for the three results would be listed side-by-side in column cells rather than sequentially in rows.

```
column (category1) (category2)
       (calories) (mincal)
       (fiber) (maxfiber);
```

Declare a symbol as a header in the table.

```
header table_header_1;
```

Specify a definition for the symbol TABLE_HEADER_1, which is the header for the table.

```
define table_header_1;
```

Specify the text of the header. When the definition executes, insert the resolved value of the macro variable TITLEONE in the text. (The macro variable TITLEONE was referenced above on the MVAR statement.) Note that in this context, do not precede the macro variable name with an ampersand so that the macro variable will resolve whenever the definition executes. An ampersand used with a macro variable in a definition causes the macro variable to be resolved when the definition is *compiled*

```
   text 'Results ' titleone;
end;
```

instead of when the definition
executes.

**Specify a definition for the symbol
CATEGORY1, which is the first
column in the table definition.**

```
define category1;
```

**Designate that the column definition
can be used by more than one
column definition.**

```
    generic=on;
```

**Specify that the text for the header
associated with CATEGORY1 is the
dynamic symbol
CATEGORYHEADER, which will
be resolved when the DATA step
executes.**

```
    header=categoryheader;
  end;
```

**Specify a definition for the symbol
CATEGORY2, which is the second
column in the table definition.**

```
  define category2;
```

**Designate that the column definition
can be used by more than one
column definition.**

```
    generic=on;
```

**Specify that the text for the header
associated with CATEGORY2 is the
dynamic symbol
CATEGORYHEADER, which will
be resolved when the DATA step
executes.**

```
    header=categoryheader;
  end;
```

**Specify the definitions for the
remaining columns in the table.**
Supply text for the headings and add
the attribute of center justification to
two of the columns.

```
  define calories;
    generic=on;
    header='Lowest Calories';
  end;
  define mincal;
    generic=on;
    header='kcal';
    style={just=center};
  end;
  define fiber;
    generic=on;
    header='Highest Fiber';
  end;
  define maxfiber;
    generic=on;
    header='grams';
    style={just=center};
  end;
 end;
run;
```

**Do not send results to the LISTING
destination.**

```
ods listing close;
```

**Send subsequent results to the RTF
destination and save the results in a
file.**

```
ods rtf file='c:\reports\example32b.rtf'
```

Suppress the automatic insertion of new pages at the start of each procedure.

```
        startpage=no;
```

Display the first table, which contains the overall statistics and no classification columns.

```
/* Start Table 1 */
```

Assign a value to the macro variable that is referenced on the MVAR statement in the CATEGORIES table definition, which in turn places the resolved value of the macro variable in the table header.

```
%let titleone=Overall;
```

Do not create a data set and instead just process the observations in the BREADSTATS data set.

```
data _null_;
```

Select results from the data set that was created in Example 3.2 by referencing the automatic variable _TYPE_ that PROC MEANS creates. Select the overall results, which correspond to _TYPE_=0.

```
set breadstats(where=(_type_=0));
```

Define six character variables that will contain the identifiers of the three products with the lowest calories and the three products with the highest fiber. For each of the three products with the lowest calories and for each of the three products with the highest fiber create one variable that fully identifies a product by concatenating the three identifiers.

```
length fullcal1 fullcal2 fullcal3
       fullfiber1 fullfiber2 fullfiber3 $ 50;
fullcal1=catx(' ',wherecal_1,flourcal_1,typecal_1);
fullcal2=catx(' ',wherecal_2,flourcal_2,typecal_2);
fullcal3=catx(' ',wherecal_3,flourcal_3,typecal_3);
fullfiber1=catx(' ',
    wherefiber_1,flourfiber_1,typefiber_1);
fullfiber2=catx(' ',
    wherefiber_2,flourfiber_2,typefiber_2);
fullfiber3=catx(' ',
    wherefiber_3,flourfiber_3,typefiber_3);
```

Create an ODS output object by binding the variables in the data set to the CATEGORIES table definition.

```
file print ods=(template='categories'
```

Repeat the column symbols three times and assign a different variable each time to the symbol. For the CALORIES and MINCAL symbols, list the product identifiers and calories for the three products with the lowest calories. For the FIBER and MAXFIBER symbols, list the product identifiers and fiber values for the three products with the highest fiber. Since each of these symbols was enclosed in parentheses in the table definition, ODS stacks the three values

```
columns=(calories=fullcal1(generic=on)
         calories=fullcal2(generic=on)
         calories=fullcal3(generic=on)
         mincal=mincal_1(generic=on)
         mincal=mincal_2(generic=on)
         mincal=mincal_3(generic=on)
         fiber=fullfiber1(generic=on)
         fiber=fullfiber2(generic=on)
         fiber=fullfiber3(generic=on)
         maxfiber=maxfiber_1(generic=on)
         maxfiber=maxfiber_2(generic=on)
         maxfiber=maxfiber_3(generic=on))));
```

for each symbol in the same column.

Write the observation's data to the report using the template specified on the FILE PRINT statement.	`put _ods_;` `run;`

Display the second table, which contains statistics for one classification variable, SOURCE, the source of the product.	`/* Start Table 2 */`
	`%let titleone=by Source;`
	`data _null_;`

Select the results for the categories of SOURCE, which correspond to _TYPE_=8.	`set breadstats(where=(_type_=8));`

Repeat the process of defining identifiers as was shown in the DATA step that created the first table.	`length fullcal1 fullcal2 fullcal3`
	`      fullfiber1 fullfiber2 fullfiber3 $ 50;`
	`fullcal1=catx(' ',wherecal_1,flourcal_1,typecal_1);`
	`fullcal2=catx(' ',wherecal_2,flourcal_2,typecal_2);`
	`fullcal3=catx(' ',wherecal_3,flourcal_3,typecal_3);`
	`fullfiber1=catx(' ',`
	`    wherefiber_1,flourfiber_1,typefiber_1);`
	`fullfiber2=catx(' ',`
	`    wherefiber_2,flourfiber_2,typefiber_2);`
	`fullfiber3=catx(' ',`
	`    wherefiber_3,flourfiber_3,typefiber_3);`

Create an ODS output object by binding the variables in the data set to the CATEGORIES table definition.	`file print ods=(template='categories'`
Place the values of the classification variable, SOURCE, in the column that corresponds to CATEGORY2.	`columns=(category2=source(generic=on`
Assign a heading to the column that contains the values of the classification variable SOURCE.	`dynamic=(categoryheader='Source'))`

Repeat the column symbols three times as was described for the same code for the first table.	`calories=fullcal1(generic=on)`
	`calories=fullcal2(generic=on)`
	`calories=fullcal3(generic=on)`
	`mincal=mincal_1(generic=on)`
	`mincal=mincal_2(generic=on)`
	`mincal=mincal_3(generic=on)`
	`fiber=fullfiber1(generic=on)`
	`fiber=fullfiber2(generic=on)`
	`fiber=fullfiber3(generic=on)`
	`maxfiber=maxfiber_1(generic=on)`
	`maxfiber=maxfiber_2(generic=on)`
	`maxfiber=maxfiber_3(generic=on)));`

Write the observation's data to the report using the template specified on the FILE PRINT statement.	`put _ods_;` `run;`

Display the third table, which contains statistics for one classification variable, TYPE, the bread type.	`/* Start Table 3 */`
	`%let titleone=by Type;`
	`data _null_;`

<table>
<tr><td>

Select the results for the categories of TYPE, which correspond to _TYPE_=1.

</td><td>

```
set breadstats(where=(_type_=1));
```

</td></tr>
<tr><td>

Repeat the process of defining identifiers as was shown in the DATA step that created the first table. Do not include TYPE in the identifier, since its values will be placed instead in the CATEGORY2 column.

</td><td>

```
length fullcal1 fullcal2 fullcal3
       fullfiber1 fullfiber2 fullfiber3 $ 30;

fullcal1=catx(' ',wherecal_1,flourcal_1);
fullcal2=catx(' ',wherecal_2,flourcal_2);
fullcal3=catx(' ',wherecal_3,flourcal_3);
fullfiber1=catx(' ',wherefiber_1,flourfiber_1);
fullfiber2=catx(' ',wherefiber_2,flourfiber_2);
fullfiber3=catx(' ',wherefiber_3,flourfiber_3);
```

</td></tr>
<tr><td>

Create an ODS output object by binding the variables in the data set to the CATEGORIES table definition.

</td><td>

```
file print ods=(template='categories'
```

</td></tr>
<tr><td>

Place the values of the classification variable, TYPE, in the column that corresponds to CATEGORY2.

</td><td>

```
columns=(category2=type(generic=on
```

</td></tr>
<tr><td>

Assign a heading to the column that contains the values of the classification variable TYPE.

</td><td>

```
dynamic=(categoryheader='Type'))
```

</td></tr>
<tr><td>

Repeat the column symbols three times as was described for the same code for the first table.

</td><td>

```
calories=fullcal1(generic=on)
calories=fullcal2(generic=on)
calories=fullcal3(generic=on)
mincal=mincal_1(generic=on)
mincal=mincal_2(generic=on)
mincal=mincal_3(generic=on)
fiber=fullfiber1(generic=on)
fiber=fullfiber2(generic=on)
fiber=fullfiber3(generic=on)
maxfiber=maxfiber_1(generic=on)
maxfiber=maxfiber_2(generic=on)
maxfiber=maxfiber_3(generic=on)));
```

</td></tr>
<tr><td>

Write the observation's data to the report using the template specified on the FILE PRINT statement.

</td><td>

```
  put _ods_;
run;
```

</td></tr>
<tr><td>

Force the next table to start on a new page.

</td><td>

```
ods rtf startpage=now;
```

</td></tr>
<tr><td>

Display the fourth table, which should contain statistics for two classification variables, SOURCE and BRAND.

</td><td>

```
/* Start Table 4 */
%let titleone=by Source and Brand;
data _null_;
```

</td></tr>
<tr><td>

Select the results for the categories of the combinations of the two variables, SOURCE and BRAND, which correspond to _TYPE_=12.

</td><td>

```
  set breadstats(where=(_type_=12));
  length fullcal1 fullcal2 fullcal3
         fullfiber1 fullfiber2 fullfiber3 $ 30;
```

</td></tr>
<tr><td>

Repeat the process of defining identifiers as was shown in the DATA step that created the first table. Do not include BRAND in the

</td><td>

```
fullcal1=catx(' ',flourcal_1,typecal_1);
fullcal2=catx(' ',flourcal_2,typecal_2);
fullcal3=catx(' ',flourcal_3,typecal_3);
fullfiber1=catx(' ',flourfiber_1,typefiber_1);
fullfiber2=catx(' ',flourfiber_2,typefiber_2);
```

</td></tr>
</table>

identifier, since its values will be placed instead in the CATEGORY2 column.	```fullfiber3=catx(' ',flourfiber_3,typefiber_3);```
Create an ODS output object by binding the variables in the data set to the CATEGORIES table definition.	```file print ods=(template='categories'```

Place the values of the classification variable SOURCE in the column that corresponds to CATEGORY1.	```columns=(category1=source(generic=on```
	 ```dynamic=(categoryheader='Source'))```
	 ``` category2=brand(generic=on```

Place the values of the classification variable BRAND in the column that corresponds to CATEGORY2.	```dynamic=(categoryheader='Brand'))```

Repeat the column symbols three times as was described for the same code for the first table.	```calories=fullcal1(generic=on)```
	```calories=fullcal2(generic=on)```
	```calories=fullcal3(generic=on)```
	```mincal=mincal_1(generic=on)```
	```mincal=mincal_2(generic=on)```
	```mincal=mincal_3(generic=on)```
	```fiber=fullfiber1(generic=on)```
	```fiber=fullfiber2(generic=on)```
	```fiber=fullfiber3(generic=on)```
	```maxfiber=maxfiber_1(generic=on)```
	```maxfiber=maxfiber_2(generic=on)```
	```maxfiber=maxfiber_3(generic=on)));```

Write the observation's data to the report using the template specified on the FILE PRINT statement.	``` put _ods_;``` ```run;```
Terminate sending output to the RTF destination.	```ods rtf close;```
Send subsequent output to the LISTING destination.	```ods listing;```

🔍 A Closer Look

Doing More with ODS

This example demonstrates that when you use ODS, the more difficult part of programming your analyses can be the presentation of the output rather than the production of the analyses. ODS provides you with many ways to present your reports. This example showed you that you can create a template that can be reused.

A thorough discussion of ODS features is beyond the scope of this book. For more information, consult these references:

❑ *SAS 9.1 Output Delivery System: User's Guide* (support.sas.com/v9doc)

❑ SAS Press books (support.sas.com/saspress)

❑ SUGI conference proceedings (support.sas.com)

Creating the Example Data Sets

This appendix presents information about the example data sets that are used in this book. Many of the data sets are used in multiple examples. Table A.1 below links the data sets to the examples where they're analyzed. The remaining sections describe each of the example data sets. The data set information is presented in the order in which the data sets are analyzed in this book.

The description for each example data set includes the DATA step that creates the data set, a few lines of raw data, and an excerpt of the PROC CONTENTS of the data set.

Refer to the SAS Press Web site for links to download the data files and programs (support.sas.com/companionsites).

Linking the Example Data Sets to the Examples in This Book

Table A.1 presents a list of the data sets and the examples in which they're analyzed. The list of data set names is presented in the order in which the data sets are analyzed in this book.

Table A.1 Data Sets Used in the Examples in This Book

Data Set	Examples				
HOUSING	2.1	2.2	6.1		
FEEDERBIRDS	2.3				
POWERUSE	2.4	2.5	2.6	6.10	
LIPIDS	2.7	3.3	6.4	6.8	6.9
TOWNSURVEY	2.8	3.9			
MARATHON	2.9				
PHONDATA	3.1				
BREAD	3.2	6.5	6.15		
JOBCLASS	3.4	3.5	3.6	6.3	6.7
LIBRARIES	3.7				
CARSALES	3.8	6.2	6.6		
CUSTRESP	3.10	6.13	6.14		
SERVICE	4.1				
DEMOG	4.2	6.12			
FITNESS	4.3				
INVENTORY	5.1	6.11			
STUDENTS	5.2				

HOUSING Data Set

DATA Step That Creates the HOUSING Data Set

```
data housing;
   input zone $1. +1 type : $9. bedr bath sqfeet age
         schools : $15. / address & $25. price;
datalines;
4 capecod 4 2.5 2538 6 920:340/400/368
211 Whitehall Way  354900
1 colonial 4 2.5 2700 7 920:470/360/552
1800 Bridgeport  369900
...more datalines....
;;;;
```

Figure A.1 Partial PROC CONTENTS Output of the HOUSING Data Set

```
                        The CONTENTS Procedure

        Data Set Name       WORK.HOUSING              Observations           50
        Member Type         DATA                      Variables              9
        Engine              V9                        Indexes                0
        Created             Thu, Feb 03, 2005 04:07:49 PM   Observation Length   96
        Last Modified       Thu, Feb 03, 2005 04:07:49 PM   Deleted Observations 0
        Protection                                    Compressed             NO
        Data Set Type                                 Sorted                 NO
        Label
        Data Representation WINDOWS_32
        Encoding            wlatin1  Western (Windows)


              Alphabetic List of Variables and Attributes

                 #     Variable    Type    Len

                 8     address     Char     25
                 6     age         Num       8
                 4     bath        Num       8
                 3     bedr        Num       8
                 9     price       Num       8
                 7     schools     Char     15
                 5     sqfeet      Num       8
                 2     type        Char      9
                 1     zone        Char      1
```

FEEDERBIRDS Data Set

DATA Step That Creates the FEEDERBIRDS Data Set

```
data feederbirds;
  infile datalines dsd;
  attrib id       length=$8 label='Study ID'
         species length=$6 label='Bird Species'
         p1       length=3  label='Birds Seen Period 1'
         p2       length=3  label='Birds Seen Period 2'
         p3       length=3  label='Birds Seen Period 3'
         p4       length=3  label='Birds Seen Period 4'
         p5       length=3  label='Birds Seen Period 5'
         p6       length=3  label='Birds Seen Period 6'
         p7       length=3  label='Birds Seen Period 7'
         p8       length=3  label='Birds Seen Period 8'
         p9       length=3  label='Birds Seen Period 9'
         p10      length=3  label='Birds Seen Period 10'
         countsitesize length=3 label='Size of feeder count site'
         countsitedesc length=3 label='Decscription of count site'
         pop      length=3  label='Population of city or town'
         density length=3   label='Housing density in neighborhood'
         seedground      length=3 label='Number of seed feeders on
                                        ground'
```

```
                       seedhang         length=3 label='Number of hanging seed
                                                         feeders'
                       seedplat         length=3 label='Number of raised platform
                                                         feeders'
                       thistle          length=3 label='Number of thistle feeders'
                       suetfat          length=3 label='Number of suet or fat
                                                         feeders'
                       water            length=3 label='Number of water dispensers'
                       everseen         length=3 label='Species seen at least once
                                                         during season';
          input id $ species $ p1-p10 countsitesize countsitedesc pop
                    density seedground seedhang seedplat thistle suetfat
                    water everseen;
     datalines;
     MN1001,amecro,,,,1,2,,2,,,,2,4,2,3,1,2,1,1,3,1,1
     MN1001,amegfi,2,2,3,6,9,7,6,8,7,6,2,4,2,3,1,2,1,1,3,1,1
     MN1001,amerob,1,20,1,,,,1,,,3,2,4,2,3,1,2,1,1,3,1,1
     MN1001,amtspa,,,,,,,,,,,2,4,2,3,1,2,1,1,3,1,0
     MN1001,bkcchi,3,2,2,2,1,1,2,2,1,2,2,4,2,3,1,2,1,1,3,1,1
     MN1001,blujay,2,2,1,4,2,2,1,4,3,2,2,4,2,3,1,2,1,1,3,1,1
     MN1001,borchi,,,,,,,,,,,2,4,2,3,1,2,1,1,3,1,0
     …more datalines….
     ;;;;
```

Figure A.2 Partial PROC CONTENTS Output of the FEEDERBIRDS Data Set

```
                          The CONTENTS Procedure

     Data Set Name          WORK.FEEDERBIRDS          Observations          370
     Member Type            DATA                      Variables             23
     Engine                 V9                        Indexes               0
     Created                Thu, Feb 03, 2005 04:12:42 PM   Observation Length    77
     Last Modified          Thu, Feb 03, 2005 04:12:42 PM   Deleted Observations  0
     Protection                                       Compressed            NO
     Data Set Type                                    Sorted                NO
     Label
     Data Representation    WINDOWS_32
     Encoding               wlatin1  Western (Windows)


                 Alphabetic List of Variables and Attributes

      #    Variable       Type    Len    Label

     14    countsitedesc  Num      3     Decscription of count site
     13    countsitesize  Num      3     Size of feeder count site
     16    density        Num      3     Housing density in neighborhood
     23    everseen       Num      3     Species seen at least once during season
      1    id             Char     8     Study ID
      3    p1             Num      3     Birds Seen Period 1
      4    p2             Num      3     Birds Seen Period 2
      5    p3             Num      3     Birds Seen Period 3
      6    p4             Num      3     Birds Seen Period 4
      7    p5             Num      3     Birds Seen Period 5
      8    p6             Num      3     Birds Seen Period 6
      9    p7             Num      3     Birds Seen Period 7
     10    p8             Num      3     Birds Seen Period 8
     11    p9             Num      3     Birds Seen Period 9
     12    p10            Num      3     Birds Seen Period 10
     15    pop            Num      3     Population of city or town
     17    seedground     Num      3     Number of seed feeders on ground
     18    seedhang       Num      3     Number of hanging seed feeders
     19    seedplat       Num      3     Number of raised platform feeders
      2    species        Char     6     Bird Species
     21    suetfat        Num      3     Number of suet or fat feeders
     20    thistle        Num      3     Number of thistle feeders
     22    water          Num      3     Number of water dispensers
```

POWERUSE
Data Set

DATA Step That Creates the POWERUSE Data Set

```
data poweruse;
   input type $3. +1 service $4. jan feb mar apr may jun;
datalines;
com area 6526 11999 17533 10221 17218 8857
com fld  10911 12648 15502 9120 8624 18338
com gen  1203 641 728 1039 1156 782
com op   15062 15635 9509 11717 11456 12461
com oth  1390 1672 1638 1282 1654 1915
com spc  111 85 121 109 125 103
com wtr  160 168 130 187 101 101
res area 118 116 91 92 95 137
res fld  96 89 75 87 75 82
res gen  22281 21505 22556 22784 25977 25371
res op   1152 1362 698 1047 534 1492
res oth  286 238 109 33 158 465
res spc  8280 10984 10111 13234 13723 11072
res wtr  9589 10625 14160 18130 8592 7654
;;;;
```

Figure A.3 Partial PROC CONTENTS Output of the POWERUSE Data Set

```
                         The CONTENTS Procedure

        Data Set Name        WORK.POWERUSE              Observations          14
        Member Type          DATA                       Variables             8
        Engine               V9                         Indexes               0
        Created              Thu, Feb 03, 2005 04:13:36 PM   Observation Length    56
        Last Modified        Thu, Feb 03, 2005 04:13:36 PM   Deleted Observations  0
        Protection                                      Compressed            NO
        Data Set Type                                   Sorted                NO
        Label
        Data Representation  WINDOWS_32
        Encoding             wlatin1  Western (Windows)


             Alphabetic List of Variables and Attributes

                #     Variable    Type    Len

                6     apr         Num      8
                4     feb         Num      8
                3     jan         Num      8
                8     jun         Num      8
                5     mar         Num      8
                7     may         Num      8
                2     service     Char     4
                1     type        Char     3
```

LIPIDS Data Set

DATA Step That Creates the LIPIDS Data Set

```
data lipids;
   input studyid gender $ testperiod :$4. chol hdl tri;
datalines;
1001 F Pre  156  48 134
1001 F Post 150  50 127
1002 F Pre  151  50 102
1002 F Post 139  54  81
1003 F Pre  165  51 114
1003 F Post 149  51 101
...more datalines....
;;;;
```

Figure A.4 Partial PROC CONTENTS Output of the LIPIDS Data Set

```
                        The CONTENTS Procedure

       Data Set Name        WORK.LIPIDS              Observations          52
       Member Type          DATA                     Variables             6
       Engine               V9                       Indexes               0
       Created              Thu, Feb 03, 2005 04:15:16 PM   Observation Length    48
       Last Modified        Thu, Feb 03, 2005 04:15:16 PM   Deleted Observations  0
       Protection                                    Compressed            NO
       Data Set Type                                 Sorted                NO
       Label
       Data Representation  WINDOWS_32
       Encoding             wlatin1  Western (Windows)


             Alphabetic List of Variables and Attributes

                  #    Variable    Type    Len

                  4    chol        Num      8
                  2    gender      Char     8
                  5    hdl         Num      8
                  1    studyid     Num      8
                  3    testperiod  Char     4
                  6    tri         Num      8
```

TOWNSURVEY Data Set

DATA Step That Creates the TOWNSURVEY Data Set

```
data townsurvey;
  infile datalines truncover dsd;
  length area kids seniors $ 1 comments $ 100;
  input surveyid area $ yrslived kids $ seniors $ q1-q9
comments;

datalines;
1,N,1,N,N,4,4,,4,2,2,3,4,4,
2,P,1,N,N,5,4,2,2,4,4,4,4,2,
3,T,2,N,N,4,2,1,2,3,4,4,4,5,
4,L,1,N,N,,5,4,4,1,4,4,4,2,
5,T,3,N,N,2,4,2,4,5,4,,4,,
6,T,2,N,N,3,5,3,4,3,4,4,4,3,
7,T,2,Y,N,2,1,1,3,3,3,4,2,3,"Please add more soccer fields"
8,N,2,N,N,2,4,4,3,3,,5,4,2,
9,T,3,N,Y,4,2,1,2,3,4,4,,4,"Enforce the dog barking ordinance"
…more datalines….
;;;;
```

Figure A.5 Partial PROC CONTENTS Output of the TOWNSURVEY Data Set

```
                       The CONTENTS Procedure

   Data Set Name       WORK.TOWNSURVEY            Observations          482
   Member Type         DATA                       Variables             15
   Engine              V9                         Indexes               0
   Created             Thu, Feb 03, 2005 04:18:46 PM   Observation Length    192
   Last Modified       Thu, Feb 03, 2005 04:18:46 PM   Deleted Observations  0
   Protection                                     Compressed            NO
   Data Set Type                                  Sorted                NO
   Label
   Data Representation WINDOWS_32
   Encoding            wlatin1  Western (Windows)


             Alphabetic List of Variables and Attributes

                   #    Variable    Type    Len

                   1    area        Char      1
                   4    comments    Char    100
                   2    kids        Char      1
                   7    q1          Num       8
                   8    q2          Num       8
                   9    q3          Num       8
                  10    q4          Num       8
                  11    q5          Num       8
                  12    q6          Num       8
                  13    q7          Num       8
                  14    q8          Num       8
                  15    q9          Num       8
                   3    seniors     Char      1
                   5    surveyid    Num       8
                   6    yrslived    Num       8
```

MARATHON Data Set

DATA Step That Creates the MARATHON Data Set

```
data marathon;
    input year 4. +1 gender $1. +1 winner $25. +1 country $13.
+1 time time7.;
datalines;
1980 M Bill Rodgers           United States 2:12:11
1981 M Toshihiko Seko         Japan         2:09:26
1982 M Alberto Salazar        United States 2:08:52
1983 M Greg Meyer             United States 2:09:00
1984 M Geoff Smith            Great Britain 2:10:34
…more datalines….
;;;;
```

Figure A.6 Partial PROC CONTENTS Output of the MARATHON Data Set

```
                        The CONTENTS Procedure

    Data Set Name       WORK.MARATHON           Observations         50
    Member Type         DATA                    Variables            5
    Engine              V9                      Indexes              0
    Created             Thu, Feb 03, 2005 04:21:01 PM  Observation Length   56
    Last Modified       Thu, Feb 03, 2005 04:21:01 PM  Deleted Observations 0
    Protection                                  Compressed           NO
    Data Set Type                               Sorted               NO
    Label
    Data Representation WINDOWS_32
    Encoding            wlatin1  Western (Windows)


            Alphabetic List of Variables and Attributes

                #    Variable    Type    Len

                4    country     Char     13
                2    gender      Char      1
                5    time        Num       8
                3    winner      Char     25
                1    year        Num       8
```

PHONDATA Data Set

DATA Step That Creates the PHONDATA Data Set

```
data phondata;
   input hour primtime time8. status $10. @@;
datalines;
12 0:04:20 PRIM/RES    12 0:13:29 AUTOMATED  ·10 0:08:06 PRIM/RES
13 0:06:06 PRIM/RES    11 0:04:05 PRIM/RES    14 0:02:23 PRIM/RES
16 0:01:40 NO ANSWER   15 0:00:30 PRIM/RES     9 0:08:51 LMOM
13 0:10:53 PRIM/RES    12 0:03:30 PRIM/RES    11 0:02:55 AUTOMATED
…more datalines….
;;;;
```

Figure A.7 Partial PROC CONTENTS Output of the PHONDATA Data Set

```
                        The CONTENTS Procedure

    Data Set Name       WORK.PHONDATA           Observations         581
    Member Type         DATA                    Variables            3
    Engine              V9                      Indexes              0
    Created             Thu, Feb 03, 2005 04:23:11 PM  Observation Length   32
    Last Modified       Thu, Feb 03, 2005 04:23:11 PM  Deleted Observations 0
    Protection                                  Compressed           NO
    Data Set Type                               Sorted               NO
    Label
    Data Representation WINDOWS_32
    Encoding            wlatin1  Western (Windows)


            Alphabetic List of Variables and Attributes

                #    Variable    Type    Len

                1    hour        Num       8
                2    primtime    Num       8
                3    status      Char     10
```

BREAD Data Set

DATA Step That Creates the BREAD Data Set

```
data bread;
   infile datalines dsd;
   attrib source        length=$7  label='Source'
          brand         length=$16 label='Brand'
          flour         length=$15 label='Primary Flour Ingredient'
          type          length=$20 label='Type of Bread'
          calories      label='Calories per Slice'
          total_fat     label='Total Fat(g) per Slice'
          dietary_fiber label='Dietary Fiber(g) per Slice'
          protein       label='Protein(g) per Slice'
          total_carb    label='Total Carbohydrates(g) per Slice';
   input source $ brand $ flour $ type $
         calories total_fat dietary_fiber protein total_carb;
datalines;
Grocery,Fabulous Breads,White,Sandwich,71,1.5,0.5,2.1,12.1
Grocery,Fabulous Breads,White,Egg,92,0.5,0.5,3.3,18.2
Grocery,Fabulous Breads,White,Buttertop,97,1.5,0,3.1,17.5
Grocery,Fabulous Breads,Whole Wheat,Sandwich,90,1.1,3.1,4.4,15.3
…more datalines….
;;;;
```

Figure A.8 Partial PROC CONTENTS Output of the BREAD Data Set

```
                        The CONTENTS Procedure

      Data Set Name       WORK.BREAD               Observations         124
      Member Type         DATA                     Variables            9
      Engine              V9                       Indexes              0
      Created             Thu, Feb 03, 2005 04:25:25 PM  Observation Length   104
      Last Modified       Thu, Feb 03, 2005 04:25:25 PM  Deleted Observations 0
      Protection                                   Compressed           NO
      Data Set Type                                Sorted               NO
      Label
      Data Representation WINDOWS_32
      Encoding            wlatin1  Western (Windows)


                 Alphabetic List of Variables and Attributes

        #    Variable        Type    Len    Label

        2    brand           Char    16     Brand
        5    calories        Num     8      Calories per Slice
        7    dietary_fiber   Num     8      Dietary Fiber(g) per Slice
        3    flour           Char    15     Primary Flour Ingredient
        8    protein         Num     8      Protein(g) per Slice
        1    source          Char    7      Source
        9    total_carb      Num     8      Total Carbohydrates(g) per Slice
        6    total_fat       Num     8      Total Fat(g) per Slice
        4    type            Char    20     Type of Bread
```

JOBCLASS Data Set

DATA Step That Creates the JOBCLASS Data Set

```
data jobclass;
   input gender region occupat @@;
datalines;
1 1 1   1 1 1   1 1 1   1 1 1   1 1 1   1 1 1   1 1 1
1 1 2   1 1 2   1 1 2   1 1 2   1 1 2   1 1 2   1 1 2
1 1 3   1 1 3   1 1 3   1 1 3   1 1 3   1 1 3   1 1 3
1 2 1   1 2 1   1 2 1   1 2 2   1 2 2   1 2 2   1 2 2
1 2 2   1 2 2   1 2 3   1 2 3   1 2 4   1 2 4   1 2 4
1 2 4   1 2 4   1 2 4   1 3 1   1 3 1   1 3 1   1 3 1
1 3 1   1 3 2   1 3 2   1 3 2   1 3 2   1 3 2   1 3 2
1 3 2   1 3 3   1 3 3   1 3 3   1 3 3   1 3 4   1 3 4
1 3 4   1 3 4   1 3 4   1 4 1   1 4 3   2 1 1   2 1 1
2 1 1   2 1 1   2 1 1   2 1 1   2 1 1   2 1 2   2 1 2
2 1 2   2 1 2   2 1 2   2 1 3   2 1 3   2 1 3   2 1 4
2 1 4   2 1 4   2 1 4   2 1 4   2 2 1   2 2 3
2 2 3   2 2 3   2 2 3   2 2 3   2 2 4   2 2 4   2 2 4
2 2 4   2 2 4   2 3 1   2 3 1   2 3 1   2 3 1   2 3 1
2 3 2   2 3 2   2 3 2   2 3 2   2 3 2   2 3 2   2 3 2
2 3 3   2 3 3   2 3 4   2 3 4   2 3 4   2 4 1   2 4 1
2 4 1   2 4 1   2 4 1   2 4 2   2 4 2   2 4 2   2 4 3
2 4 3   2 4 3   2 4 3   2 4 4
;;;;
```

Figure A.9 Partial PROC CONTENTS Output of the JOBCLASS Data Set

```
                         The CONTENTS Procedure

    Data Set Name      WORK.JOBCLASS               Observations          123
    Member Type        DATA                        Variables             3
    Engine             V9                          Indexes               0
    Created            Thu, Feb 03, 2005 04:28:09 PM   Observation Length    24
    Last Modified      Thu, Feb 03, 2005 04:28:09 PM   Deleted Observations  0
    Protection                                     Compressed            NO
    Data Set Type                                  Sorted                NO
    Label
    Data Representation WINDOWS_32
    Encoding           wlatin1  Western (Windows)


              Alphabetic List of Variables and Attributes

              #      Variable   Type    Len

              1      gender     Num      8
              3      occupat    Num      8
              2      region     Num      8
```

LIBRARIES Data Set

DATA Step That Creates the LIBRARIES Data Set

```
data libraries;
   infile datalines dsd;
   length media audience type category subcategory $ 20;
   input media audience type category subcategory items;
datalines;
Audio,Adult,Audiocassettes,All,General,1569
Audio,Adult,CompactDiscs,All,General,2018
Books,Adult,Hardcover,Fiction,General,5210
Books,Adult,Paperback,Fiction,General,1353
Books,Adult,Hardcover,Fiction,Mystery,1293
Books,Adult,Paperback,Fiction,Mystery,1521
Books,Adult,Hardcover,Fiction,Romance,170
Books,Adult,Paperback,Fiction,Romance,854
...more datalines....
;;;;
```

Figure A.10 Partial PROC CONTENTS Output of the LIBRARIES Data Set

```
                          The CONTENTS Procedure

        Data Set Name        WORK.LIBRARIES              Observations          61
        Member Type          DATA                        Variables             6
        Engine               V9                          Indexes               0
        Created              Thu, Feb 03, 2005 04:30:00 PM   Observation Length    112
        Last Modified        Thu, Feb 03, 2005 04:30:00 PM   Deleted Observations  0
        Protection                                       Compressed            NO
        Data Set Type                                    Sorted                NO
        Label
        Data Representation  WINDOWS_32
        Encoding             wlatin1  Western (Windows)



                 Alphabetic List of Variables and Attributes

                    #     Variable      Type    Len

                    2     audience      Char     20
                    4     category      Char     20
                    6     items         Num       8
                    1     media         Char     20
                    5     subcategory   Char     20
                    3     type          Char     20
```

CARSALES Data Set

DATA Step That Creates the CARSALES Data Set

```
data carsales;
   length name $ 18;
   input name $ month numsold amtsold @@;
datalines;
Langlois-Peele 1 3 105000 Langlois-Peele 2 2  60000
Langlois-Peele 3 1  52000 Langlois-Peele 4 4 200000
Langlois-Peele 5 7  310000 Langlois-Peele 6 9  425000
Langlois-Peele 7 3 100000 Langlois-Peele 8 4 160000
Langlois-Peele 9 3 98000 Langlois-Peele 10 8  445000
Langlois-Peele 11 1  62000 Langlois-Peele 12 4 160000
Johnson 1 2  65000 Johnson 2 1  44000
Johnson 3 3  95000 Johnson 4 2  61000
Johnson 5 2  75000 Johnson 6 6  200000
Johnson 7 3 97000 Johnson 8 2  85000
Johnson 9 2 73000 Johnson 10 5 195000
Johnson 11 3 140000 Johnson 12 2 72000
;;;;
```

Figure A.11 Partial PROC CONTENTS Output of the CARSALES Data Set

```
                         The CONTENTS Procedure

    Data Set Name        WORK.CARSALES              Observations        24
    Member Type          DATA                       Variables           4
    Engine               V9                         Indexes             0
    Created              Thu, Feb 03, 2005 04:31:52 PM  Observation Length  48
    Last Modified        Thu, Feb 03, 2005 04:31:52 PM  Deleted Observations 0
    Protection                                      Compressed          NO
    Data Set Type                                   Sorted              NO
    Label
    Data Representation  WINDOWS_32
    Encoding             wlatin1  Western (Windows)


             Alphabetic List of Variables and Attributes

             #    Variable   Type    Len

             4    amtsold    Num      8
             2    month      Num      8
             1    name       Char    18
             3    numsold    Num      8
```

CUSTRESP Data Set

DATA Step That Creates the CUSTRESP Data Set

```
data custresp;
   input customer factor1-factor4 source1-source3 website
store;
datalines;
 1 . . 1 1 1 1 . 0  1
 2 1 1 . 1 1 1 . 0  8
 3 . . 1 1 1 1 . 0  4
 4 1 1 . 1 . 1 . 10 3
 5 . 1 . 1 1 . . 1  0
 6 . 1 . 1 1 . . 3  0
 7 . 1 . 1 1 . . 0  6
…more datalines….
;;;;
```

Figure A.12 Partial PROC CONTENTS Output of the CUSTRESP Data Set

```
                         The CONTENTS Procedure

    Data Set Name        WORK.CUSTRESP             Observations        120
    Member Type          DATA                      Variables           10
    Engine               V9                        Indexes             0
    Created              Thu, Feb 03, 2005 04:31:52 PM  Observation Length  80
    Last Modified        Thu, Feb 03, 2005 04:31:52 PM  Deleted Observations 0
    Protection                                     Compressed          NO
    Data Set Type                                  Sorted              NO
    Label
    Data Representation  WINDOWS_32
    Encoding             wlatin1  Western (Windows)


             Alphabetic List of Variables and Attributes

             #    Variable   Type    Len

             1    customer   Num      8
             2    factor1    Num      8
             3    factor2    Num      8
             4    factor3    Num      8
             5    factor4    Num      8
             6    source1    Num      8
             7    source2    Num      8
             8    source3    Num      8
            10    store      Num      8
             9    website    Num      8
```

SERVICE Data Set

DATA Step That Creates the SERVICE Data Set

```
data service;
   input @1 name $10. @12 address $17. @30 city $7.
         @38 state $2. @41 zipcode $5. @47 date mmddyy8.
         @55  workdone $15. @71 hours 4.1 /
         cartype & $25. parts;
datalines;
Bert Allen 1803 Knollton Ct. Bristol NC 29345 07012005 oil change       0.5
Jeep Cherokee 2000  18.00
Bert Allen 1803 Knollton Ct. Bristol NC 29345 01102006 replace brakes 2.0
Jeep Cherokee 2000  45.00
Bert Allen 1803 Knollton Ct. Bristol NC 29345 02202006 rotate tires     1.0
Jeep Cherokee 2000  20.00
Bert Allen 1803 Knollton Ct. Bristol NC 29345 02202006 transmission     5.5
Jeep Cherokee 2000  50.00
Bert Allen 1803 Knollton Ct. Bristol NC 29345 10192005 oil change       0.5
Ford F-150 1998  18.00
Bert Allen 1803 Knollton Ct. Bristol NC 29345 01102006 replace belts    1.5
Ford F-150 1998  0  35.00
Sara Jones 202 Stargate Dr.  Dart    NC 29445 12072005 align frontend 1.5
Chrysler Voyager 2003  20.00
Sara Jones 202 Stargate Dr.  Dart    NC 29445 12072005 rotate tires     1.0
Chrysler Voyager 2003  20.00
Joe Smith  1991 Cohansey St. New Ulm NC 29545 01192006 oil change       0.5
Ford F-150 1998  18.00
Joe Smith  1991 Cohansey St. New Ulm NC 29545 02252006 rotate tires     1.0
Ford F-150 1998  0  20.00
;;;;
```

Figure A.13 Partial PROC CONTENTS Output of the SERVICE Data Set

```
                     The CONTENTS Procedure

Data Set Name      WORK.SERVICE              Observations          10
Member Type        DATA                      Variables             10
Engine             V9                        Indexes               0
Created            Thu, Feb 03, 2005 04:35:48 PM   Observation Length   112
Last Modified      Thu, Feb 03, 2005 04:35:48 PM   Deleted Observations  0
Protection                                   Compressed            NO
Data Set Type                                Sorted                NO
Label
Data Representation   WINDOWS_32
Encoding              wlatin1  Western (Windows)


             Alphabetic List of Variables and Attributes

                   #    Variable    Type    Len

                   2    address     Char     17
                   9    cartype     Char     25
                   3    city        Char      7
                   6    date        Num       8
                   8    hours       Num       8
                   1    name        Char     10
                  10    parts       Num       8
                   4    state       Char      2
                   7    workdone    Char     15
                   5    zipcode     Char      5
```

DEMOG Data Set

DATA Step That Creates the DEMOG Data Set

Creating the DEMOG data set requires that you define the TMTDGFMT format.

```
proc format;
  value tmtdgfmt 0='Active'
                 1='Placebo';
run;
data demog;
  do i=1 to 200;
    patient=put(i,z3.);
    gender=(ranuni(770)<=0.5);
    height=ranuni(22878)*20+55;
    weight=ranuni(2179)*170+110;
    age=ranuni(51602)*65+20;
    race=(ranuni(7270)<=0.66);
    tmtdg=left(put((ranuni(76517)<=0.5),tmtdgfmt.));
    output;
  end;
run;
```

Figure A.14 Partial PROC CONTENTS Output of the DEMOG Data Set

```
                          The CONTENTS Procedure

    Data Set Name          WORK.DEMOG                Observations          200
    Member Type            DATA                      Variables             8
    Engine                 V9                        Indexes               0
    Created                Thu, Feb 03, 2005 04:38:15 PM   Observation Length    64
    Last Modified          Thu, Feb 03, 2005 04:38:15 PM   Deleted Observations  0
    Protection                                       Compressed            NO
    Data Set Type                                    Sorted                NO
    Label
    Data Representation    WINDOWS_32
    Encoding               wlatin1  Western (Windows)


             Alphabetic List of Variables and Attributes

            #     Variable    Type    Len

            6     age         Num      8
            3     gender      Num      8
            4     height      Num      8
            1     i           Num      8
            2     patient     Char     3
            7     race        Num      8
            8     tmtdg       Char     7
            5     weight      Num      8
```

FITNESS Data Set

DATA Step That Creates the FITNESS Data Set

```
data fitness(label = 'Exercise/fitness study table');
  input age weight runtime rstpulse runpulse maxpulse
        oxygen group;
  label age      = 'Age in years'
        weight   = 'Weight in kg'
        runtime  = 'Min. to run 1.5 miles'
        rstpulse = 'Heart rate while resting'
        runpulse = 'Heart rate while running'
        maxpulse = 'Maximum heart rate'
        oxygen   = 'Oxygen consumption'
        group    = 'Experimental group';
  cards;
```

```
57 73.37 12.63 58 174 176 39.407    2
54 79.38 11.17 62 156 165 46.080    2
52 76.32 9.63 48 164 166 45.441    2
50 70.87 8.92 48 146 155 54.625    2
51 67.25 11.08 48 172 172 45.118    2
54 91.63 12.88 44 168 172 39.203    2
51 73.71 10.47 59 186 188 45.790    2
57 59.08 9.93 49 148 155 50.545    2
…more datalines….
;;;;
```

Figure A.15 Partial PROC CONTENTS Output of the FITNESS Data Set

```
                      The CONTENTS Procedure

Data Set Name      WORK.FITNESS              Observations        31
Member Type        DATA                      Variables            8
Engine             V9                        Indexes              0
Created            Thu, Feb 03, 2005 04:40:55 PM   Observation Length  64
Last Modified      Thu, Feb 03, 2005 04:40:55 PM   Deleted Observations 0
Protection                                   Compressed          NO
Data Set Type                                Sorted              NO
Label              Exercise/fitness study table
Data Representation WINDOWS_32
Encoding           wlatin1  Western (Windows)


            Alphabetic List of Variables and Attributes

    #   Variable   Type   Len   Label

    1   age        Num     8    Age in years
    8   group      Num     8    Experimental group
    6   maxpulse   Num     8    Maximum heart rate
    7   oxygen     Num     8    Oxygen consumption
    4   rstpulse   Num     8    Heart rate while resting
    5   runpulse   Num     8    Heart rate while running
    3   runtime    Num     8    Min. to run 1.5 miles
    2   weight     Num     8    Weight in kg
```

INVENTORY Data Set

DATA Step That Creates the INVENTORY Data Set

```
data inventory;
   input partnmbr $ quantity price @@;
datalines;
B01-03/06 100   5.75 B02-03/08 100   6.60 B03-03/10  79   7.25
B04-03/12  37   7.80 B05-03/14   3   8.40 B06-03/16  15   7.95
B07-03/20  97   8.80 B08-03/25  24   4.25 B09-03/30  18   7.40
B10-03/06  92   7.10 B11-03/08  12   7.20 B12-03/10   9   7.70
B13-03/12   2   8.00 B14-03/14  37   8.80 B15-03/16  22   9.05
B16-03/20  15   9.20 B17-03/25  50   5.75 B18-03/30  50   8.00
B19-04/06 100  10.10 B20-04/08  33   5.90 B21-04/10  41   6.40
B22-04/12   7   6.80 B23-04/14  11   7.50 B24-04/16  17   6.95
B25-04/18  26   7.95 B26-04/20  31   7.20 B27-04/22  99   9.60
B28-04/25  50   3.95 B29-04/30  42   4.60 B30-04/06  87  11.60
B31-04/08  31   6.70 B32-04/10  11   7.10 B33-04/12   8   7.70
B34-04/14  14   8.80 B35-04/16  19   9.05 B36-04/18  17   9.60
B37-04/20  33   8.80 B38-04/22  51  11.20 B39-04/25  50   5.25
B40-04/30  47   5.50 B41-05/06  97  11.80 B42-05/08  13   6.40
B43-05/10  17   6.60 B44-05/12  15   6.80 B45-05/14   2   7.70
B46-05/16   4   6.60 B47-05/18  77   7.95 B48-05/20  11   7.20
B49-05/22  81   8.80 B50-05/25  50   4.15 B51-05/30  31   4.60
B52-05/06 100  13.75 B53-05/08  23   7.05 B54-05/10  59   7.10
```

```
B55-05/12  87  7.70 B56-05/14  22  7.95 B57-05/16  83  8.15
B58-05/18  16  8.45 B59-05/20  18  8.90 B60-05/22  29 10.40
B61-05/25  50  4.85 B62-05/30  31  5.25 B63-06/06 100 12.20
B64-06/08 100  7.00 B65-06/10  52  7.20 B66-06/12  43  7.45
B67-06/14  66  7.95 B68-06/16  69  8.05
;;;;
```

Figure A.16 Partial PROC CONTENTS Output of the INVENTORY Data Set

```
                        The CONTENTS Procedure

   Data Set Name        WORK.INVENTORY          Observations        68
   Member Type          DATA                    Variables            3
   Engine               V9                      Indexes              0
   Created              Thu, Feb 03, 2005 04:42:38 PM  Observation Length  24
   Last Modified        Thu, Feb 03, 2005 04:42:38 PM  Deleted Observations 0
   Protection                                   Compressed          NO
   Data Set Type                                Sorted              NO
   Label
   Data Representation  WINDOWS_32
   Encoding             wlatin1  Western (Windows)


               Alphabetic List of Variables and Attributes

          #    Variable    Type    Len

          1    partnmbr    Char     8
          3    price       Num      8
          2    quantity    Num      8
```

STUDENTS Data Set

DATA Step That Creates the STUDENTS Data Set

```
data students;
   length fullname $ 30 department $ 20 class $ 2;

   keep fullname department extension class;

   array dn{7} $ 20 _temporary_
              ('Biochemistry' 'Biophysics'
               'Microbiology' 'Ecology' 'Zoology and Behavior'
               'Plant Sciences' 'Neurobiology');

   array ln{125} $ 15 _temporary_ (
'smith     '  'johnson   '  'williams  '  'jones     '
'brown     '  'davis     '  'miller    '  'wilson    '
'moore     '  'taylor    '  'anderson  '  'thomas    '
'jackson   '  'white     '  'harris    '  'martin    '
'thompson  '  'garcia    '  'martinez  '  'robinson  '
'clark     '  'rodriguez '  'lewis     '  'lee       '
'walker    '  'hall      '  'allen     '  'young     '
'hernandez '  'king      '  'wright    '  'lopez     '
'hill      '  'scott     '  'green     '  'adams     '
'baker     '  'gonzalez  '  'nelson    '  'carter    '
'mitchell  '  'perez     '  'roberts   '  'turner    '
'phillips  '  'campbell  '  'parker    '  'evans     '
'edwards   '  'collins   '  'stewart   '  'sanchez   '
'morris    '  'rogers    '  'reed      '  'cook      '
'morgan    '  'bell      '  'murphy    '  'bailey    '
'rivera    '  'cooper    '  'richardson'  'cox       '
'howard    '  'ward      '  'torres    '  'peterson  '
'gray      '  'ramirez   '  'james     '  'watson    '
'brooks    '  'kelly     '  'sanders   '  'price     '
'bennett   '  'wood      '  'barnes    '  'ross      '
'henderson '  'coleman   '  'jenkins   '  'perry     '
'powell    '  'long      '  'patterson '  'hughes    '
'flores    '  'washington'  'butler    '  'simmons   '
'foster    '  'gonzales  '  'bryant    '  'alexander '
'russell   '  'griffin   '  'diaz      '  'hayes     '
```

```
'myers         '  'ford         '  'hamilton     '  'graham       '
'sullivan      '  'wallace      '  'woods        '  'cole         '
'west          '  'jordan       '  'owens        '  'reynolds     '
'fisher        '  'ellis        '  'harrison     '  'gibson       '
'mcdonald      '  'cruz         '  'marshall     '  'ortiz        '
'gomez         '  'murray       '  'freeman      '  'wells        '
'webb          ');

   array fnm{35} $ 11 _temporary_ (
'James         '  'John         '  'Robert       '  'Michael      '
'William       '  'David        '  'Richard      '  'Charles      '
'Joseph        '  'Thomas       '  'Christopher'  'Daniel       '
'Paul          '  'Mark         '  'Donald       '  'George       '
'Kenneth       '  'Steven       '  'Edward       '  'Brian        '
'Ronald        '  'Anthony      '  'Kevin        '  'Jason        '
'Matthew       '  'Gary         '  'Timothy      '  'Jose         '
'Larry         '  'Jeffrey      '  'Jacob        '  'Joshua       '
'Ethan         '  'Andrew       '  'Nicholas     ');

   array fnf{35} $ 11 _temporary_ (
'Mary          '  'Patricia     '  'Linda        '  'Barbara      '
'Elizabeth     '  'Jennifer     '  'Maria        '  'Susan        '
'Margaret      '  'Dorothy      '  'Lisa         '  'Nancy        '
'Karen         '  'Betty        '  'Helen        '  'Sandra       '
'Donna         '  'Carol        '  'Ruth         '  'Sharon       '
'Michelle      '  'Laura        '  'Sarah        '  'Kimberly     '
'Deborah       '  'Jessica      '  'Shirley      '  'Cynthia      '
'Angela        '  'Melissa      '  'Emily        '  'Hannah       '
'Emma          '  'Ashley       '  'Abigail      ');

  do i=1 to 149;
    lnptr=round(125*(uniform(38284)),1.);

    if lnptr=0 then lnptr=1;
    lastname=ln{lnptr};

    fnptr=round(35*(uniform(61961)),1.);
    if fnptr=0 then fnptr=1;
    if i le 90 then firstname=fnf{fnptr};
    else firstname=fnm{fnptr};

    fullname=trim(lastname) || ', ' || trim(firstname);
    substr(fullname,1,1)=upcase(substr(fullname,1,1));

    if mod(i,2)=0 then class='JR';
    else class='SR';

    if i le 35 then department=dn{1};
    else if 36 le i le 49 then department=dn{2};
    else if 50 le i le 77 then department=dn{3};
    else if 78 le i le 100 then department=dn{4};
    else if 101 le i le 123 then department=dn{5};
    else if 124 le i le 136 then department=dn{6};
    else if i ge 137 then department=dn{7};

    extension=5000+round(1000*uniform(10438),1.);
    output;
  end;
run;
```

Figure A.17 Partial PROC CONTENTS Output of the STUDENTS Data Set

```
                          The CONTENTS Procedure

        Data Set Name      WORK.STUDENTS              Observations          149
        Member Type        DATA                       Variables             4
        Engine             V9                         Indexes               0
        Created            Thu, Feb 03, 2005 04:44:47 PM  Observation Length    64
        Last Modified      Thu, Feb 03, 2005 04:44:47 PM  Deleted Observations  0
        Protection                                    Compressed            NO
        Data Set Type                                 Sorted                NO
        Label
        Data Representation  WINDOWS_32
        Encoding           wlatin1  Western (Windows)



                   Alphabetic List of Variables and Attributes

                      #    Variable     Type    Len

                      3    class        Char      2
                      2    department   Char     20
                      4    extension    Num       8
                      1    fullname     Char     30
```

APPENDIX B
Cross-Reference of the Examples in This Book

Table B.1 in this appendix presents a cross-reference of the examples in this book to the type of report, procedures used, data sets used, and ODS enhanced versions of the examples.

The examples in Chapter 6 are derived from the examples in Chapters 2 through 5, and Table B.2 links the examples in Chapter 6 to their original versions.

Table B.1 Cross-Reference of Examples in This Book

Example	REPORT	TABULATE	PRINT	DATA Step	MEANS	FREQ	ODS Enhanced Version	Data Set	Example Title	Title of ODS Enhanced Version
Detail										
2.1			X					HOUSING	Listing Selected Observations in a Specific Order	
2.2	X		Related Technique				6.1	HOUSING	Ordering the Rows of a Report	Customizing a PROC REPORT Detail Report
2.3			X					FEEDERBIRDS	Placing Data That is Constant for a Category in Titles	
2.4	X		Related Technique				6.10	POWERUSE	Summarizing the Rows of a Report	Customizing the Appearance of a Detail Report Created by PROC PRINT
2.5	X							POWERUSE	Summarizing Columns and Rows	
2.6	X							POWERUSE	Suppressing the Display of Specific Columns	
2.7	X						6.4	LIPIDS	Presenting Multiple Observations per Report Row	Adding "Traffic Lighting" to a Report Created by PROC REPORT
2.8	X							TOWNSURVEY	Presenting Long Text Fields in a Report	
2.9	X							MARATHON	Listing the Rank and Percentile for Each Observation	
Summary										
3.1	X	Related Technique						PHONDATA	Summarizing Data	
3.2		Related Technique			X		6.5, 6.15	BREAD	Computing Descriptive Statistics for Specific Groups	Adding "Traffic Lighting" to a Report Created by PROC TABULATE (6.5); Organizing Results into Tables Using ODS (6.15)
3.3	Related Technique	X					6.8, 6.9	LIPIDS	Displaying Descriptive Statistics in a Tabular Format	Presenting Graphics and Tables in the Same Report (6.8); Placing Hyperlinks in a Report (6.9)

(continued)

Example				Related Technique	Data Set	Example Title	Related Technique	Related Technique Title
3.4		X			JOBCLASS	Displaying Basic Frequency Counts and Percentages		
3.5		X			JOBCLASS	Producing a Hierarchical Tabular Report	6.3, 6.7	Customizing a PROC TABULATE Report (6.3); Including Images in a Report Created by PROC TABULATE (6.7)
3.6		X			JOBCLASS	Creating Multipage Summary Tables		
3.7		X			LIBRARIES	Assigning Multiple Labels to Categories		
3.8		X	X		CARSALES	Writing Customized Lines in Summary Reports	6.2, 6.6	Customizing a PROC REPORT Summary Report (6.2); Including Images in a Report Created by PROC REPORT (6.6)
3.9		X	Related Technique		TOWNSURVEY	Reporting on Multiple-Choice Survey Data		
3.10		X			CUSTRESP	Reporting on Multiple-Response Survey Data	6.13, 6.14	Condensing a Multipage, Multitable Report to One Page and Customizing the Output (6.13); Defining a Reusable Generic Style (6.14)
4.1	X				SERVICE	Customizing a Detail Report with Individualized Page Headers		
4.2			X		DEMOG	Creating a Customized Table of Descriptive Statistics	6.12	Customizing the Appearance of a Report Produced by a DATA Step
4.3	X				FITNESS	Customizing the Presentation of Analyses	4.3 (output objects)	
5.1	X				INVENTORY	Constructing a Basic Multipanel Report	6.11	Customizing a Multipanel Report Created by PROC REPORT
5.2			X		STUDENTS	Constructing an Advanced Multipanel Report		

Customized

Multipanel

Table B.2 Cross-Reference of Examples in Chapter 6

Example	Report-Writing Tool Used					Data Set	Chapter 6 Example Title	Title of Original Example	Derived from Example(s)
	REPORT	TABULATE	PRINT	DATA Step	TEMPLATE				
6.1	X					HOUSING	Customizing a PROC REPORT Detail Report	Ordering the Rows of a Report	2.2
6.2	X					CARSALES	Customizing a PROC REPORT Summary Report	Writing Customized Lines in Summary Reports	3.8
6.3		X				JOBCLASS	Customizing a PROC TABULATE Report	Producing a Hierarchical Tabular Report	3.5
6.4	X, RT*					LIPIDS	Adding "Traffic Lighting" to a Report Created by PROC REPORT	Presenting Multiple Observations per Report Row	2.7
6.5		X				BREAD	Adding "Traffic Lighting" to a Report Created by a PROC TABULATE	Computing Descriptive Statistics for Specific Groups	3.2 Related Technique
6.6	X					CARSALES	Including Images in a Report Created by PROC REPORT	Writing Customized Lines in Summary Reports	3.8, 6.2
6.7		X				JOBCLASS	Including Images in a Report Created by PROC TABULATE	Producing a Hierarchical Tabular Report	3.5, 6.3
6.8		X				LIPIDS	Presenting Graphics and Tables in the Same Report	Displaying Descriptive Statistics in a Tabular Format	3.3
6.9	RT*	X				LIPIDS	Placing Hyperlinks in a Report	Displaying Descriptive Statistics in a Tabular Format	3.3
6.10			X			POWERUSE	Customizing the Appearance of a Detail Report Created by PROC PRINT	Summarizing the Rows of a Report	2.4 Related Technique
6.11	X					INVENTORY	Customizing a Multipanel Report Created by PROC REPORT	Constructing a Basic Multipanel Report	5.1
6.12				X	X	DEMOG	Customizing the Appearance of a Report Produced by a DATA Step	Creating a Customized Table of Descriptive Statistics	4.2

(continued)

				Code	Title	RT*
6.13	X			CUSTRESP	Condensing a Multipage, Multitable Report to One Page and Customizing the Output	Reporting on Multiple-Response Survey Data — 3.10
6.14	X	X		CUSTRESP	Defining a Reusable Generic Style	Reporting on Multiple-Response Survey Data — 3.10, 6.13
6.15		X	X	BREAD	Organizing Results into Tables Using ODS	Computing Descriptive Statistics for Specific Groups — 3.2

* Note that "RT" stands for Related Technique.

Index

Books Available from SAS Press

Advanced Log-Linear Models Using SAS®
by **Daniel Zelterman**

Analysis of Clinical Trials Using SAS®: A Practical Guide
by **Alex Dmitrienko, Geert Molenberghs, Walter Offen,** and **Christy Chuang-Stein**

Annotate: Simply the Basics
by **Art Carpenter**

Applied Multivariate Statistics with SAS® Software, Second Edition
by **Ravindra Khattree** and **Dayanand N. Naik**

Applied Statistics and the SAS® Programming Language, Fourth Edition
by **Ronald P. Cody** and **Jeffrey K. Smith**

An Array of Challenges — Test Your SAS® Skills
by **Robert Virgile**

Carpenter's Complete Guide to the SAS® Macro Language, Second Edition
by **Art Carpenter**

The Cartoon Guide to Statistics
by **Larry Gonick** and **Woollcott Smith**

Categorical Data Analysis Using the SAS® System, Second Edition
by **Maura E. Stokes, Charles S. Davis,** and **Gary G. Koch**

Cody's Data Cleaning Techniques Using SAS® Software
by **Ron Cody**

Common Statistical Methods for Clinical Research with SAS® Examples, Second Edition
by **Glenn A. Walker**

Debugging SAS® Programs: A Handbook of Tools and Techniques
by **Michele M. Burlew**

Efficiency: Improving the Performance of Your SAS® Applications
by **Robert Virgile**

The Essential PROC SQL Handbook for SAS® Users
by **Katherine Prairie**

Fixed Effects Regression Methods for Longitudinal Data Using SAS®
by **Paul D. Allison**

Genetic Analysis of Complex Traits Using SAS®
Edited by **Arnold M. Saxton**

A Handbook of Statistical Analyses Using SAS®, Second Edition
by **B.S. Everitt** and **G. Der**

Health Care Data and SAS®
by **Marge Scerbo, Craig Dickstein,** and **Alan Wilson**

The How-To Book for SAS/GRAPH® Software
by **Thomas Miron**

In the Know ... SAS® Tips and Techniques From Around the Globe
by **Phil Mason**

Instant ODS: Style Templates for the Output Delivery System
by **Bernadette Johnson**

Integrating Results through Meta-Analytic Review Using SAS® Software
by **Morgan C. Wang** and **Brad J. Bushman**

Learning SAS® in the Computer Lab, Second Edition
by **Rebecca J. Elliott**

The Little SAS® Book: A Primer
by **Lora D. Delwiche** and **Susan J. Slaughter**

The Little SAS® Book: A Primer, Second Edition
by **Lora D. Delwiche** and **Susan J. Slaughter**
(updated to include Version 7 features)

The Little SAS® Book: A Primer, Third Edition
by **Lora D. Delwiche** and **Susan J. Slaughter**
(updated to include SAS 9.1 features)

Logistic Regression Using the SAS® System: Theory and Application
by **Paul D. Allison**

Longitudinal Data and SAS®: A Programmer's Guide
by **Ron Cody**

Maps Made Easy Using SAS®
by **Mike Zdeb**

Models for Discrete Data
by **Daniel Zelterman**

Multiple Comparisons and Multiple Tests Using SAS®
Text and Workbook Set
(books in this set also sold separately)
by **Peter H. Westfall, Randall D. Tobias,
Dror Rom, Russell D. Wolfinger,**
and **Yosef Hochberg**

Multiple-Plot Displays: Simplified with Macros
by **Perry Watts**

*Multivariate Data Reduction and Discrimination with
SAS® Software*
by **Ravindra Khattree**
and **Dayanand N. Naik**

Output Delivery System: The Basics
by **Lauren E. Haworth**

Painless Windows: A Handbook for SAS® Users, Third Edition
by **Jodie Gilmore**
(updated to include Version 8 and SAS 9.1 features)

The Power of PROC FORMAT
by **Jonas V. Bilenas**

PROC TABULATE by Example
by **Lauren E. Haworth**

Professional SAS® Programming Shortcuts
by **Rick Aster**

Quick Results with SAS/GRAPH® Software
by **Arthur L. Carpenter**
and **Charles E. Shipp**

Quick Results with the Output Delivery System
by **Sunil K. Gupta**

Quick Start to Data Analysis with SAS®
by **Frank C. DiIorio**
and **Kenneth A. Hardy**

Reading External Data Files Using SAS®: Examples Handbook
by **Michele M. Burlew**

*Regression and ANOVA: An Integrated Approach Using
SAS® Software*
by **Keith E. Muller**
and **Bethel A. Fetterman**

SAS®Applications Programming: A Gentle Introduction
by **Frank C. DiIorio**

SAS® for Forecasting Time Series, Second Edition
by **John C. Brocklebank**
and **David A. Dickey**

SAS® for Linear Models, Fourth Edition
by **Ramon C. Littell, Walter W. Stroup,**
and **Rudolf J. Freund**

*SAS® for Monte Carlo Studies: A Guide for Quantitative
Researchers*
by **Xitao Fan, Ákos Felsővályi, Stephen A. Sivo,**
and **Sean C. Keenan**

SAS® Functions by Example
by **Ron Cody**

SAS® Guide to Report Writing, Second Edition
by **Michele M. Burlew**

SAS® Macro Programming Made Easy
by **Michele M. Burlew**

SAS® Programming by Example
by **Ron Cody**
and **Ray Pass**

*SAS® Programming for Researchers and Social Scientists,
Second Edition*
by **Paul E. Spector**

*SAS® Survival Analysis Techniques for Medical Research,
Second Edition*
by **Alan B. Cantor**

*SAS® System for Elementary Statistical Analysis,
Second Edition*
by **Sandra D. Schlotzhauer**
and **Ramon C. Littell**

SAS® System for Mixed Models
by **Ramon C. Littell, George A. Milliken, Walter W. Stroup,**
and **Russell D. Wolfinger**

SAS® System for Regression, Third Edition
by **Rudolf J. Freund**
and **Ramon C. Littell**

SAS® System for Statistical Graphics, First Edition
by **Michael Friendly**

The SAS® Workbook and *Solutions* Set
(books in this set also sold separately)
by **Ron Cody**

*Selecting Statistical Techniques for Social Science Data:
A Guide for SAS® Users*
by **Frank M. Andrews, Laura Klem, Patrick M. O'Malley,
Willard L. Rodgers, Kathleen B. Welch,**
and **Terrence N. Davidson**

Statistical Quality Control Using the SAS® System
by **Dennis W. King**

*A Step-by-Step Approach to Using the SAS® System
for Factor Analysis and Structural Equation Modeling*
by **Larry Hatcher**

*A Step-by-Step Approach to Using SAS® for Univariate and
Multivariate Statistics, Second Edition*
by **Norm O'Rourke, Larry Hatcher,**
and **Edward J. Stepanski**

Step-by-Step Basic Statistics Using SAS®: Student Guide
and *Exercises*
*(*books in this set also sold separately)
by **Larry Hatcher**

*Survival Analysis Using the SAS® System:
A Practical Guide*
by **Paul D. Allison**

support.sas.com/pubs

*Tuning SAS® Applications in the OS/390 and z/OS
Environments, Second Edition*
by **Michael A. Raithel**

*Univariate and Multivariate General Linear Models:
Theory and Applications Using SAS® Software*
by **Neil H. Timm**
and **Tammy A. Mieczkowski**

Using SAS® in Financial Research
by **Ekkehart Boehmer, John Paul Broussard,**
and **Juha-Pekka Kallunki**

Using the SAS® Windowing Environment: A Quick Tutorial
by **Larry Hatcher**

Visualizing Categorical Data
by **Michael Friendly**

Web Development with SAS® by Example
by **Frederick Pratter**

Your Guide to Survey Research Using the SAS® System
by **Archer Gravely**

JMP® Books

*JMP® for Basic Univariate and Multivariate Statistics: A Step-by-
Step Guide*
by **Ann Lehman, Norm O'Rourke, Larry Hatcher,**
and **Edward J. Stepanski**

JMP® Start Statistics, Third Edition
by **John Sall, Ann Lehman,**
and **Lee Creighton**

Regression Using JMP®
by **Rudolf J. Freund, Ramon C. Littell,**
and **Lee Creighton**